THE HELLBLAZER

VOL. 4 THE GOOD OLD DAYS

TIM SEELEY
writer

DAVIDE FABBRI * **CHRISTIAN DALLA VECCHIA**
artists

CARRIE STRACHAN
colorist

SAL CIPRIANO
letterer

TIM SEELEY with CHRIS SOTOMAYOR
collection cover art and original series covers

JOHN CONSTANTINE created by ALAN MOORE, STEVE BISSETTE,
JOHN TOTLEBEN and JAMIE DELANO & JOHN RIDGWAY

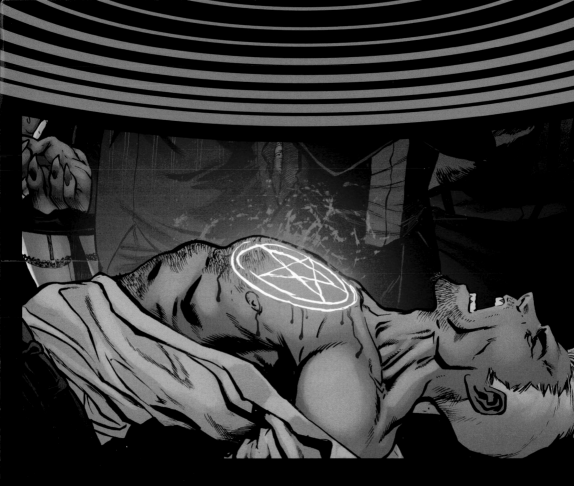

KRISTY QUINN Editor - Original Series ✳ **JEB WOODARD** Group Editor - Collected Editions
SCOTT NYBAKKEN Editor - Collected Edition ✳ **STEVE COOK** Design Director - Books

BOB HARRAS Senior VP - Editor-in-Chief, DC Comics ✳ **PAT McCALLUM** Executive Editor, DC Comics

DAN DiDIO Publisher ✳ **JIM LEE** Publisher & Chief Creative Officer ✳ **AMIT DESAI** Executive VP - Business & Marketing Strategy, Direct to Consumer & Global Franchise Management
BOBBIE CHASE VP & Executive Editor, Young Reader & Talent Development ✳ **MARK CHIARELLO** Senior VP - Art, Design & Collected Editions
JOHN CUNNINGHAM Senior VP - Sales & Trade Marketing ✳ **BRIAR DARDEN** VP - Business Affairs ✳ **ANNE DePIES** Senior VP - Business Strategy, Finance & Administration
DON FALLETTI VP - Manufacturing Operations ✳ **LAWRENCE GANEM** VP - Editorial Administration & Talent Relations ✳ **ALISON GILL** Senior VP - Manufacturing & Operations
JASON GREENBERG VP - Business Strategy & Finance ✳ **HANK KANALZ** Senior VP - Editorial Strategy & Administration ✳ **JAY KOGAN** Senior VP - Legal Affairs
NICK J. NAPOLITANO VP - Manufacturing Administration ✳ **LISETTE OSTERLOH** VP - Digital Marketing & Events ✳ **EDDIE SCANNELL** VP - Consumer Marketing
COURTNEY SIMMONS Senior VP - Publicity & Communications ✳ **JIM (SKI) SOKOLOWSKI** VP - Comic Book Specialty Sales & Trade Marketing
NANCY SPEARS VP - Mass, Book, Digital Sales & Trade Marketing ✳ **MICHELE R. WELLS** VP - Content Strategy

THE HELLBLAZER VOL. 4: THE GOOD OLD DAYS

Published by DC Comics. Compilation and all new material Copyright © 2018 DC Comics. All Rights Reserved.

Originally published in single magazine form in THE HELLBLAZER 19-24. Copyright © 2018 DC Comics. All Rights Reserved. All characters,
their distinctive likenesses and related elements featured in this publication are trademarks of DC Comics. The stories, characters and incidents
featured in this publication are entirely fictional. DC Comics does not read or accept unsolicited submissions of ideas, stories or artwork.

DC Comics, 2900 West Alameda Ave., Burbank, CA 91505
Printed by LSC Communications, Kendallville, IN, USA. 11/16/18.
First Printing. ISBN: 978-1-4012-8627-9

Library of Congress Cataloging-in-Publication Data is available.

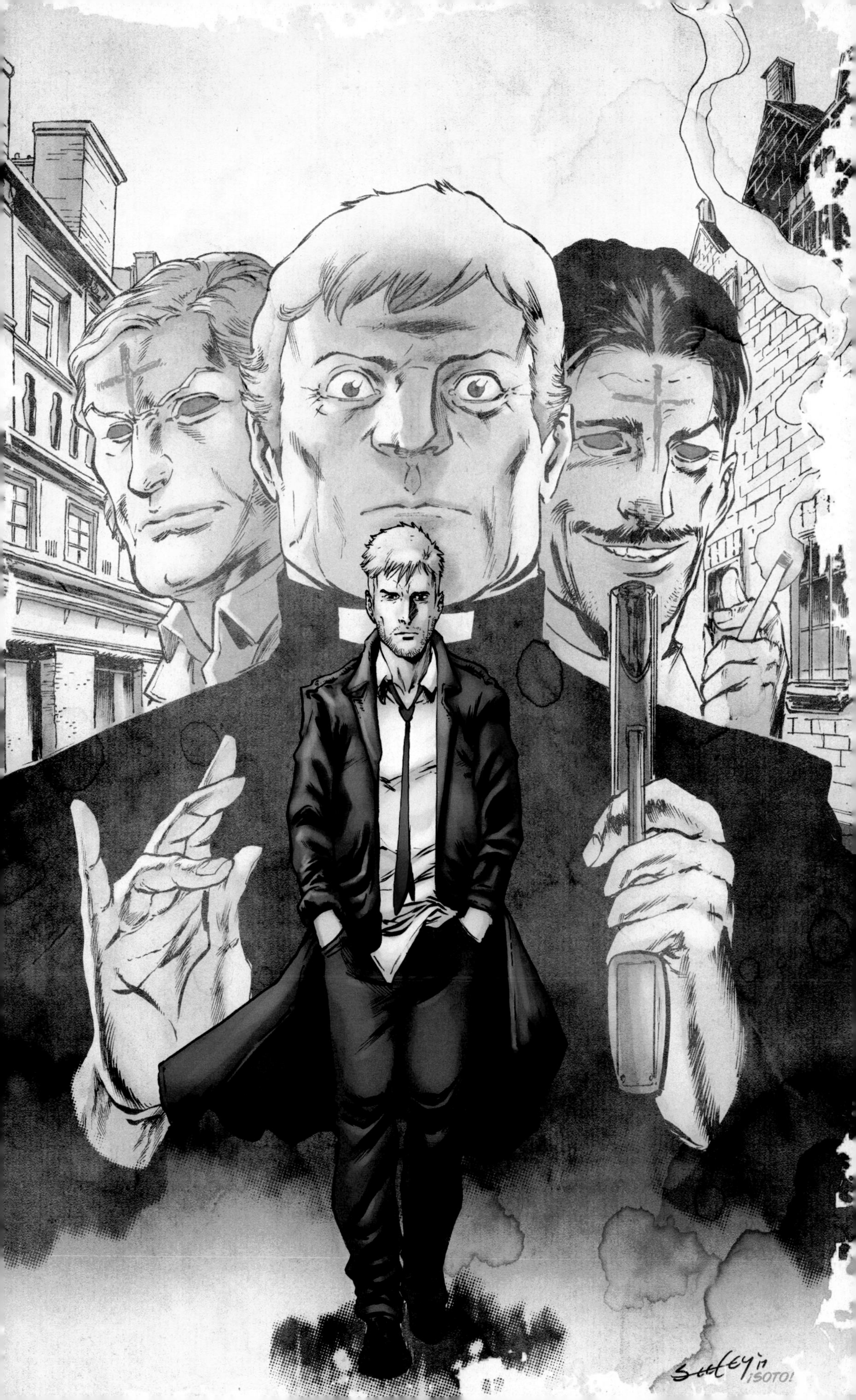
¡SOTO!

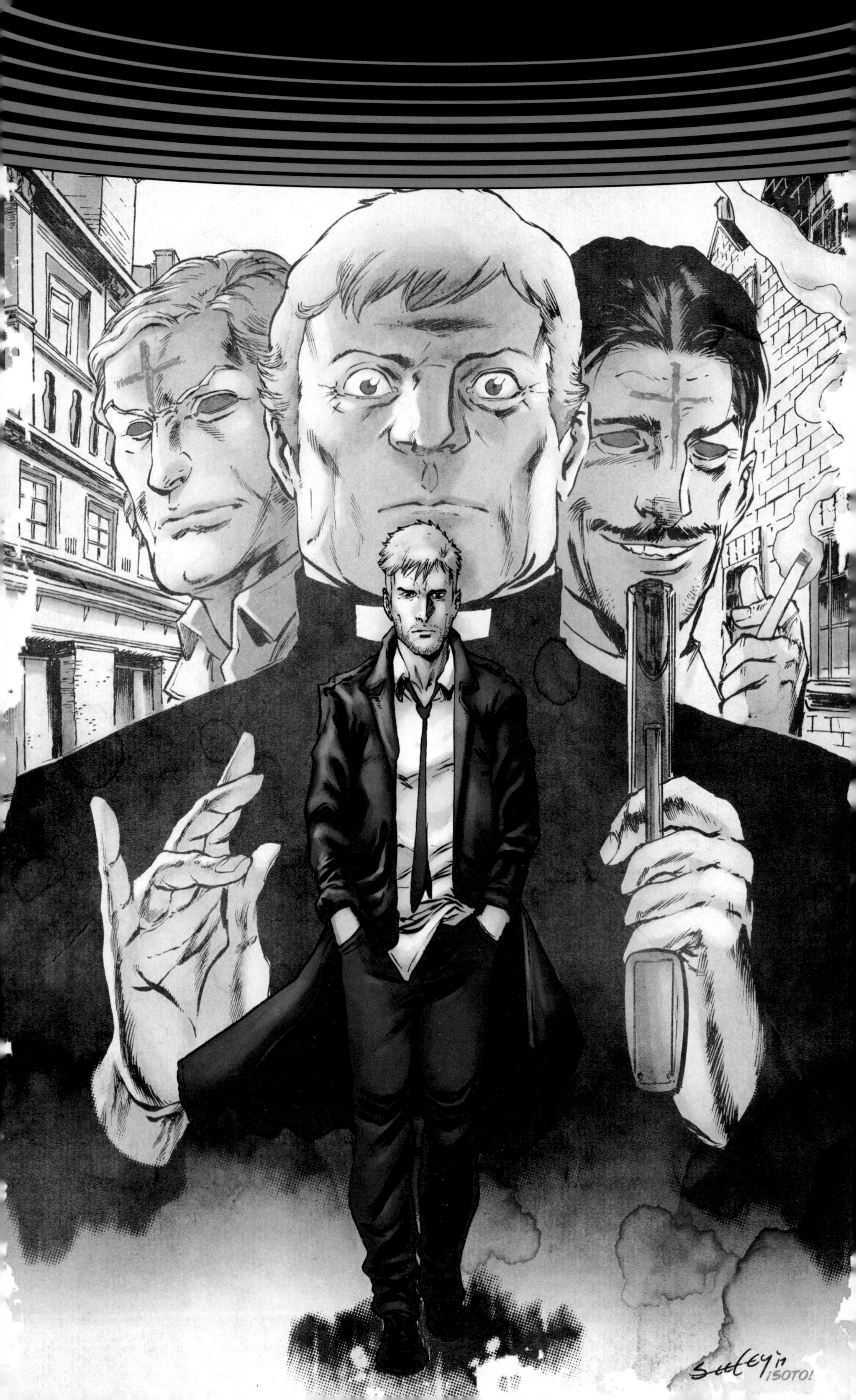
¡SOTO!

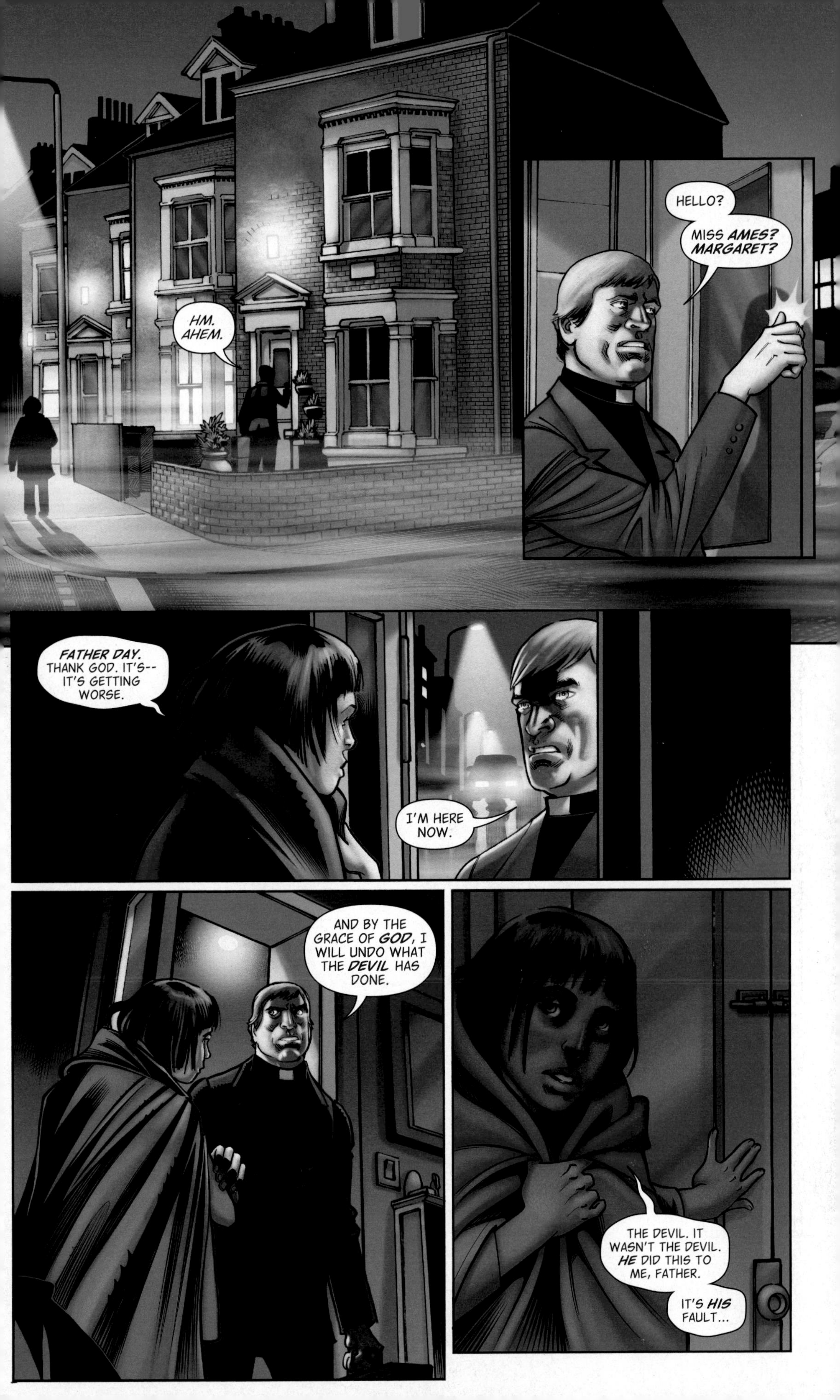
HM. AHEM.
HELLO?
MISS *AMES? MARGARET?*
FATHER DAY. THANK GOD. IT'S-- IT'S GETTING WORSE.
I'M HERE NOW.
AND BY THE GRACE OF *GOD*, I WILL UNDO WHAT THE *DEVIL* HAS DONE.
THE DEVIL. IT WASN'T THE DEVIL. *HE* DID THIS TO ME, FATHER.
IT'S *HIS* FAULT...

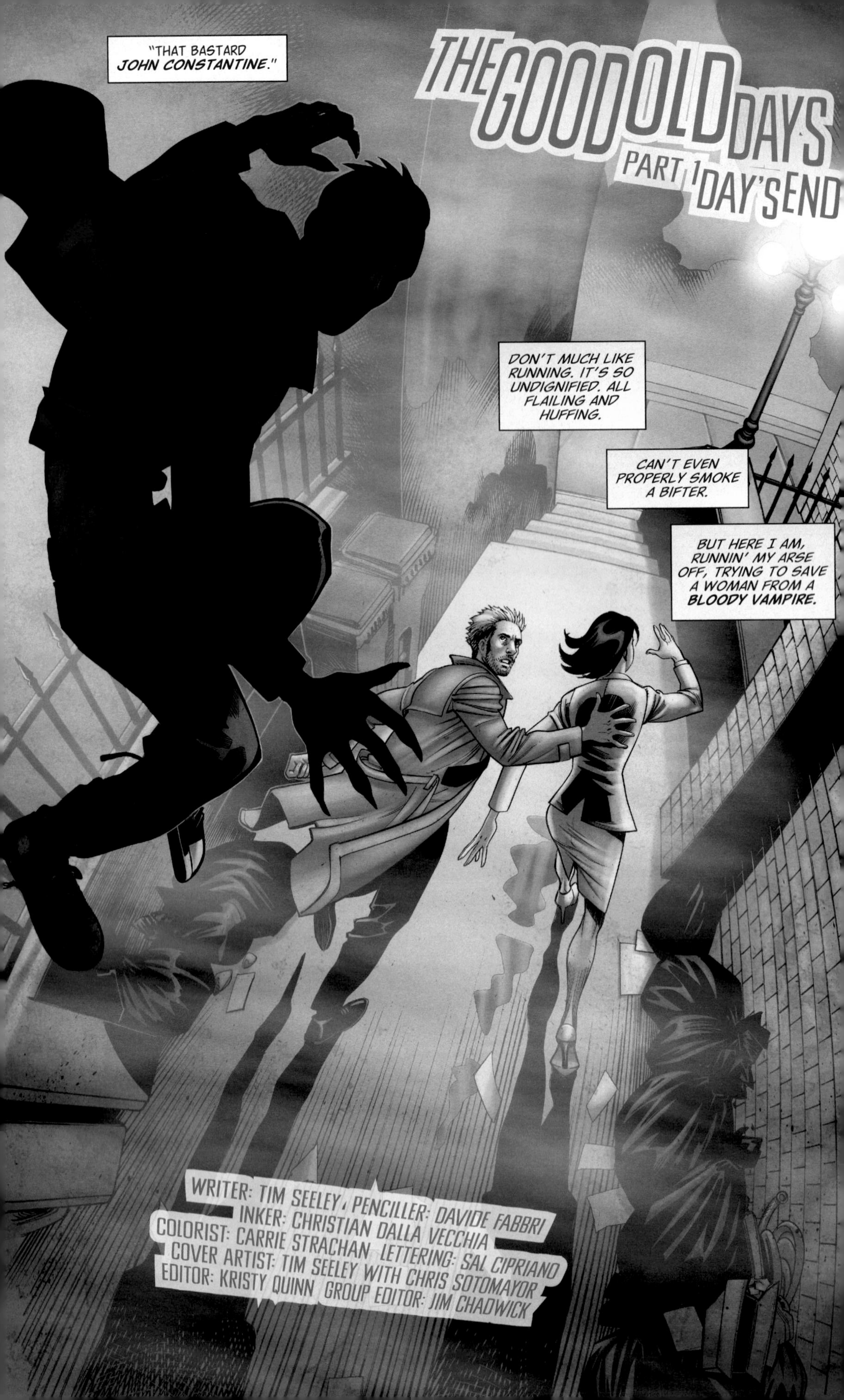
"THAT BASTARD JOHN CONSTANTINE."
THE GOOD OLD DAYS PART 1 DAY'S END
DON'T MUCH LIKE RUNNING. IT'S SO UNDIGNIFIED. ALL FLAILING AND HUFFING.
CAN'T EVEN PROPERLY SMOKE A BIFTER.
BUT HERE I AM, RUNNIN' MY ARSE OFF, TRYING TO SAVE A WOMAN FROM A BLOODY VAMPIRE.
WRITER: TIM SEELEY PENCILLER: DAVIDE FABBRI
INKER: CHRISTIAN DALLA VECCHIA
COLORIST: CARRIE STRACHAN LETTERING: SAL CIPRIANO
COVER ARTIST: TIM SEELEY WITH CHRIS SOTOMAYOR
EDITOR: KRISTY QUINN GROUP EDITOR: JIM CHADWICK

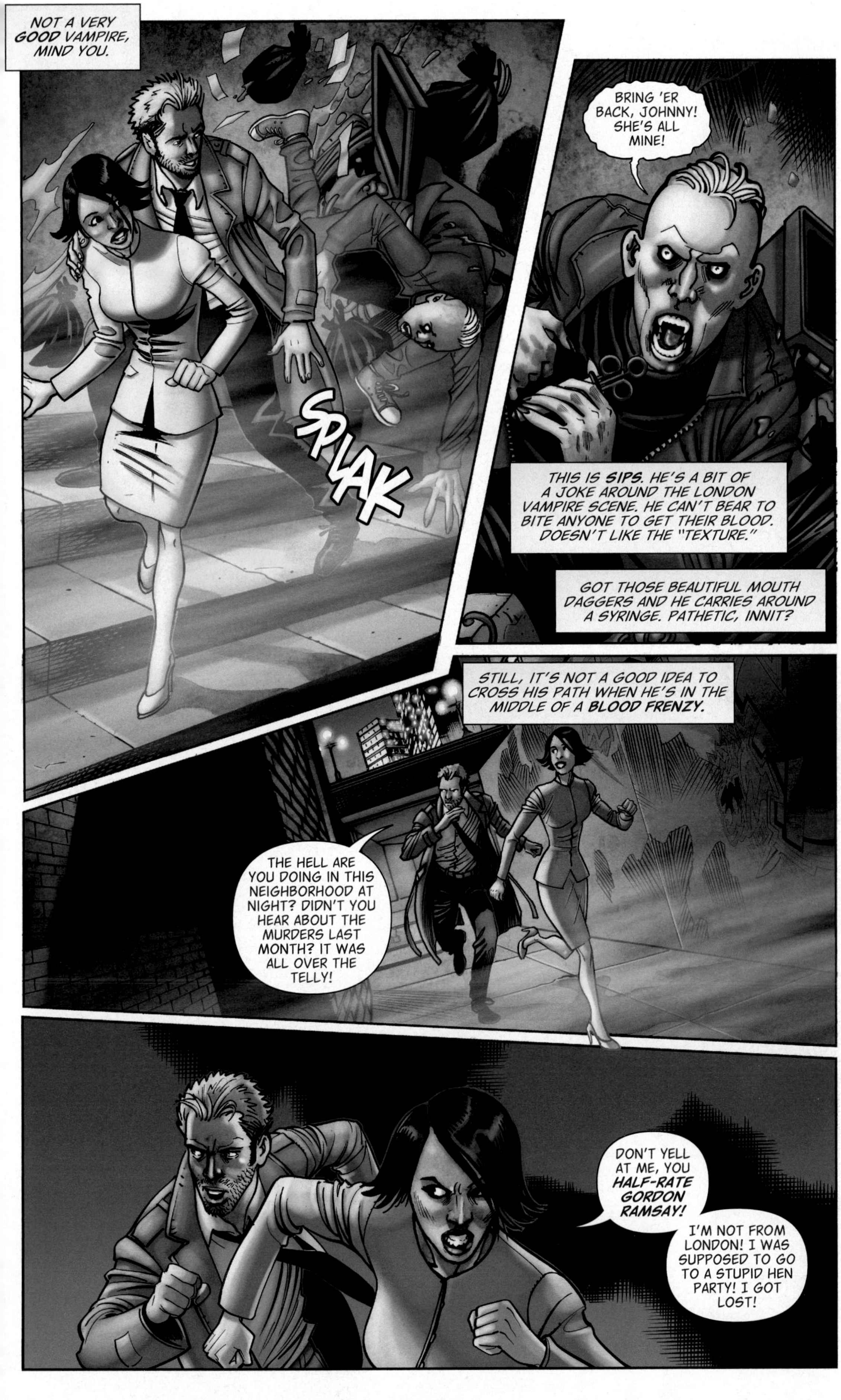
NOT A VERY GOOD VAMPIRE, MIND YOU.
SPLAK
BRING 'ER BACK, JOHNNY! SHE'S ALL MINE!
THIS IS SIPS. HE'S A BIT OF A JOKE AROUND THE LONDON VAMPIRE SCENE. HE CAN'T BEAR TO BITE ANYONE TO GET THEIR BLOOD. DOESN'T LIKE THE "TEXTURE."
GOT THOSE BEAUTIFUL MOUTH DAGGERS AND HE CARRIES AROUND A SYRINGE. PATHETIC, INNIT?
STILL, IT'S NOT A GOOD IDEA TO CROSS HIS PATH WHEN HE'S IN THE MIDDLE OF A BLOOD FRENZY.
THE HELL ARE YOU DOING IN THIS NEIGHBORHOOD AT NIGHT? DIDN'T YOU HEAR ABOUT THE MURDERS LAST MONTH? IT WAS ALL OVER THE TELLY!
DON'T YELL AT ME, YOU HALF-RATE GORDON RAMSAY!
I'M NOT FROM LONDON! I WAS SUPPOSED TO GO TO A STUPID HEN PARTY! I GOT LOST!

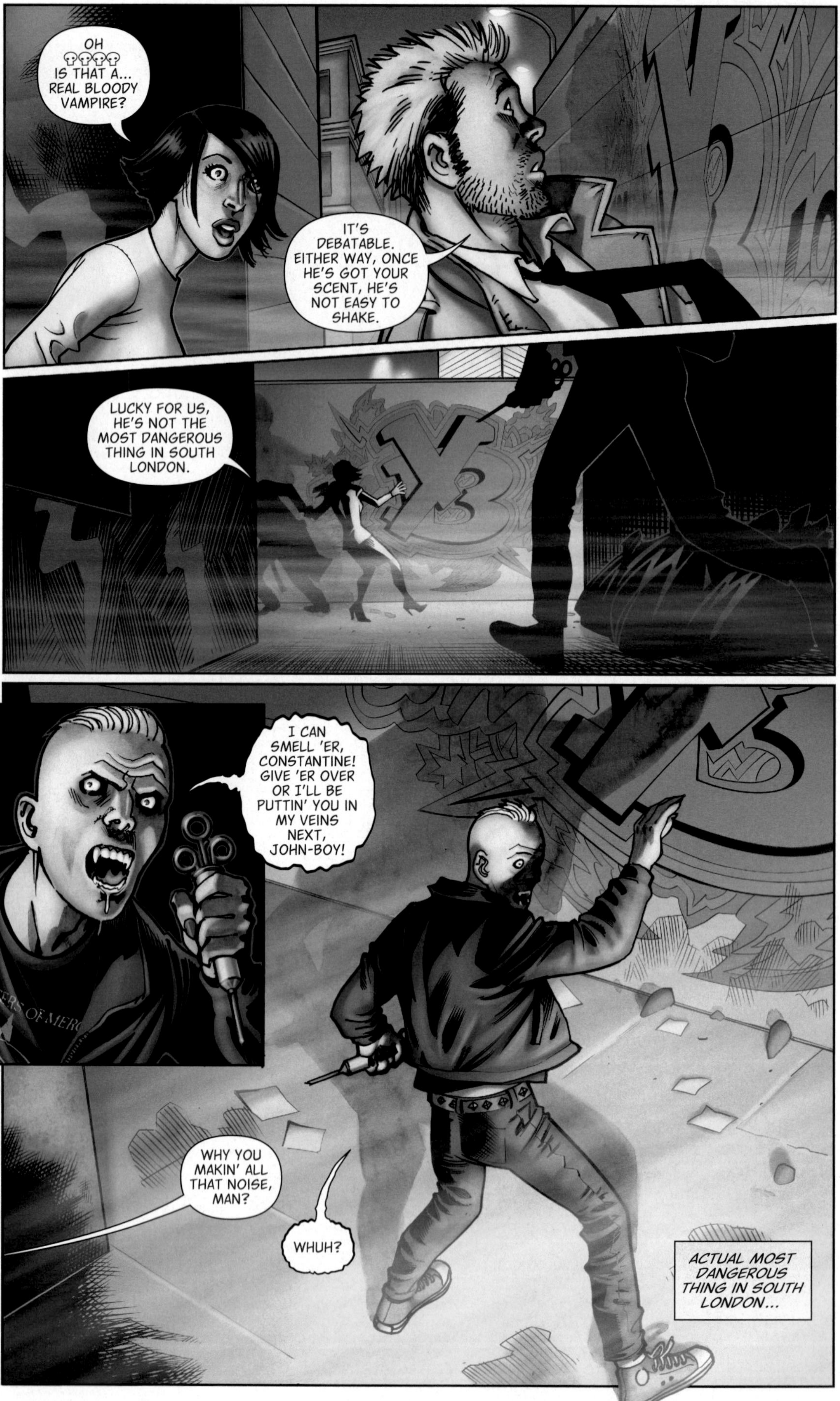
OH ☠☠☠☠ IS THAT A... REAL BLOODY VAMPIRE?
IT'S DEBATABLE. EITHER WAY, ONCE HE'S GOT YOUR SCENT, HE'S NOT EASY TO SHAKE.
LUCKY FOR US, HE'S NOT THE MOST DANGEROUS THING IN SOUTH LONDON.
I CAN SMELL 'ER, CONSTANTINE! GIVE 'ER OVER OR I'LL BE PUTTIN' YOU IN MY VEINS NEXT, JOHN-BOY!
SISTERS OF MERC
WHY YOU MAKIN' ALL THAT NOISE, MAN?
WHUH?
ACTUAL MOST DANGEROUS THING IN SOUTH LONDON...

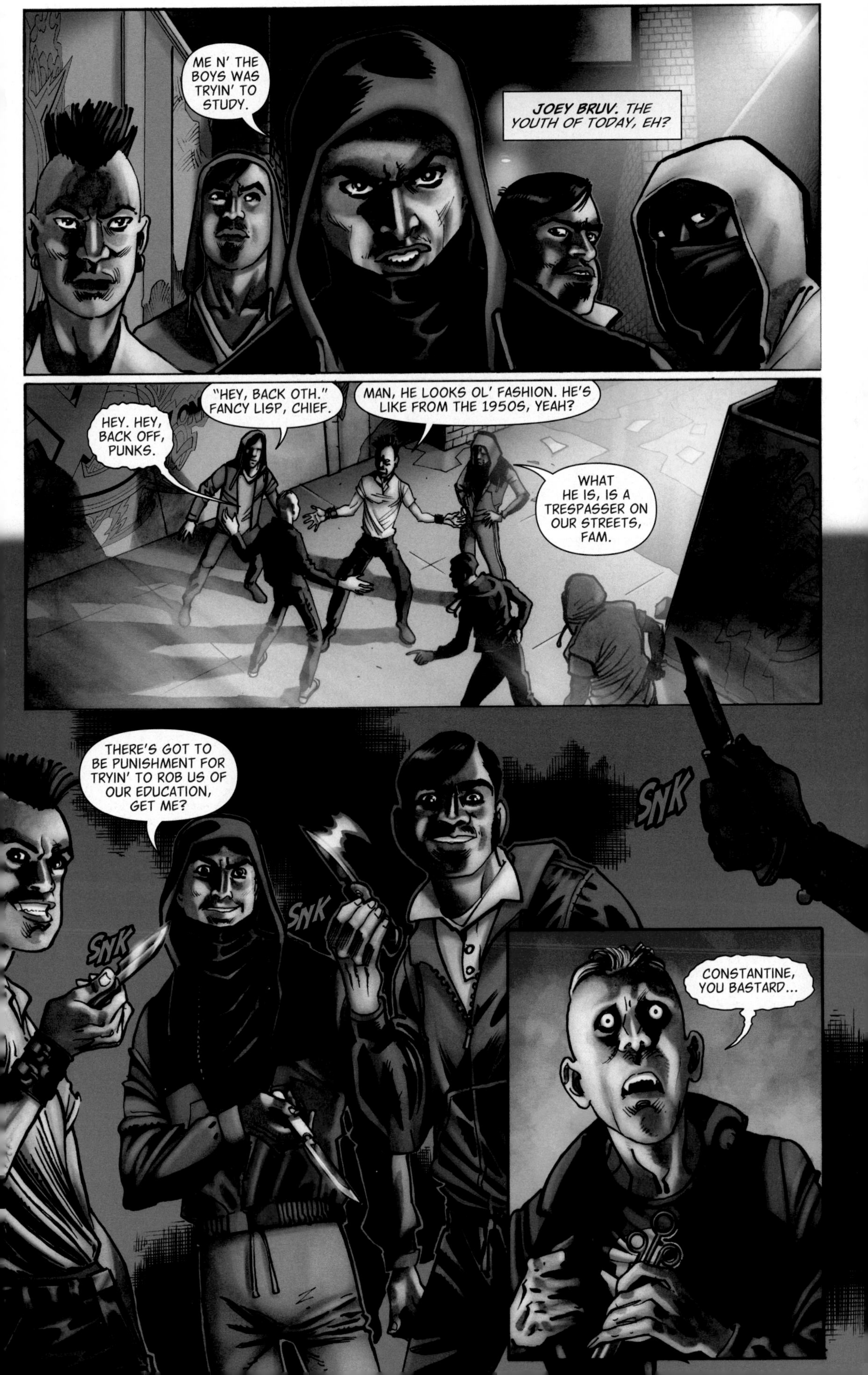
ME N' THE BOYS WAS TRYIN' TO STUDY.
JOEY BRUV. THE YOUTH OF TODAY, EH?
HEY. HEY, BACK OFF, PUNKS.
"HEY, BACK OTH." FANCY LISP, CHIEF.
MAN, HE LOOKS OL' FASHION. HE'S LIKE FROM THE 1950S, YEAH?
WHAT HE IS, IS A TRESPASSER ON OUR STREETS, FAM.
THERE'S GOT TO BE PUNISHMENT FOR TRYIN' TO ROB US OF OUR EDUCATION, GET ME?
SNK
SNK
SNK
CONSTANTINE, YOU BASTARD...

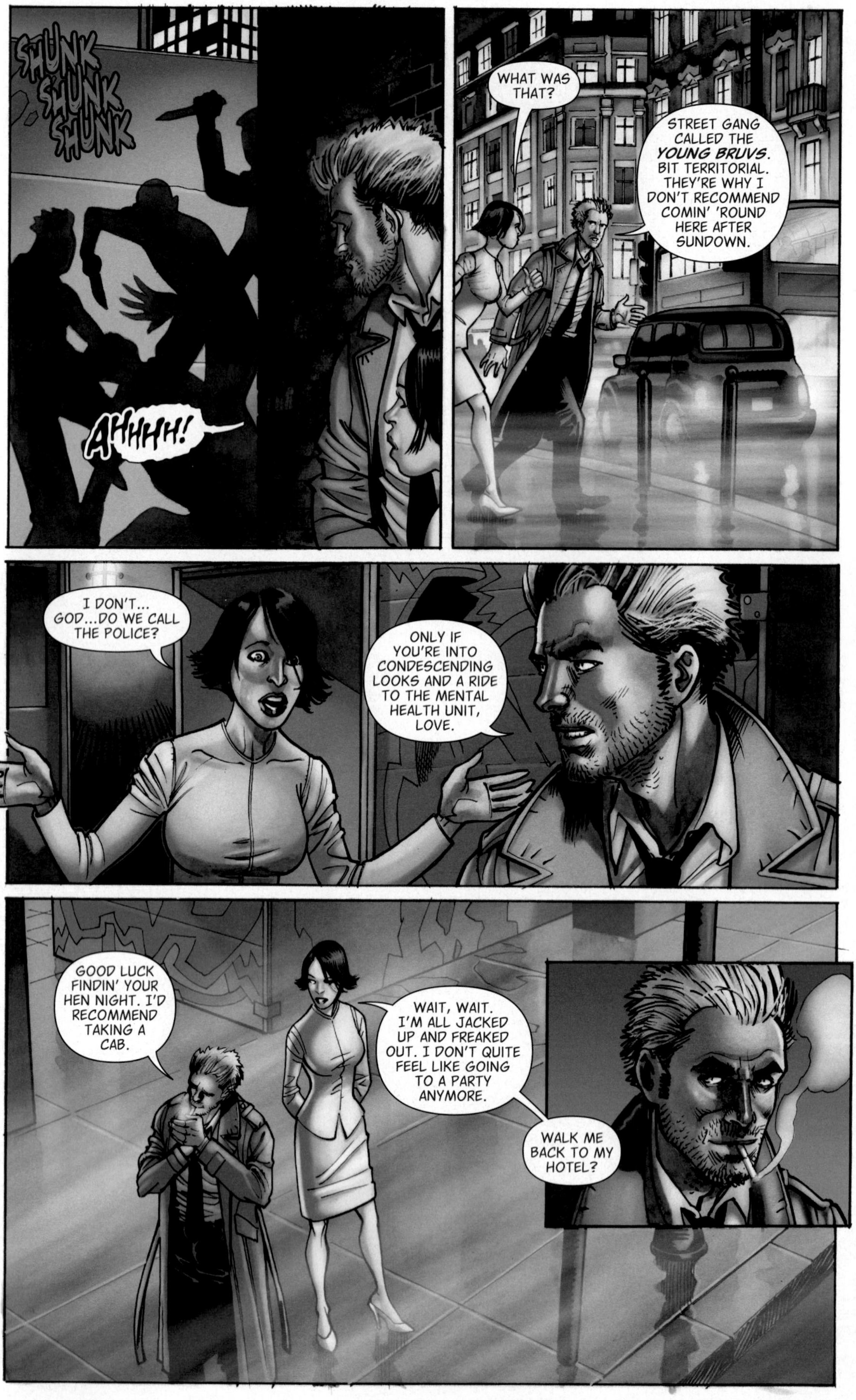

SHUNK SHUNK SHUNK
AHHHH!
WHAT WAS THAT?
STREET GANG CALLED THE *YOUNG BRUVS*. BIT TERRITORIAL. THEY'RE WHY I DON'T RECOMMEND COMIN' 'ROUND HERE AFTER SUNDOWN.
I DON'T... GOD...DO WE CALL THE POLICE?
ONLY IF YOU'RE INTO CONDESCENDING LOOKS AND A RIDE TO THE MENTAL HEALTH UNIT, LOVE.
GOOD LUCK FINDIN' YOUR HEN NIGHT. I'D RECOMMEND TAKING A CAB.
WAIT, WAIT. I'M ALL JACKED UP AND FREAKED OUT. I DON'T QUITE FEEL LIKE GOING TO A PARTY ANYMORE.
WALK ME BACK TO MY HOTEL?

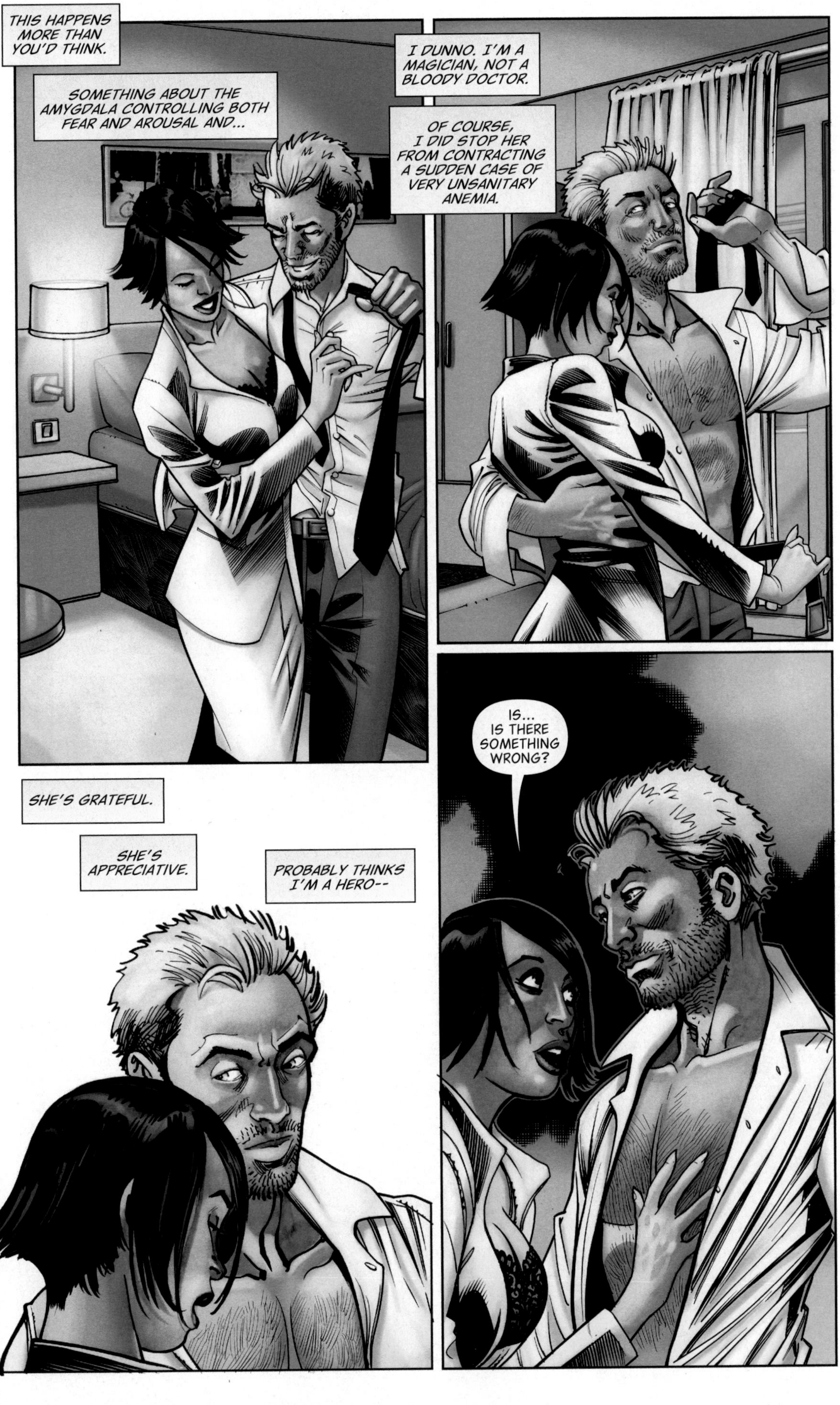
THIS HAPPENS MORE THAN YOU'D THINK.
SOMETHING ABOUT THE AMYGDALA CONTROLLING BOTH FEAR AND AROUSAL AND...
I DUNNO. I'M A MAGICIAN, NOT A BLOODY DOCTOR.
OF COURSE, I DID STOP HER FROM CONTRACTING A SUDDEN CASE OF VERY UNSANITARY ANEMIA.
SHE'S GRATEFUL.
SHE'S APPRECIATIVE.
PROBABLY THINKS I'M A HERO--
IS... IS THERE SOMETHING WRONG?

YEAH. THERE'S SOMETHING WRONG.

THAT'S HAPPENED MORE OFTEN LATELY THAN I'D LIKE TO ADMIT.

MORE OFTEN THAN NOT REALLY.

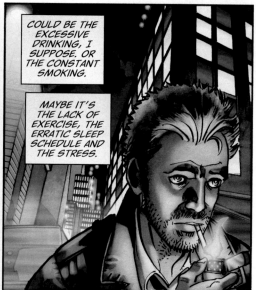

COULD BE THE EXCESSIVE DRINKING, I SUPPOSE. OR THE CONSTANT SMOKING.

MAYBE IT'S THE LACK OF EXERCISE, THE ERRATIC SLEEP SCHEDULE AND THE STRESS.

BUT THAT'S NEVER STOPPED ME BEFORE. ALWAYS SEEMED TO ME MY ENGINE'S BEEN CONVERTED TO RUN ON GARBAGE.

YOU CAN STICK YOUR KALE AND SPINNING CLASSES IN YOUR TAUT, CELLULITE-FREE END, I SAY.

COULD BE THE **BLACK MAGIC**, I GUESS.

NOT LIKE THERE'VE BEEN GOOD STUDIES ON THE LONG-TERM EFFECTS OF DEMON BLOOD ON TESTOSTERONE.

AND IT GOES WITHOUT SAYING, THAT SEEING THE THINGS I CAN SEE WOULD MAKE ANY NORMAL PERSON LOSE THEIR SANITY, MUCH LESS THEIR LIBIDO.

DO GO EASY ON HIM, LOVE.

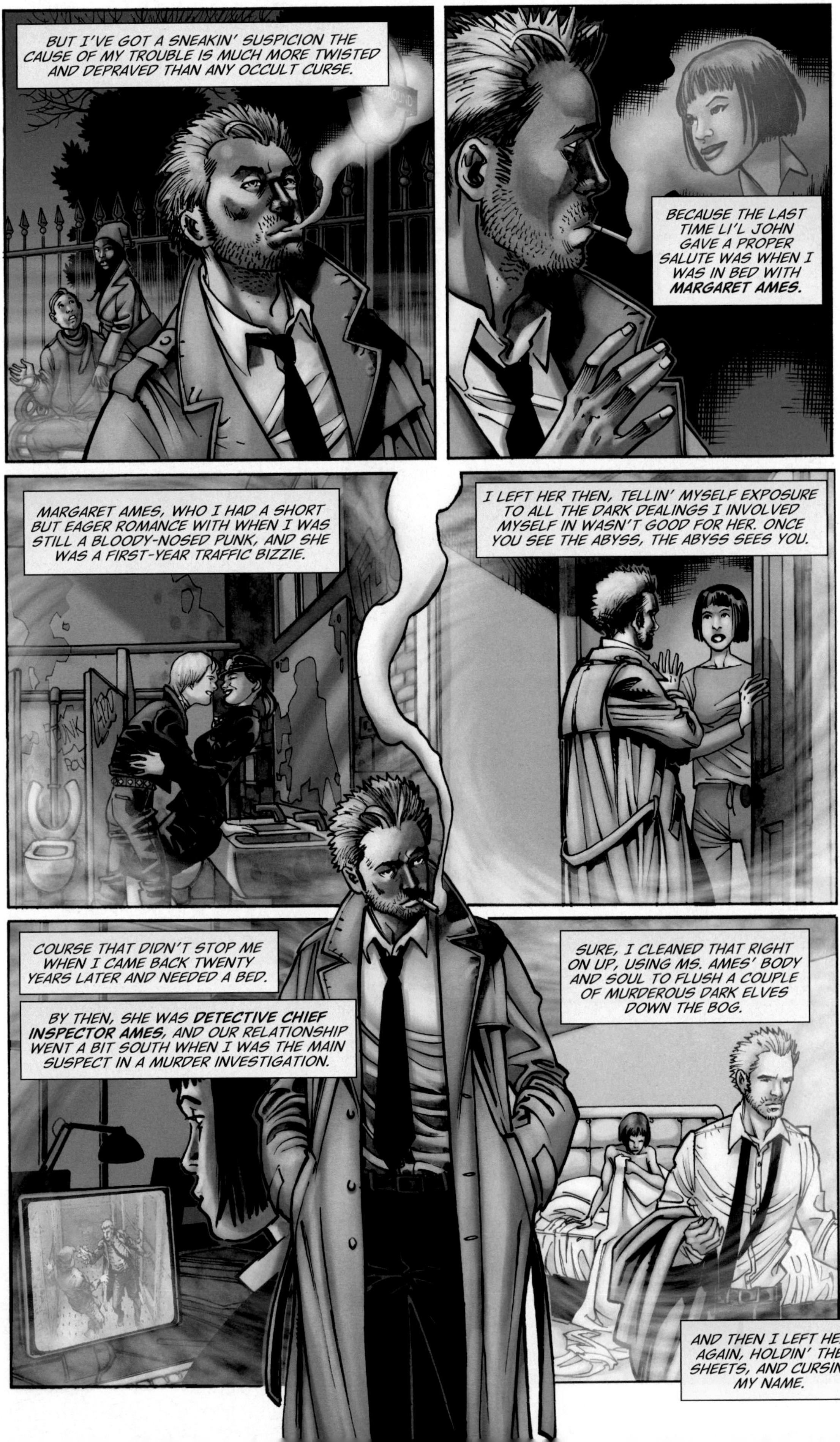
BUT I'VE GOT A SNEAKIN' SUSPICION THE CAUSE OF MY TROUBLE IS MUCH MORE TWISTED AND DEPRAVED THAN ANY OCCULT CURSE.
BECAUSE THE LAST TIME LI'L JOHN GAVE A PROPER SALUTE WAS WHEN I WAS IN BED WITH MARGARET AMES.
MARGARET AMES, WHO I HAD A SHORT BUT EAGER ROMANCE WITH WHEN I WAS STILL A BLOODY-NOSED PUNK, AND SHE WAS A FIRST-YEAR TRAFFIC BIZZIE.
I LEFT HER THEN, TELLIN' MYSELF EXPOSURE TO ALL THE DARK DEALINGS I INVOLVED MYSELF IN WASN'T GOOD FOR HER. ONCE YOU SEE THE ABYSS, THE ABYSS SEES YOU.
COURSE THAT DIDN'T STOP ME WHEN I CAME BACK TWENTY YEARS LATER AND NEEDED A BED.
BY THEN, SHE WAS DETECTIVE CHIEF INSPECTOR AMES, AND OUR RELATIONSHIP WENT A BIT SOUTH WHEN I WAS THE MAIN SUSPECT IN A MURDER INVESTIGATION.
SURE, I CLEANED THAT RIGHT ON UP, USING MS. AMES' BODY AND SOUL TO FLUSH A COUPLE OF MURDEROUS DARK ELVES DOWN THE BOG.
AND THEN I LEFT HER AGAIN, HOLDIN' THE SHEETS, AND CURSIN' MY NAME.

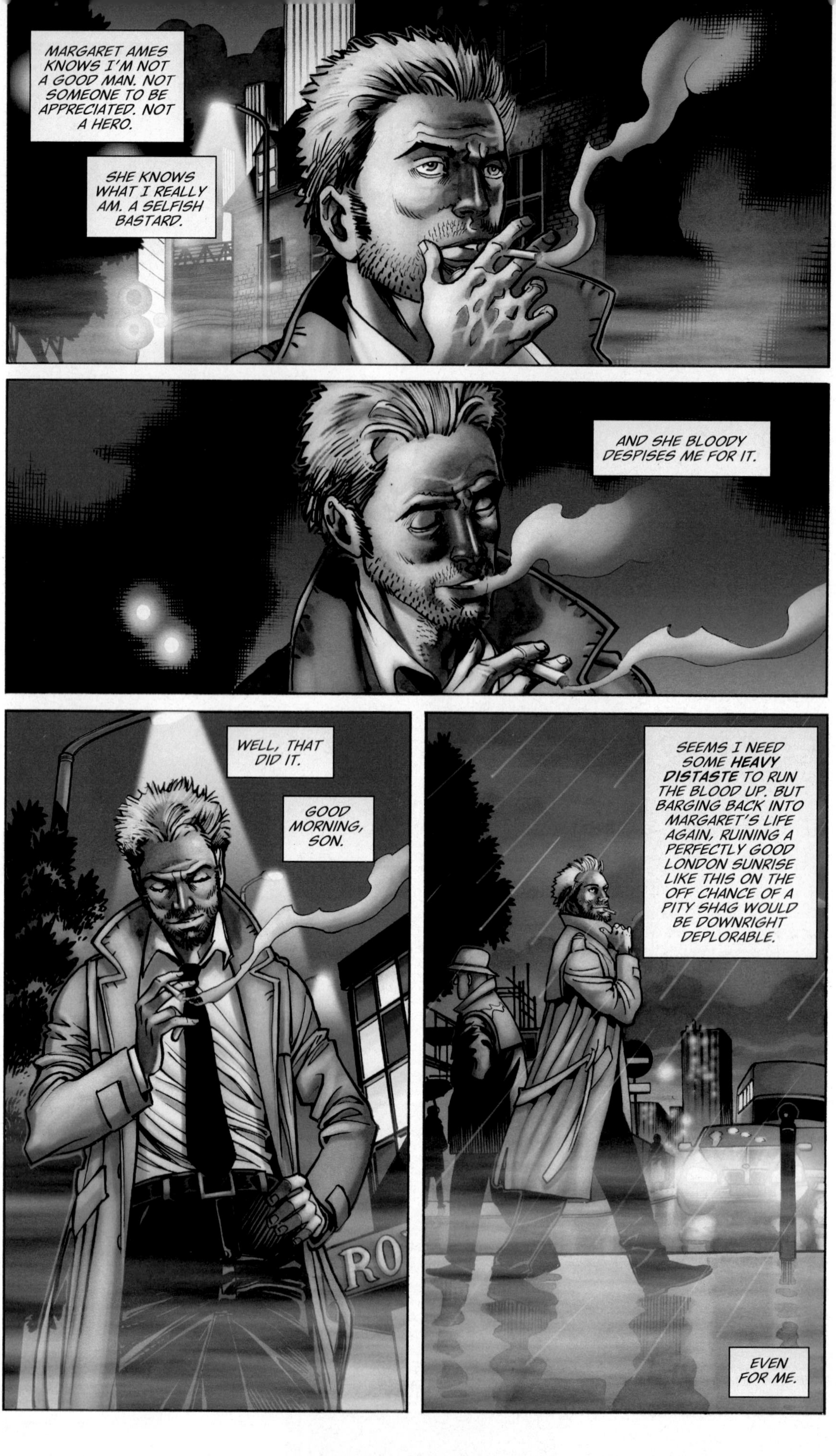
MARGARET AMES KNOWS I'M NOT A GOOD MAN. NOT SOMEONE TO BE APPRECIATED. NOT A HERO.
SHE KNOWS WHAT I REALLY AM. A SELFISH BASTARD.
AND SHE BLOODY DESPISES ME FOR IT.
WELL, THAT DID IT.
GOOD MORNING, SON.
SEEMS I NEED SOME **HEAVY DISTASTE** TO RUN THE BLOOD UP. BUT BARGING BACK INTO MARGARET'S LIFE AGAIN, RUINING A PERFECTLY GOOD LONDON SUNRISE LIKE THIS ON THE OFF CHANCE OF A PITY SHAG WOULD BE DOWNRIGHT DEPLORABLE.
EVEN FOR ME.

MARGARET? YOU ABOUT, **DETECTIVE CHIEF INSPECTOR?** FANCY SOME BREAKFAST?

ALRIGHT. IT WAS A BIT OF A LONG SHOT. EVEN IF SHE WEREN'T ALREADY UP AND CHASING MURDERERS AND RAPISTS, THERE'S NOT MUCH CHANCE SHE'D RUN SKIPPING TO OPEN THE DOOR FOR ME.

COME ON, JOHN. GET YOURSELF OUT OF HERE. YOU'VE DONE ENOUGH DARKENING OF DOORSTEPS--

EH. WHAT'S THIS?

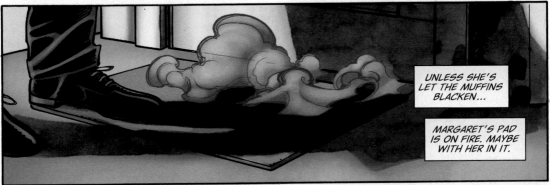

UNLESS SHE'S LET THE MUFFINS BLACKEN...

MARGARET'S PAD IS ON FIRE. MAYBE WITH HER IN IT.

IT MIGHT BE A TOSS-UP, BUT I HAVE TO ASSUME BURNING IN HER SLEEP IS ONE THING SHE'D LIKE LESS THAN SEEING ME.

MARGARET!

KRAK

THERE WERE SEVERAL POSSIBILITIES IN MY MIND AS TO WHAT STARTED THE BLAZE, FROM A CAT KNOCKING OVER CANDLES TO SPONTANEOUS HUMAN COMBUSTION...

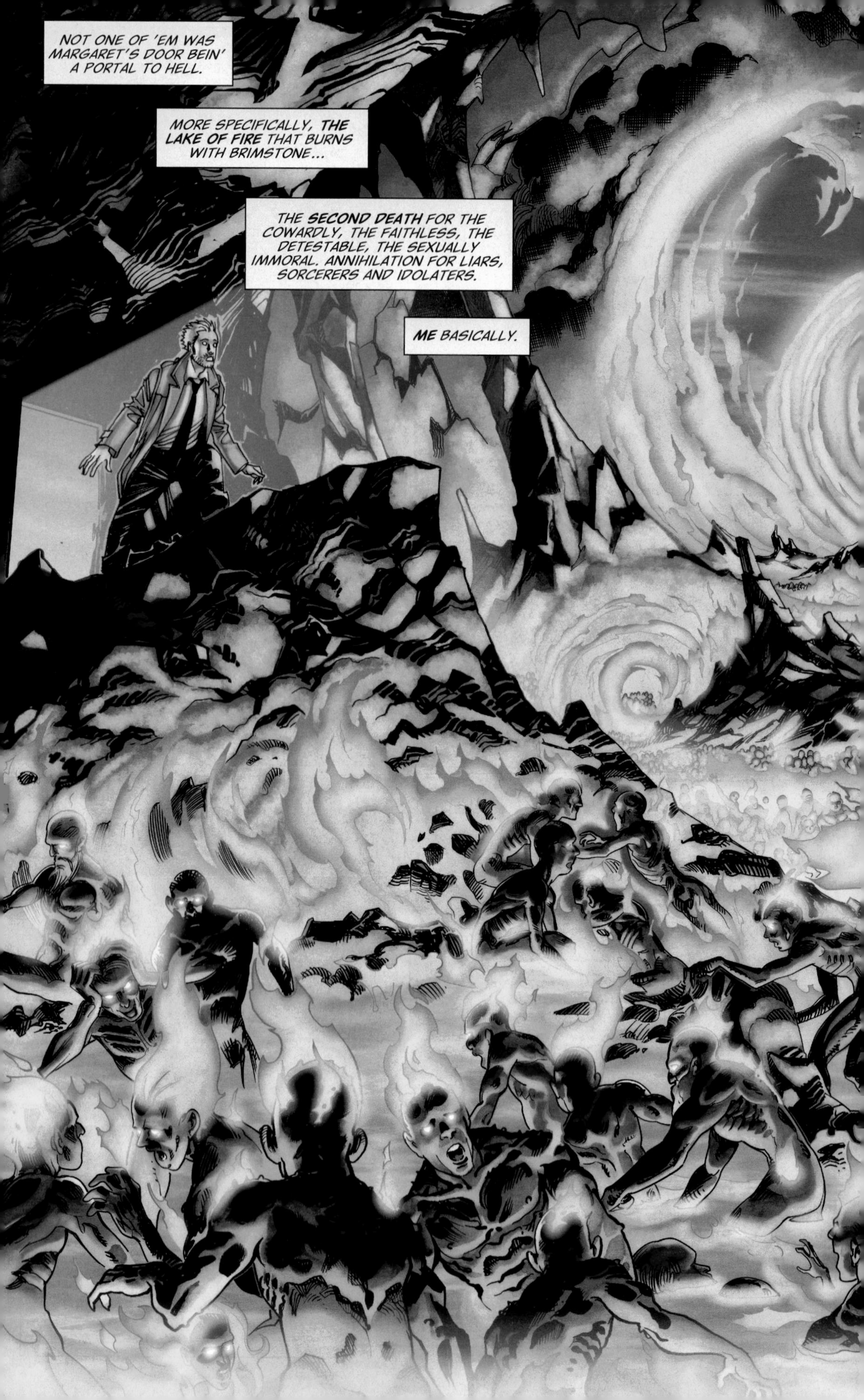
NOT ONE OF 'EM WAS MARGARET'S DOOR BEIN' A PORTAL TO HELL.
MORE SPECIFICALLY, THE LAKE OF FIRE THAT BURNS WITH BRIMSTONE...
THE SECOND DEATH FOR THE COWARDLY, THE FAITHLESS, THE DETESTABLE, THE SEXUALLY IMMORAL. ANNIHILATION FOR LIARS, SORCERERS AND IDOLATERS.
ME BASICALLY.

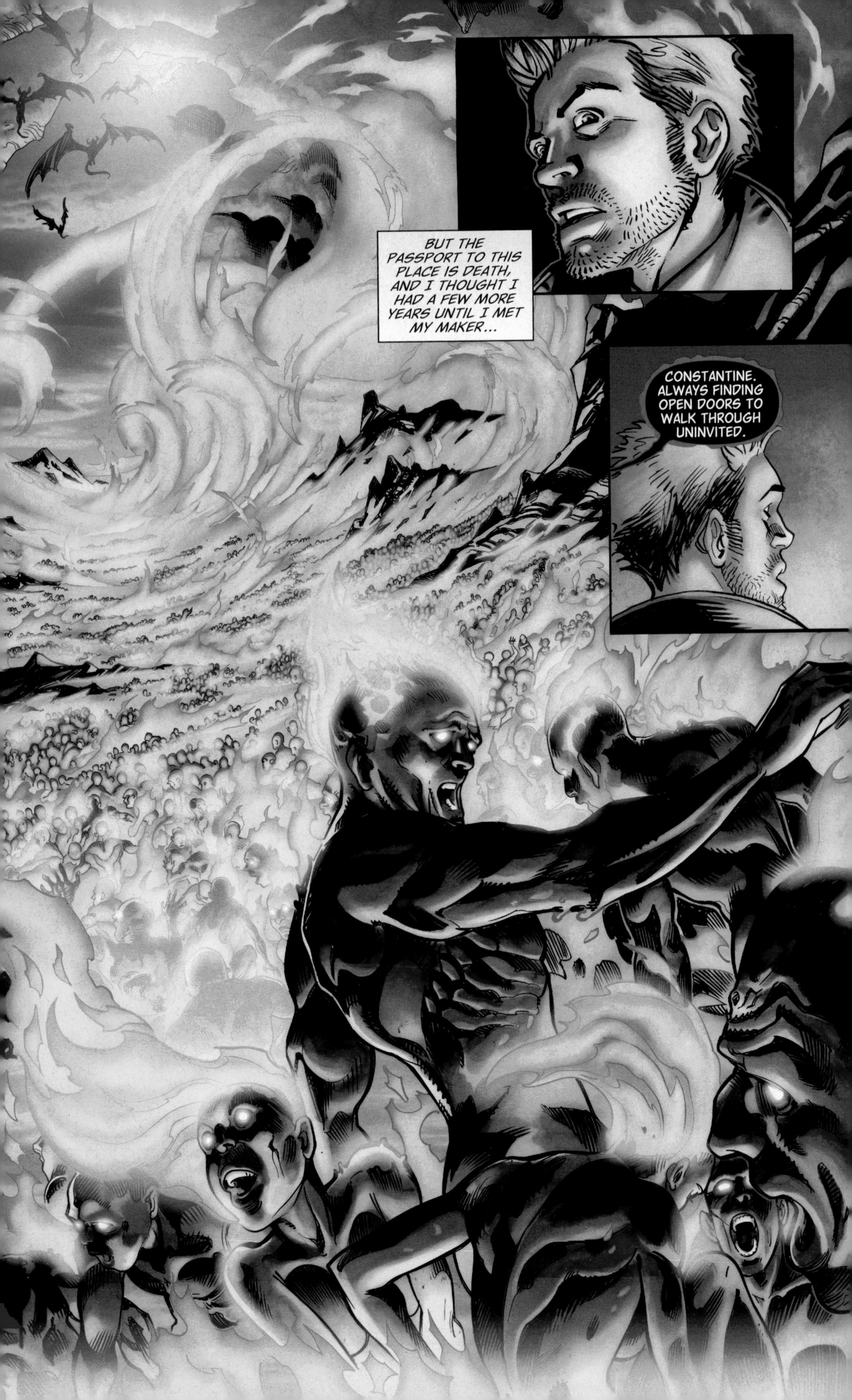
BUT THE PASSPORT TO THIS PLACE IS DEATH, AND I THOUGHT I HAD A FEW MORE YEARS UNTIL I MET MY MAKER...
CONSTANTINE. ALWAYS FINDING OPEN DOORS TO WALK THROUGH UNINVITED.

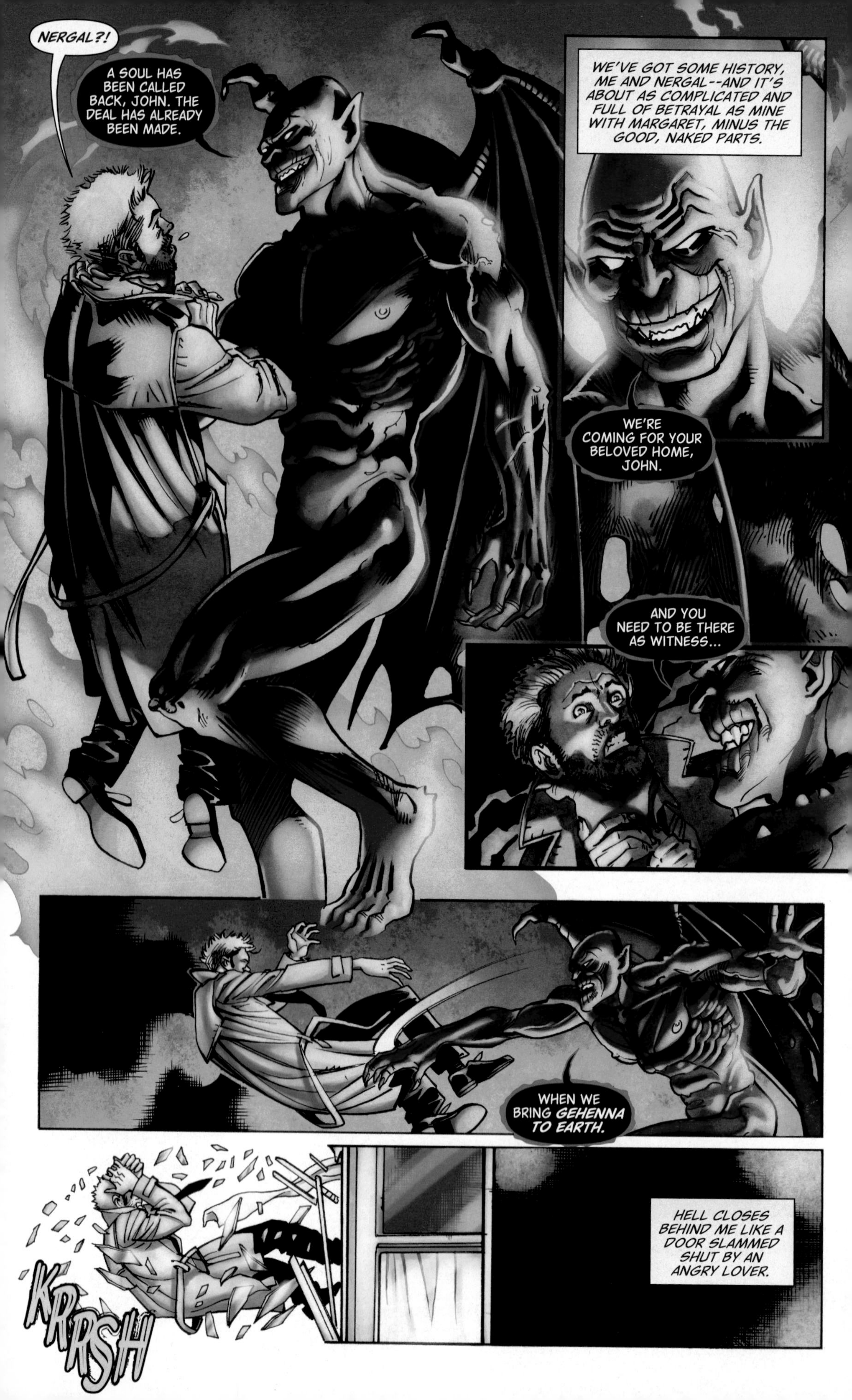
NERGAL?!
A SOUL HAS BEEN CALLED BACK, JOHN. THE DEAL HAS ALREADY BEEN MADE.
WE'VE GOT SOME HISTORY, ME AND NERGAL--AND IT'S ABOUT AS COMPLICATED AND FULL OF BETRAYAL AS MINE WITH MARGARET, MINUS THE GOOD, NAKED PARTS.
WE'RE COMING FOR YOUR BELOVED HOME, JOHN.
AND YOU NEED TO BE THERE AS WITNESS...
WHEN WE BRING *GEHENNA* TO EARTH.
KRRSH
HELL CLOSES BEHIND ME LIKE A DOOR SLAMMED SHUT BY AN ANGRY LOVER.

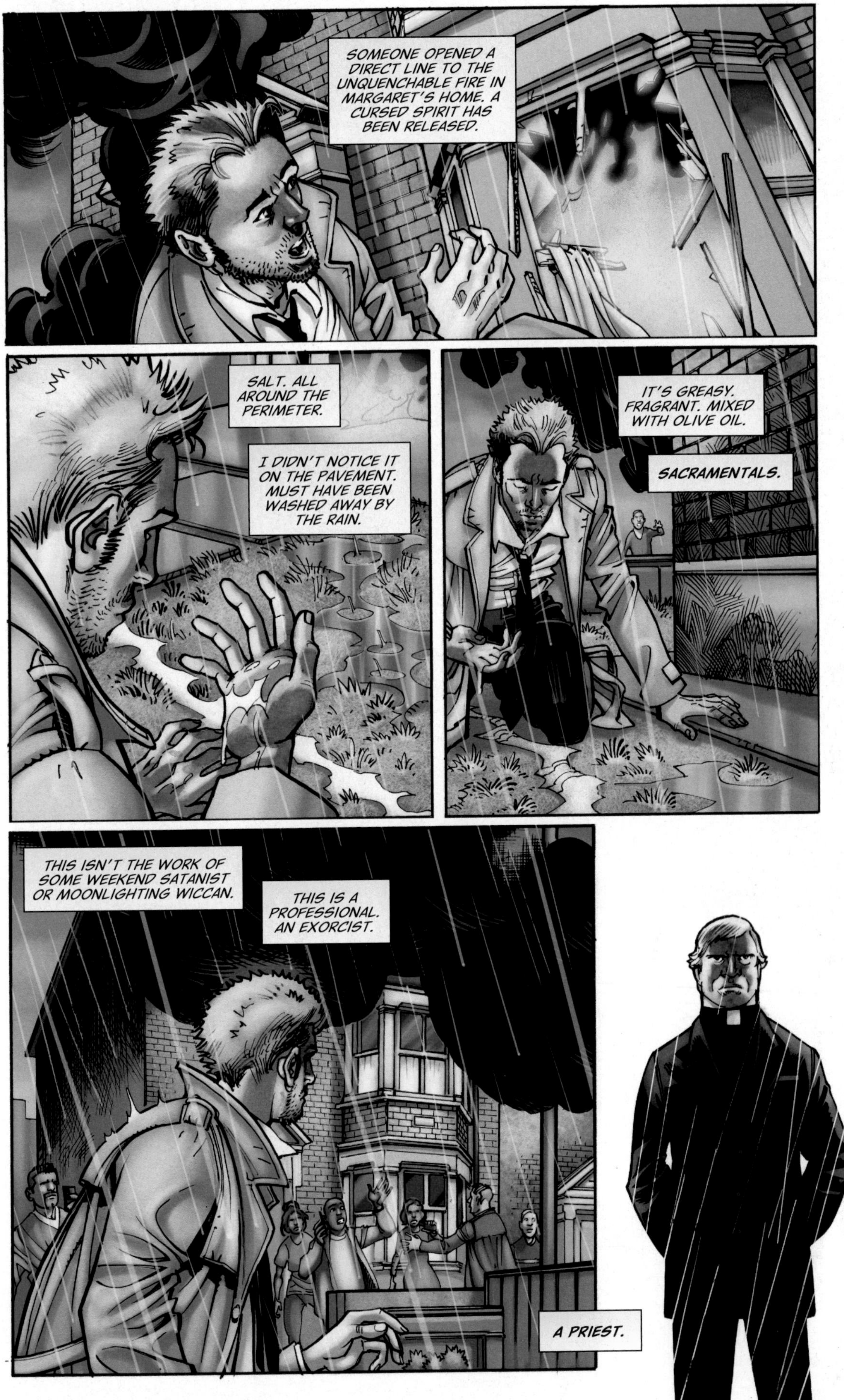
SOMEONE OPENED A DIRECT LINE TO THE UNQUENCHABLE FIRE IN MARGARET'S HOME. A CURSED SPIRIT HAS BEEN RELEASED.
SALT. ALL AROUND THE PERIMETER.
I DIDN'T NOTICE IT ON THE PAVEMENT. MUST HAVE BEEN WASHED AWAY BY THE RAIN.
IT'S GREASY. FRAGRANT. MIXED WITH OLIVE OIL.
SACRAMENTALS.
THIS ISN'T THE WORK OF SOME WEEKEND SATANIST OR MOONLIGHTING WICCAN.
THIS IS A PROFESSIONAL. AN EXORCIST.
A PRIEST.

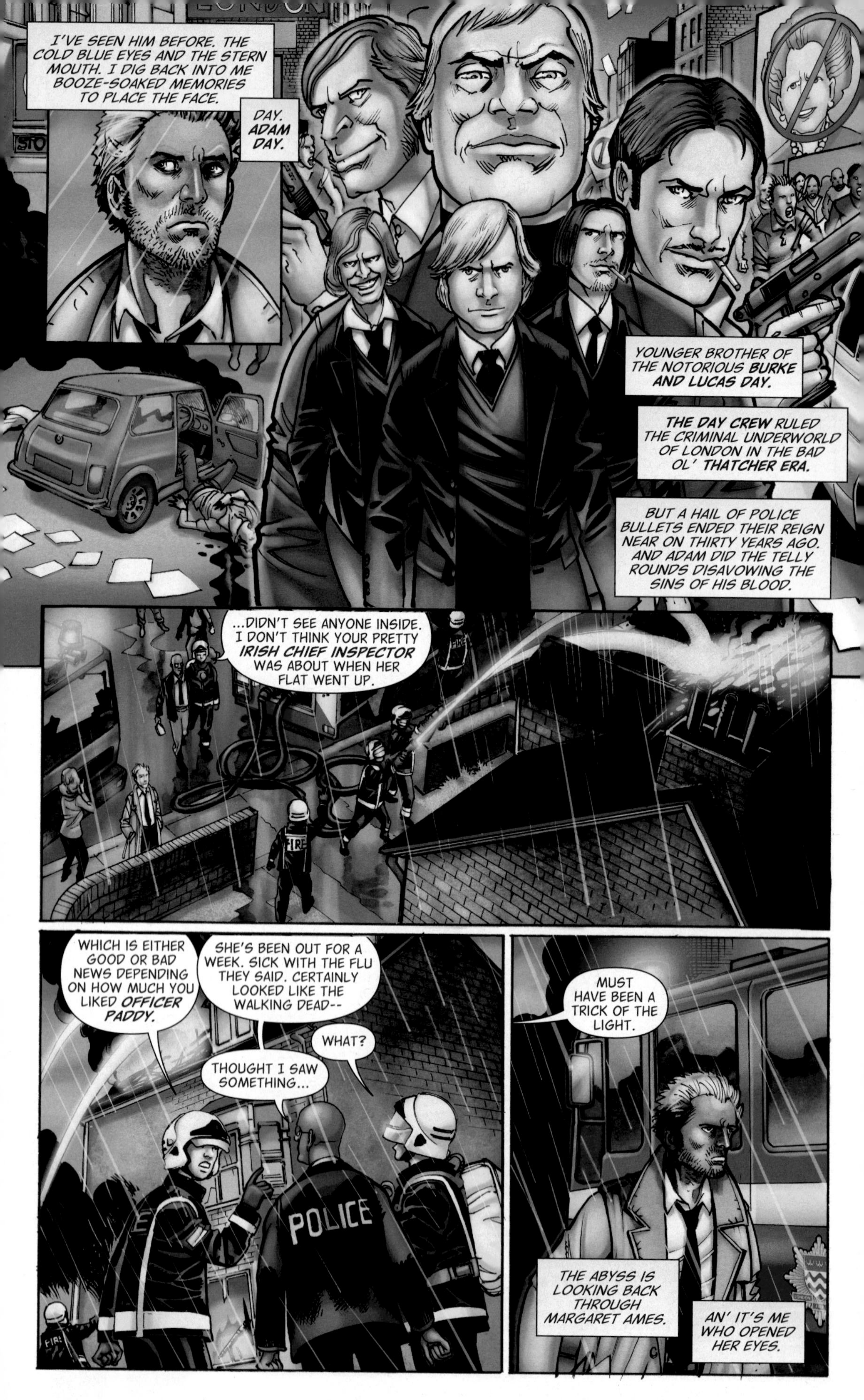
I'VE SEEN HIM BEFORE. THE COLD BLUE EYES AND THE STERN MOUTH. I DIG BACK INTO ME BOOZE-SOAKED MEMORIES TO PLACE THE FACE.
DAY. ADAM DAY.
YOUNGER BROTHER OF THE NOTORIOUS BURKE AND LUCAS DAY.
THE DAY CREW RULED THE CRIMINAL UNDERWORLD OF LONDON IN THE BAD OL' THATCHER ERA.
BUT A HAIL OF POLICE BULLETS ENDED THEIR REIGN NEAR ON THIRTY YEARS AGO. AND ADAM DID THE TELLY ROUNDS DISAVOWING THE SINS OF HIS BLOOD.
...DIDN'T SEE ANYONE INSIDE. I DON'T THINK YOUR PRETTY IRISH CHIEF INSPECTOR WAS ABOUT WHEN HER FLAT WENT UP.
WHICH IS EITHER GOOD OR BAD NEWS DEPENDING ON HOW MUCH YOU LIKED OFFICER PADDY.
SHE'S BEEN OUT FOR A WEEK. SICK WITH THE FLU THEY SAID. CERTAINLY LOOKED LIKE THE WALKING DEAD--
WHAT?
THOUGHT I SAW SOMETHING...
POLICE
MUST HAVE BEEN A TRICK OF THE LIGHT.
THE ABYSS IS LOOKING BACK THROUGH MARGARET AMES.
AN' IT'S ME WHO OPENED HER EYES.

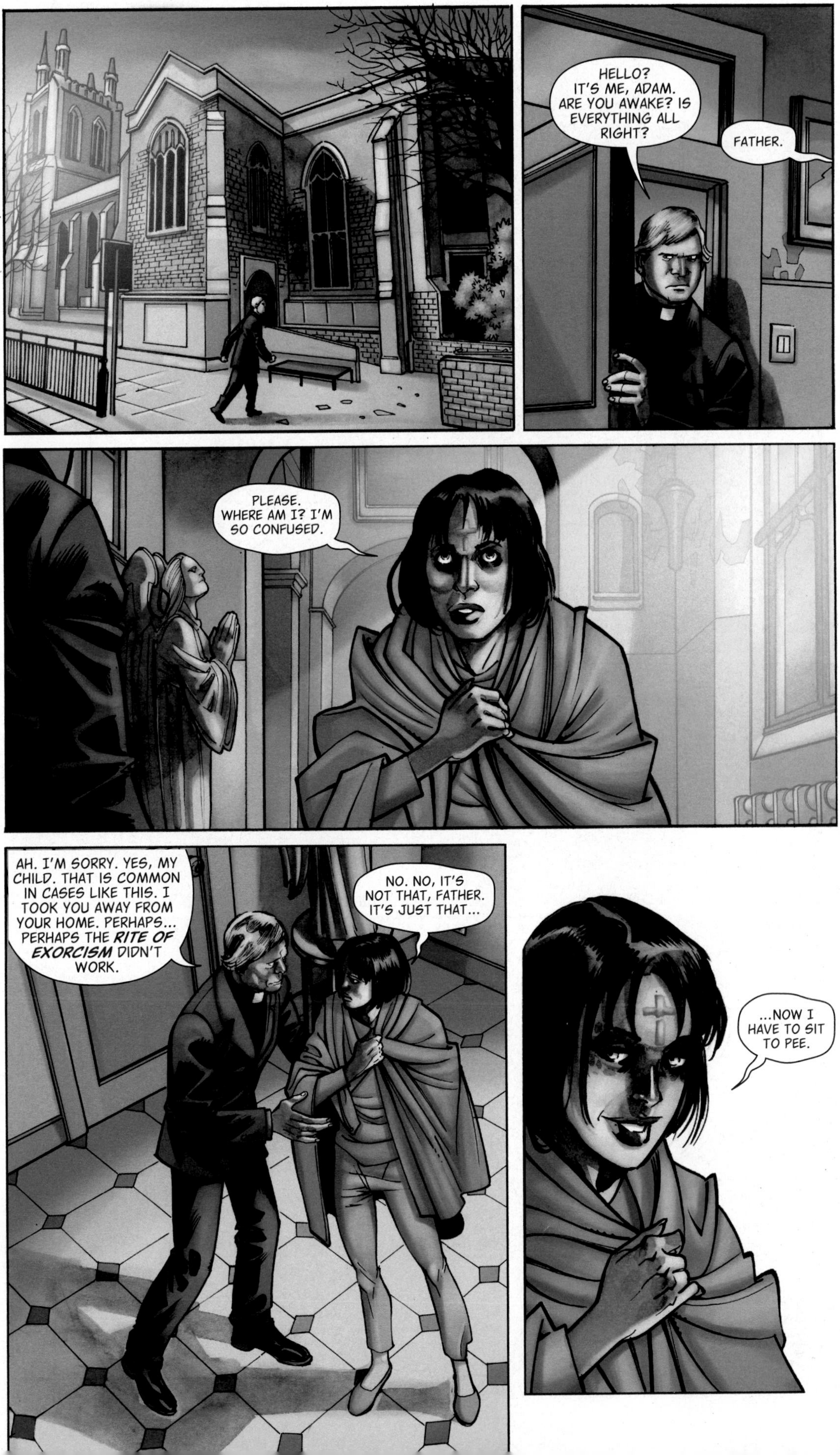
HELLO? IT'S ME, ADAM. ARE YOU AWAKE? IS EVERYTHING ALL RIGHT?
FATHER.
PLEASE. WHERE AM I? I'M SO CONFUSED.
AH. I'M SORRY. YES, MY CHILD. THAT IS COMMON IN CASES LIKE THIS. I TOOK YOU AWAY FROM YOUR HOME. PERHAPS... PERHAPS THE ***RITE OF EXORCISM*** DIDN'T WORK.
NO. NO, IT'S NOT THAT, FATHER. IT'S JUST THAT...
...NOW I HAVE TO SIT TO PEE.

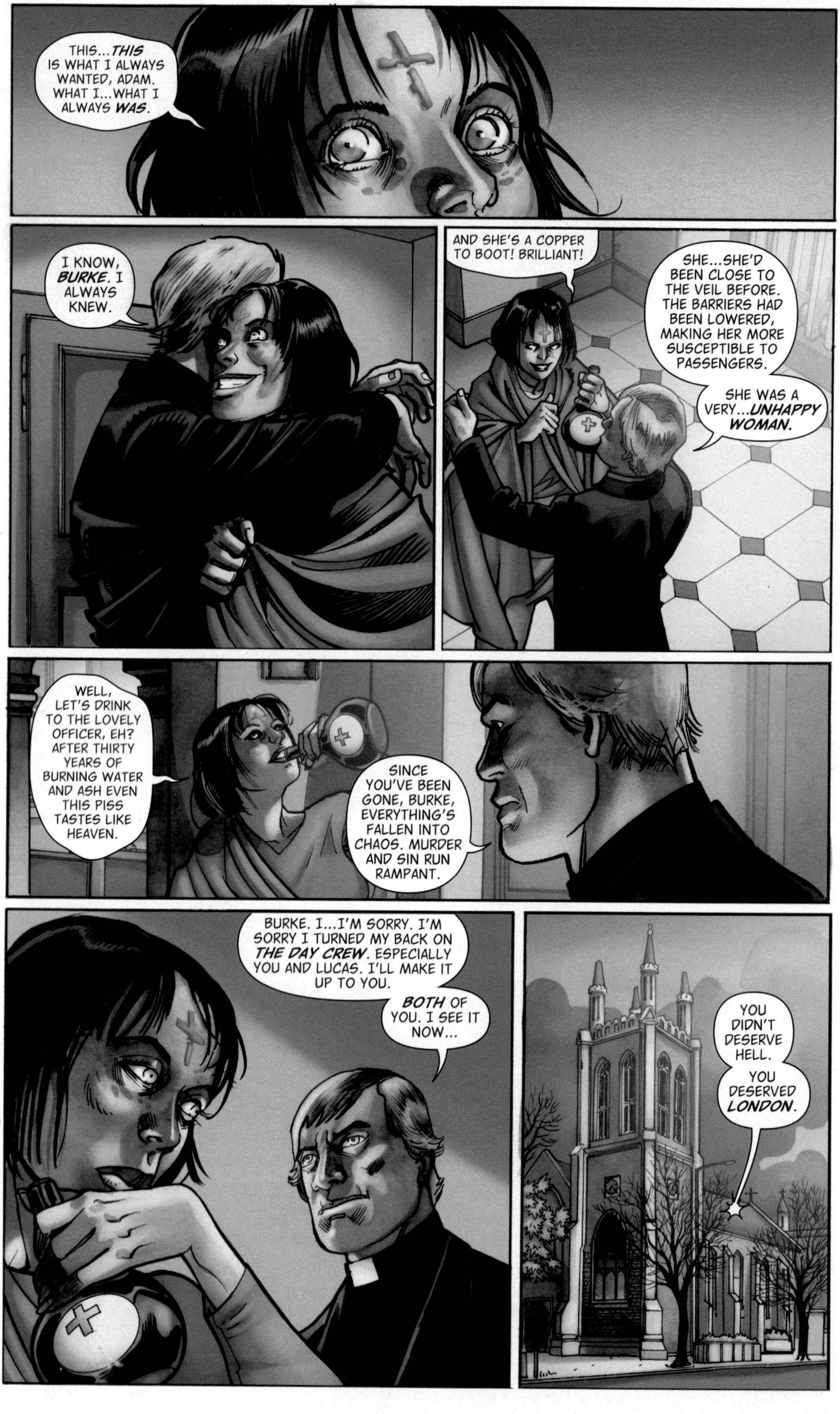
THIS...THIS IS WHAT I ALWAYS WANTED, ADAM. WHAT I...WHAT I ALWAYS WAS.
I KNOW, BURKE. I ALWAYS KNEW.
AND SHE'S A COPPER TO BOOT! BRILLIANT!
SHE...SHE'D BEEN CLOSE TO THE VEIL BEFORE. THE BARRIERS HAD BEEN LOWERED, MAKING HER MORE SUSCEPTIBLE TO PASSENGERS.
SHE WAS A VERY...UNHAPPY WOMAN.
WELL, LET'S DRINK TO THE LOVELY OFFICER, EH? AFTER THIRTY YEARS OF BURNING WATER AND ASH EVEN THIS PISS TASTES LIKE HEAVEN.
SINCE YOU'VE BEEN GONE, BURKE, EVERYTHING'S FALLEN INTO CHAOS. MURDER AND SIN RUN RAMPANT.
BURKE. I...I'M SORRY. I'M SORRY I TURNED MY BACK ON THE DAY CREW. ESPECIALLY YOU AND LUCAS. I'LL MAKE IT UP TO YOU.
BOTH OF YOU. I SEE IT NOW...
YOU DIDN'T DESERVE HELL.
YOU DESERVED LONDON.

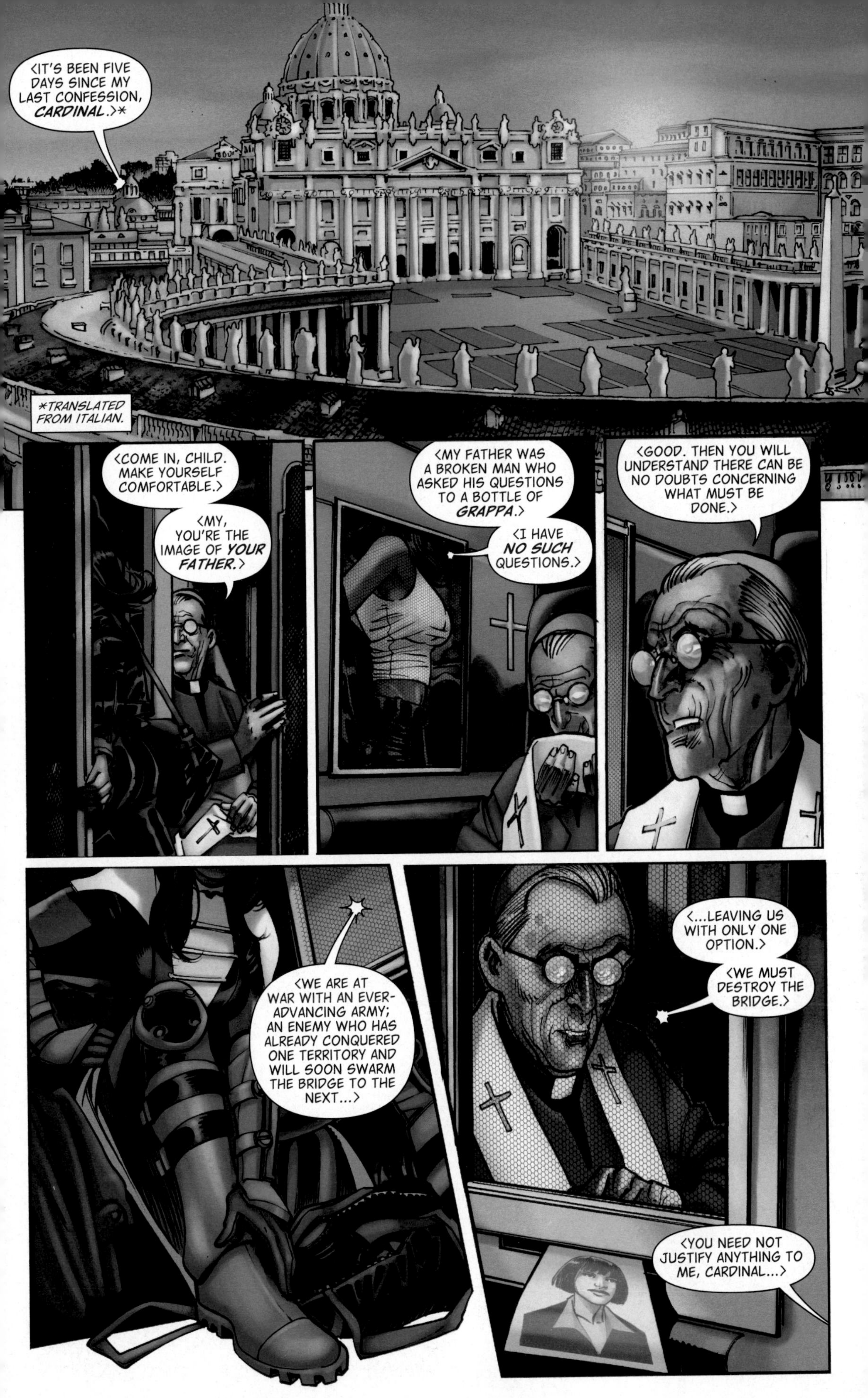
<IT'S BEEN FIVE DAYS SINCE MY LAST CONFESSION, CARDINAL.>*
*TRANSLATED FROM ITALIAN.
<COME IN, CHILD. MAKE YOURSELF COMFORTABLE.>
<MY, YOU'RE THE IMAGE OF YOUR FATHER.>
<MY FATHER WAS A BROKEN MAN WHO ASKED HIS QUESTIONS TO A BOTTLE OF GRAPPA.>
<I HAVE NO SUCH QUESTIONS.>
<GOOD. THEN YOU WILL UNDERSTAND THERE CAN BE NO DOUBTS CONCERNING WHAT MUST BE DONE.>
<WE ARE AT WAR WITH AN EVER-ADVANCING ARMY; AN ENEMY WHO HAS ALREADY CONQUERED ONE TERRITORY AND WILL SOON SWARM THE BRIDGE TO THE NEXT...>
<...LEAVING US WITH ONLY ONE OPTION.>
<WE MUST DESTROY THE BRIDGE.>
<YOU NEED NOT JUSTIFY ANYTHING TO ME, CARDINAL...>

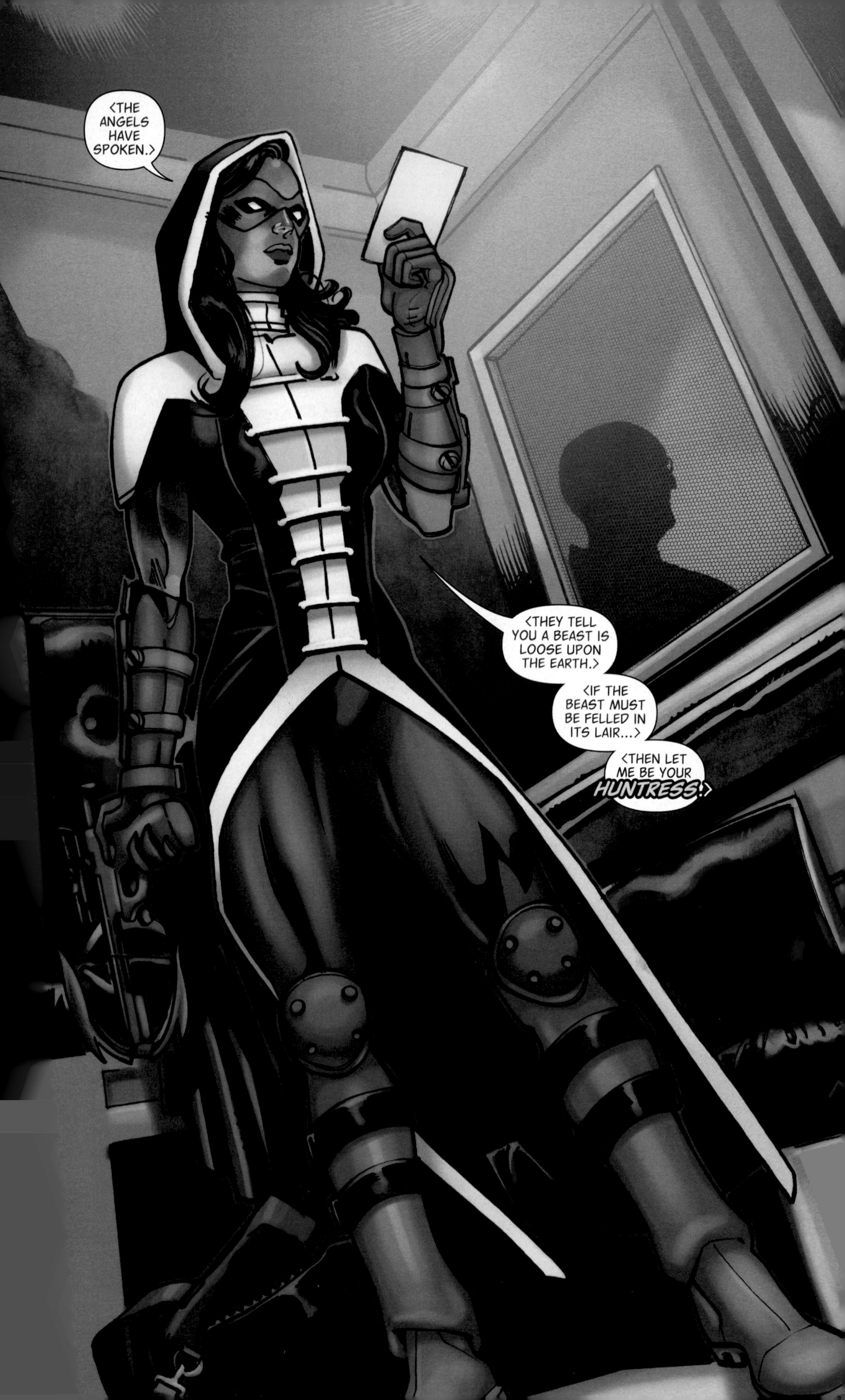
<THE ANGELS HAVE SPOKEN.>
<THEY TELL YOU A BEAST IS LOOSE UPON THE EARTH.>
<IF THE BEAST MUST BE FELLED IN ITS LAIR...>
<THEN LET ME BE YOUR HUNTRESS!>

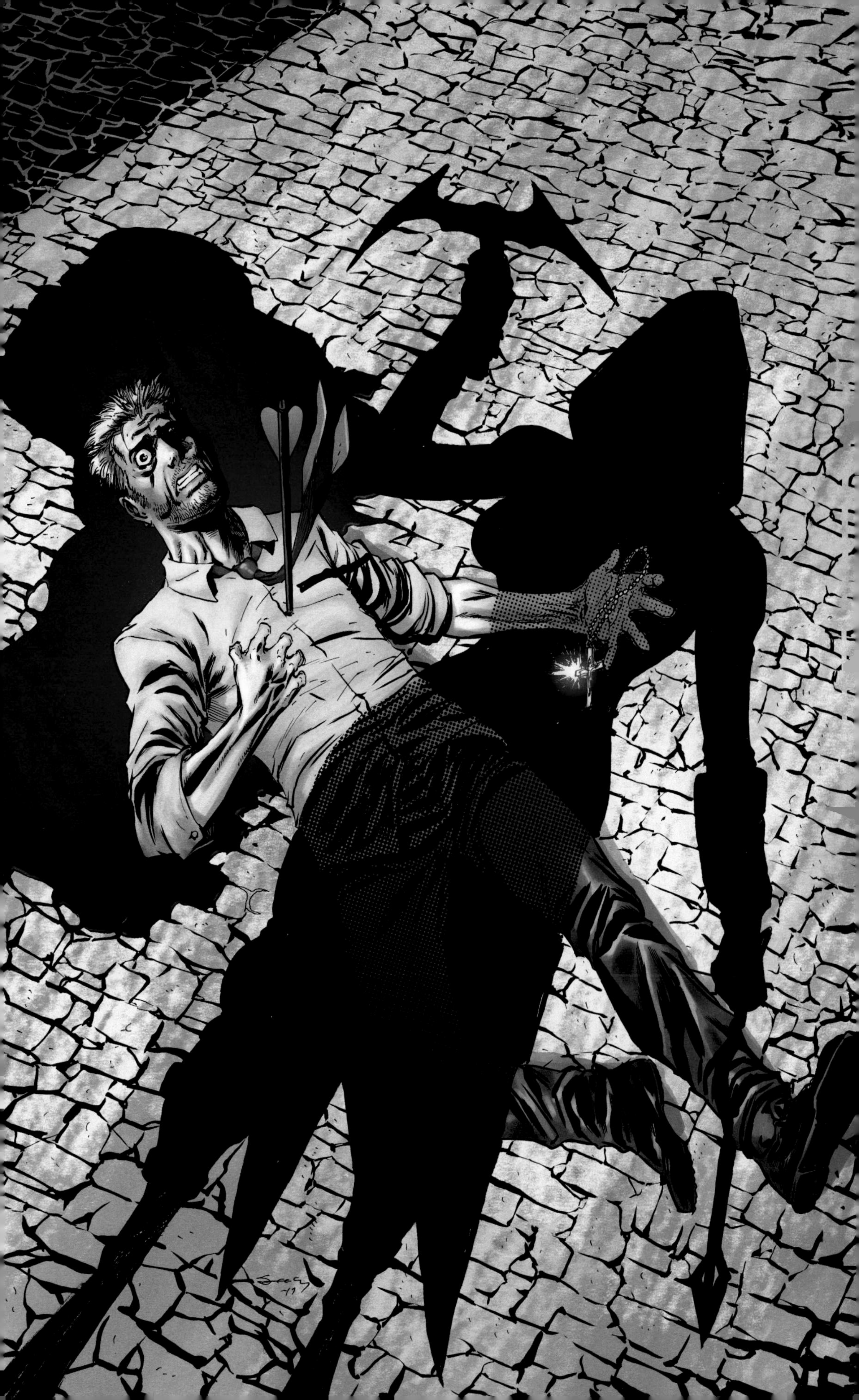

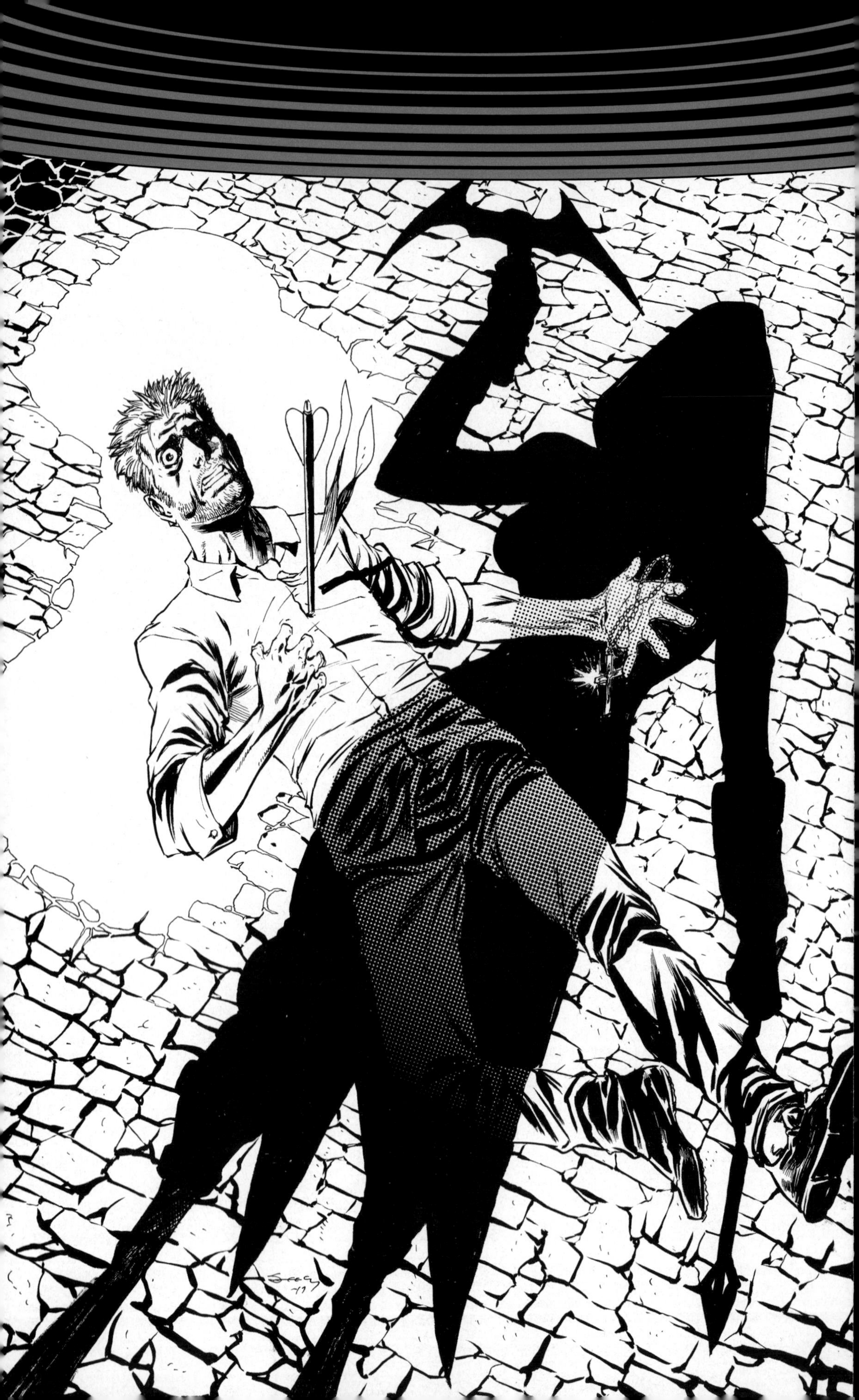

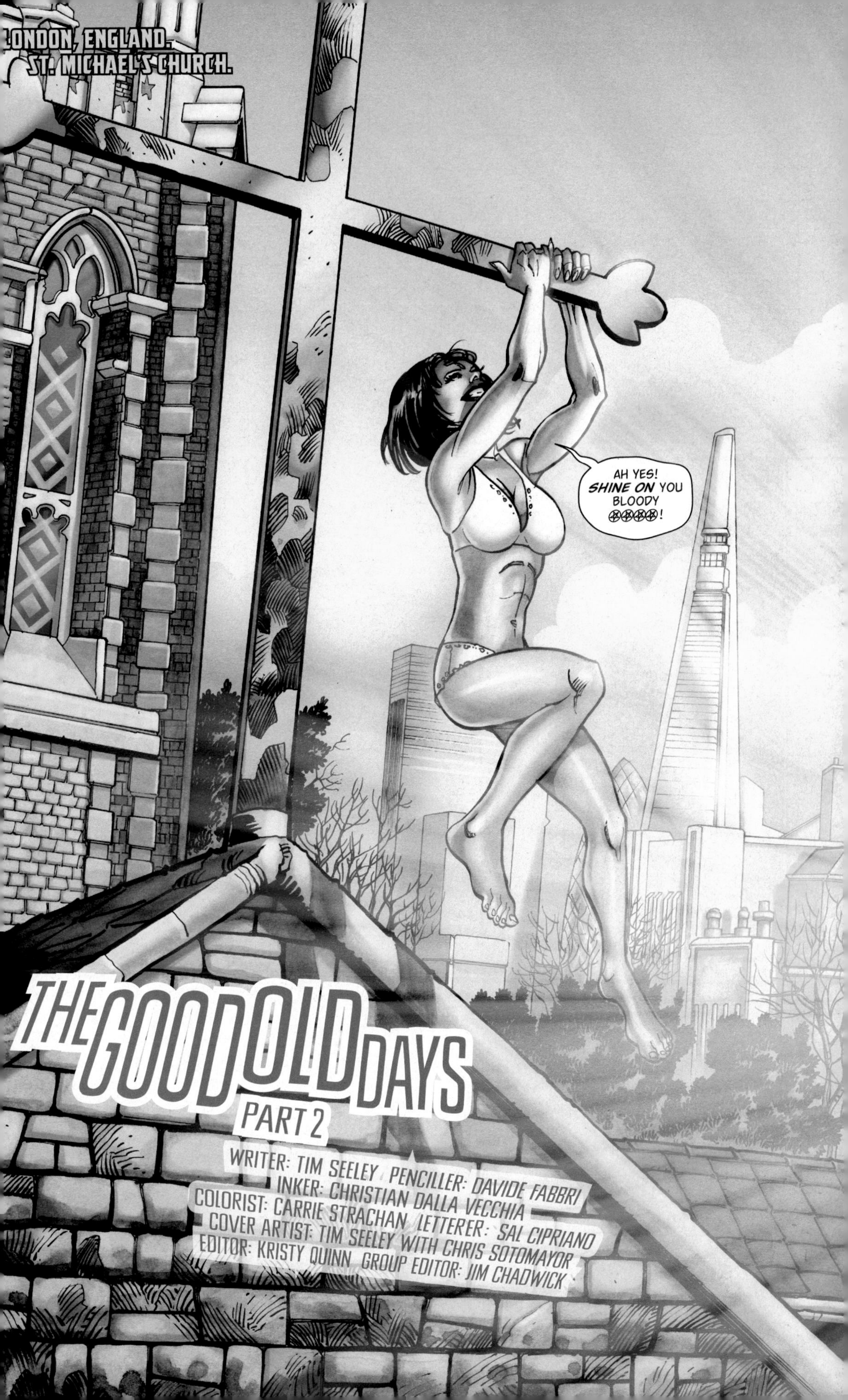
LONDON, ENGLAND.
ST. MICHAEL'S CHURCH.
AH YES! SHINE ON YOU BLOODY ⊗⊗⊗⊗!
THE GOOD OLD DAYS
PART 2
WRITER: TIM SEELEY PENCILLER: DAVIDE FABBRI
INKER: CHRISTIAN DALLA VECCHIA
COLORIST: CARRIE STRACHAN LETTERER: SAL CIPRIANO
COVER ARTIST: TIM SEELEY WITH CHRIS SOTOMAYOR
EDITOR: KRISTY QUINN GROUP EDITOR: JIM CHADWICK

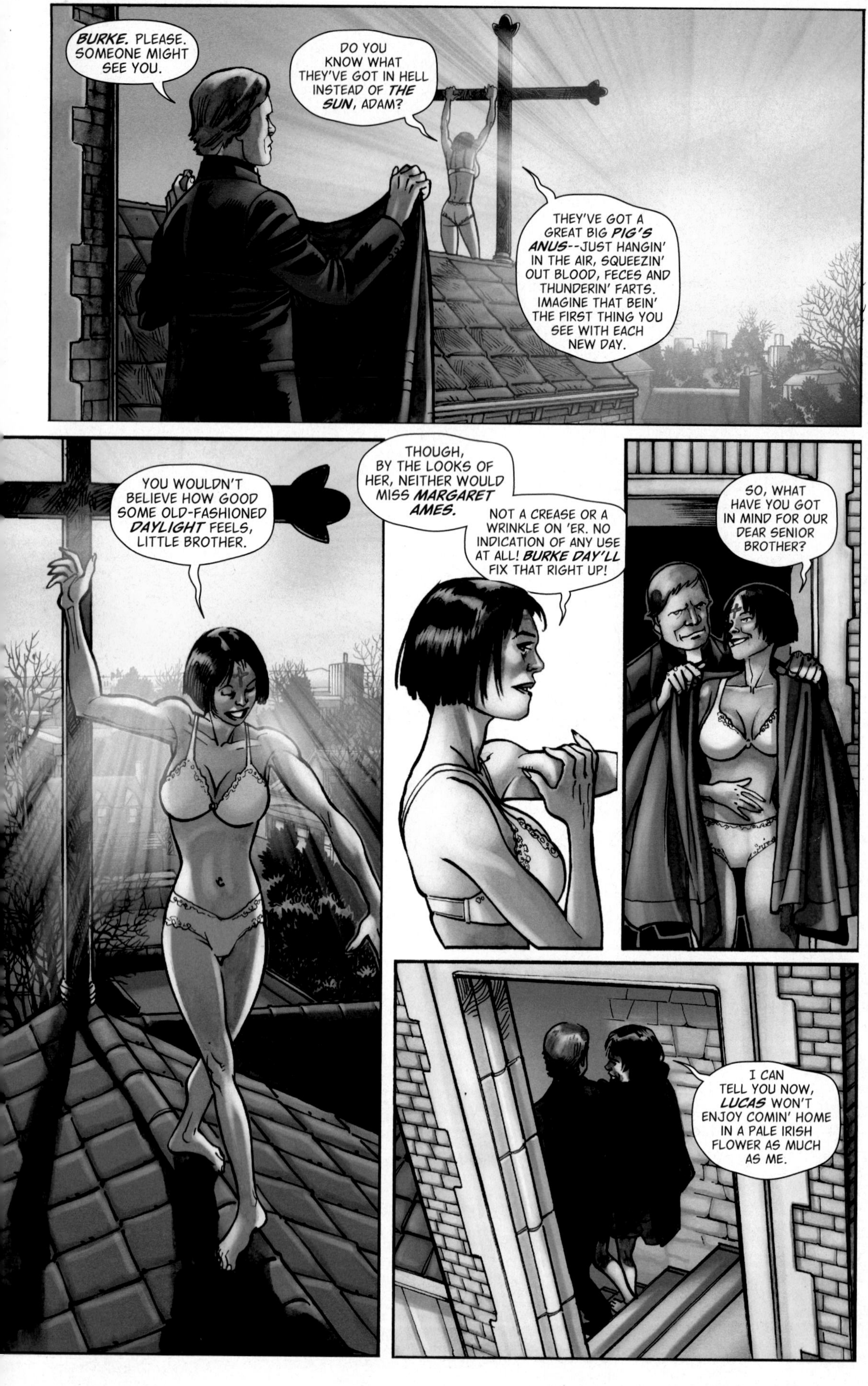
BURKE. PLEASE. SOMEONE MIGHT SEE YOU.
DO YOU KNOW WHAT THEY'VE GOT IN HELL INSTEAD OF THE SUN, ADAM?
THEY'VE GOT A GREAT BIG PIG'S ANUS--JUST HANGIN' IN THE AIR, SQUEEZIN' OUT BLOOD, FECES AND THUNDERIN' FARTS. IMAGINE THAT BEIN' THE FIRST THING YOU SEE WITH EACH NEW DAY.
YOU WOULDN'T BELIEVE HOW GOOD SOME OLD-FASHIONED DAYLIGHT FEELS, LITTLE BROTHER.
THOUGH, BY THE LOOKS OF HER, NEITHER WOULD MISS MARGARET AMES.
NOT A CREASE OR A WRINKLE ON 'ER. NO INDICATION OF ANY USE AT ALL! BURKE DAY'LL FIX THAT RIGHT UP!
SO, WHAT HAVE YOU GOT IN MIND FOR OUR DEAR SENIOR BROTHER?
I CAN TELL YOU NOW, LUCAS WON'T ENJOY COMIN' HOME IN A PALE IRISH FLOWER AS MUCH AS ME.

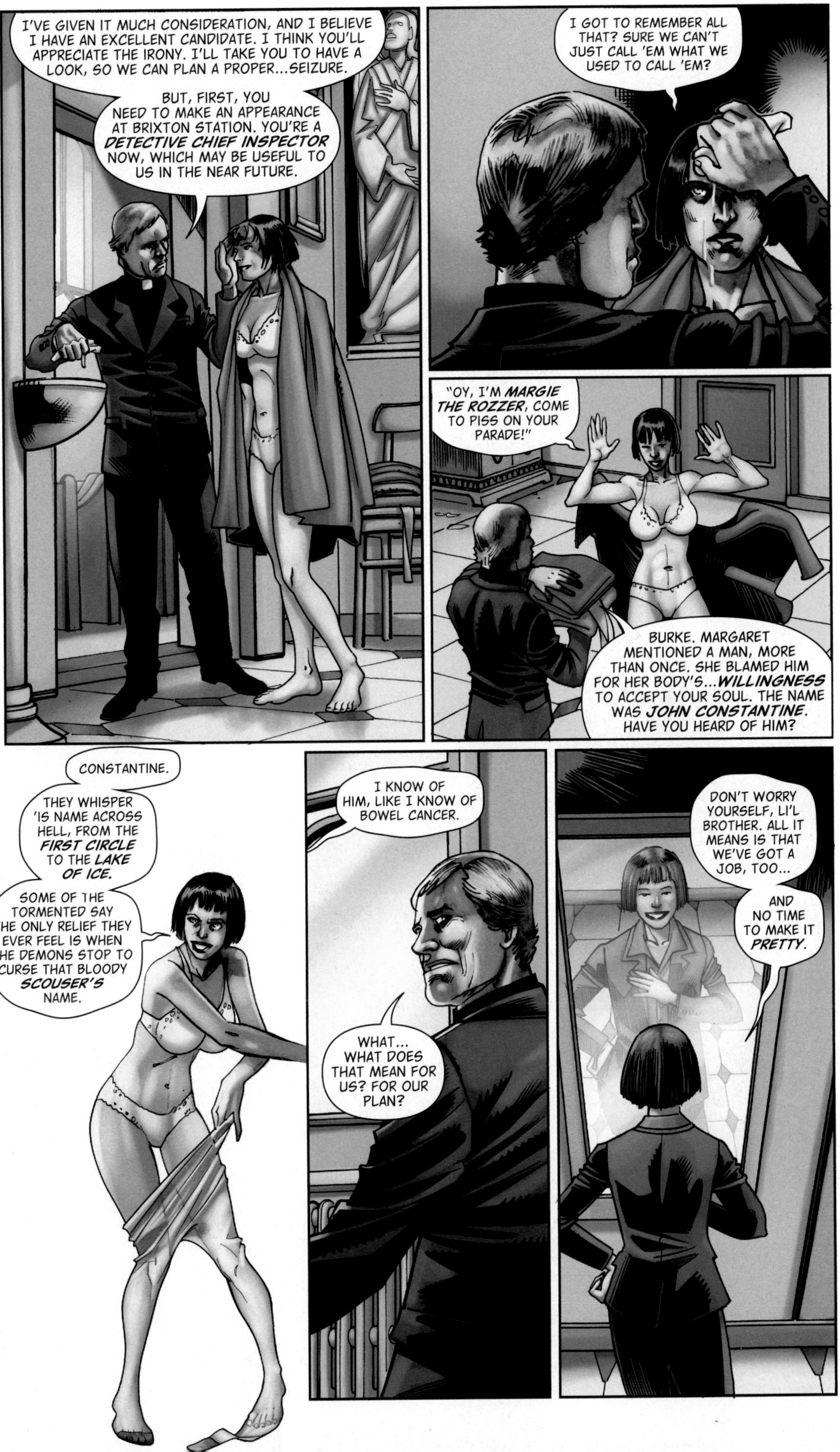
I'VE GIVEN IT MUCH CONSIDERATION, AND I BELIEVE I HAVE AN EXCELLENT CANDIDATE. I THINK YOU'LL APPRECIATE THE IRONY. I'LL TAKE YOU TO HAVE A LOOK, SO WE CAN PLAN A PROPER...SEIZURE.
BUT, FIRST, YOU NEED TO MAKE AN APPEARANCE AT BRIXTON STATION. YOU'RE A DETECTIVE CHIEF INSPECTOR NOW, WHICH MAY BE USEFUL TO US IN THE NEAR FUTURE.
I GOT TO REMEMBER ALL THAT? SURE WE CAN'T JUST CALL 'EM WHAT WE USED TO CALL 'EM?
"OY, I'M MARGIE THE ROZZER, COME TO PISS ON YOUR PARADE!"
BURKE. MARGARET MENTIONED A MAN, MORE THAN ONCE. SHE BLAMED HIM FOR HER BODY'S...WILLINGNESS TO ACCEPT YOUR SOUL. THE NAME WAS JOHN CONSTANTINE. HAVE YOU HEARD OF HIM?
CONSTANTINE.
THEY WHISPER 'IS NAME ACROSS HELL, FROM THE FIRST CIRCLE TO THE LAKE OF ICE.
SOME OF THE TORMENTED SAY THE ONLY RELIEF THEY EVER FEEL IS WHEN THE DEMONS STOP TO CURSE THAT BLOODY SCOUSER'S NAME.
I KNOW OF HIM, LIKE I KNOW OF BOWEL CANCER.
WHAT... WHAT DOES THAT MEAN FOR US? FOR OUR PLAN?
DON'T WORRY YOURSELF, LI'L BROTHER. ALL IT MEANS IS THAT WE'VE GOT A JOB, TOO...
AND NO TIME TO MAKE IT PRETTY.

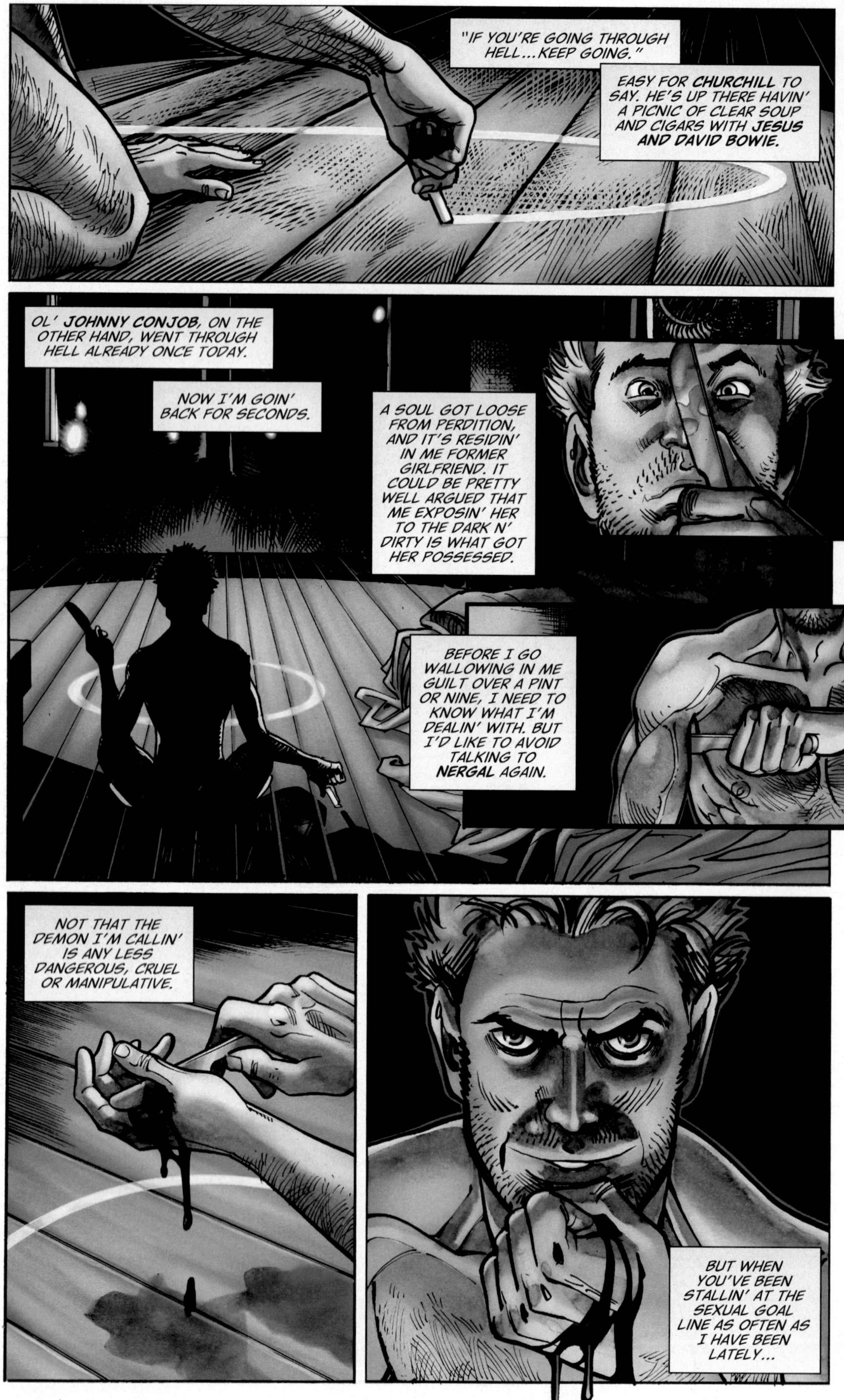
"IF YOU'RE GOING THROUGH HELL...KEEP GOING."
EASY FOR CHURCHILL TO SAY. HE'S UP THERE HAVIN' A PICNIC OF CLEAR SOUP AND CIGARS WITH JESUS AND DAVID BOWIE.
OL' JOHNNY CONJOB, ON THE OTHER HAND, WENT THROUGH HELL ALREADY ONCE TODAY.
NOW I'M GOIN' BACK FOR SECONDS.
A SOUL GOT LOOSE FROM PERDITION, AND IT'S RESIDIN' IN ME FORMER GIRLFRIEND. IT COULD BE PRETTY WELL ARGUED THAT ME EXPOSIN' HER TO THE DARK N' DIRTY IS WHAT GOT HER POSSESSED.
BEFORE I GO WALLOWING IN ME GUILT OVER A PINT OR NINE, I NEED TO KNOW WHAT I'M DEALIN' WITH. BUT I'D LIKE TO AVOID TALKING TO NERGAL AGAIN.
NOT THAT THE DEMON I'M CALLIN' IS ANY LESS DANGEROUS, CRUEL OR MANIPULATIVE.
BUT WHEN YOU'VE BEEN STALLIN' AT THE SEXUAL GOAL LINE AS OFTEN AS I HAVE BEEN LATELY...

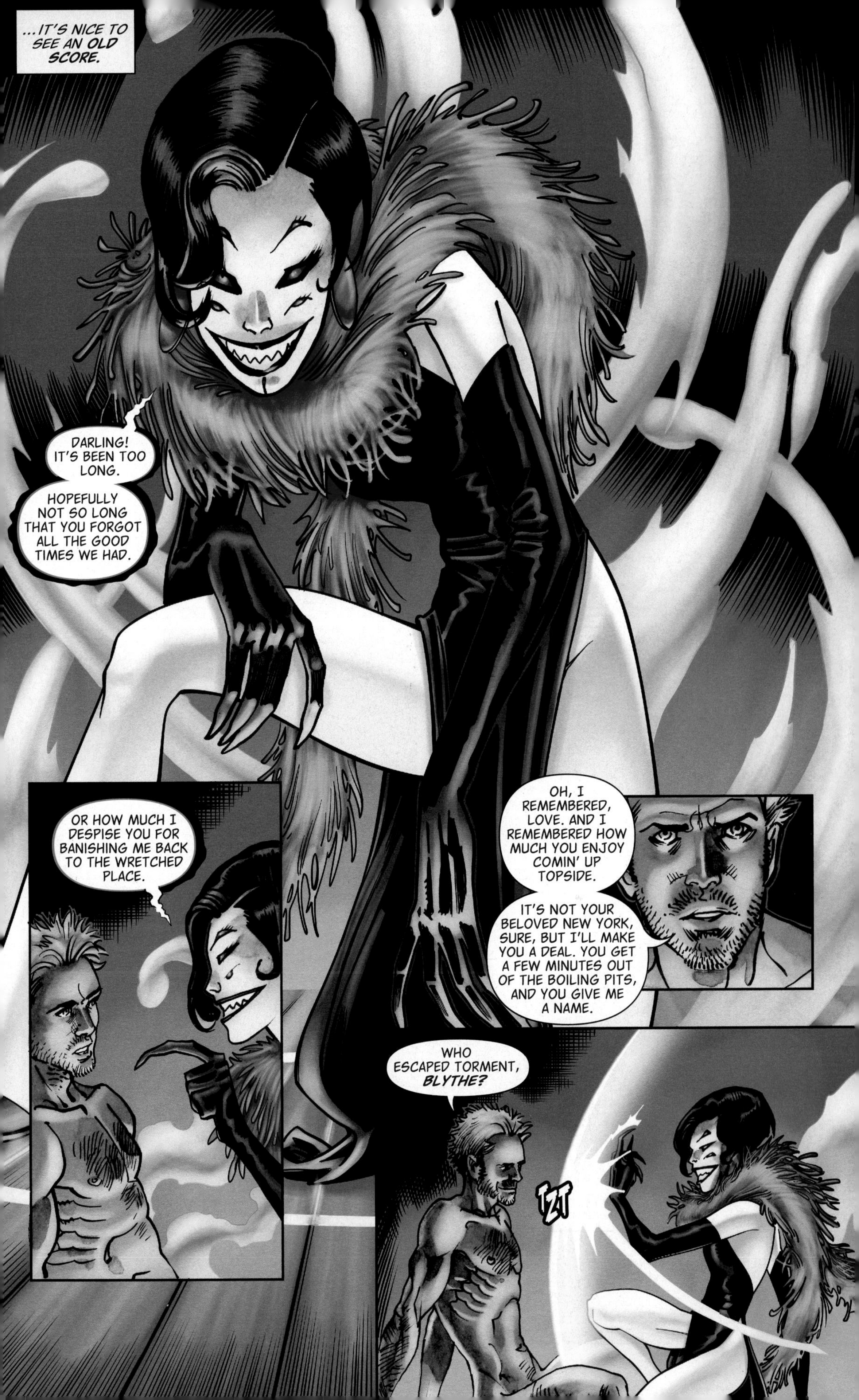

...IT'S NICE TO SEE AN OLD SCORE.
DARLING! IT'S BEEN TOO LONG.
HOPEFULLY NOT SO LONG THAT YOU FORGOT ALL THE GOOD TIMES WE HAD.
OR HOW MUCH I DESPISE YOU FOR BANISHING ME BACK TO THE WRETCHED PLACE.
OH, I REMEMBERED, LOVE. AND I REMEMBERED HOW MUCH YOU ENJOY COMIN' UP TOPSIDE.
IT'S NOT YOUR BELOVED NEW YORK, SURE, BUT I'LL MAKE YOU A DEAL. YOU GET A FEW MINUTES OUT OF THE BOILING PITS, AND YOU GIVE ME A NAME.
WHO ESCAPED TORMENT, BLYTHE?
TZT

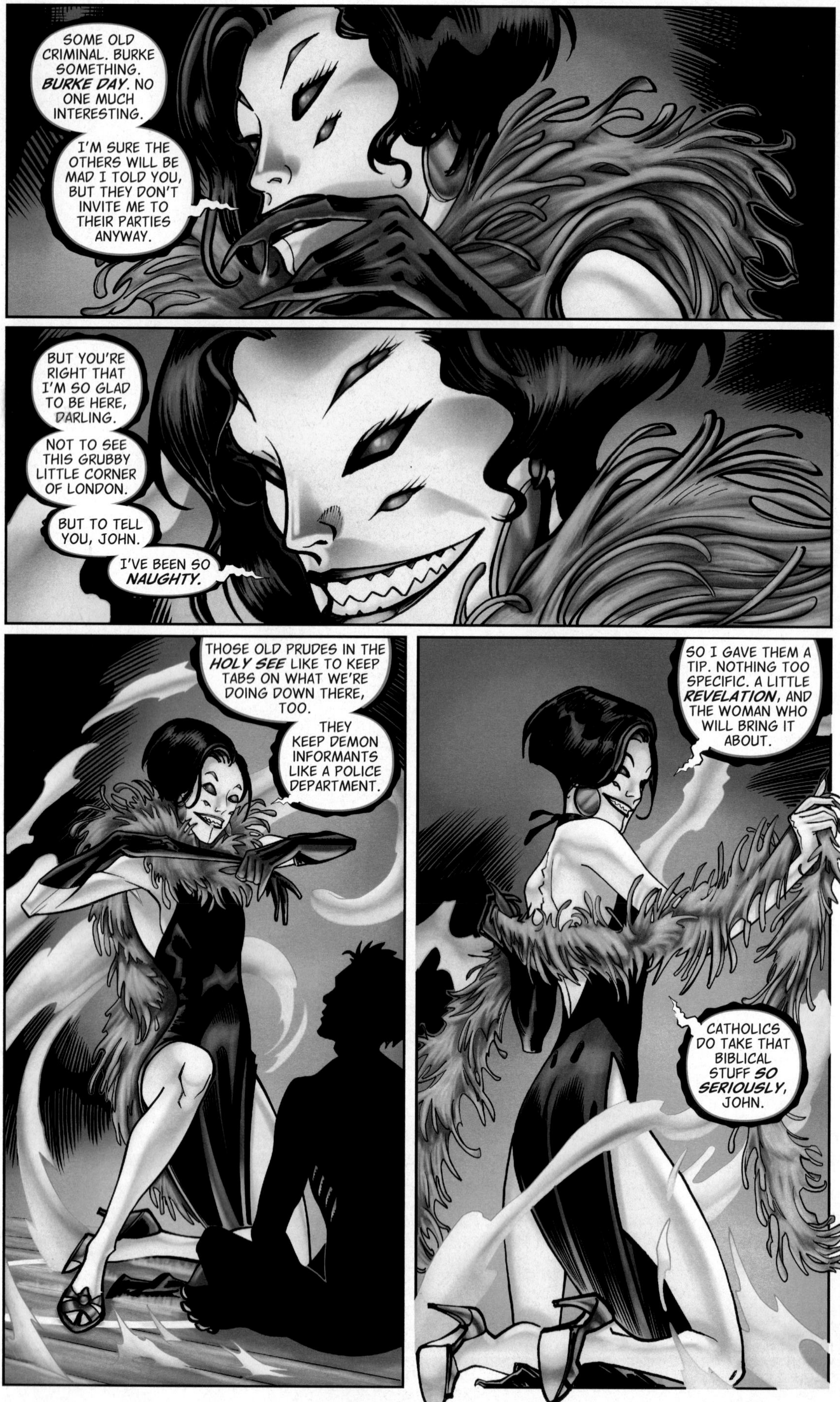

SOME OLD CRIMINAL. BURKE SOMETHING. BURKE DAY. NO ONE MUCH INTERESTING.
I'M SURE THE OTHERS WILL BE MAD I TOLD YOU, BUT THEY DON'T INVITE ME TO THEIR PARTIES ANYWAY.
BUT YOU'RE RIGHT THAT I'M SO GLAD TO BE HERE, DARLING.
NOT TO SEE THIS GRUBBY LITTLE CORNER OF LONDON.
BUT TO TELL YOU, JOHN.
I'VE BEEN SO NAUGHTY.
THOSE OLD PRUDES IN THE HOLY SEE LIKE TO KEEP TABS ON WHAT WE'RE DOING DOWN THERE, TOO.
THEY KEEP DEMON INFORMANTS LIKE A POLICE DEPARTMENT.
SO I GAVE THEM A TIP. NOTHING TOO SPECIFIC. A LITTLE REVELATION, AND THE WOMAN WHO WILL BRING IT ABOUT.
CATHOLICS DO TAKE THAT BIBLICAL STUFF SO SERIOUSLY, JOHN.

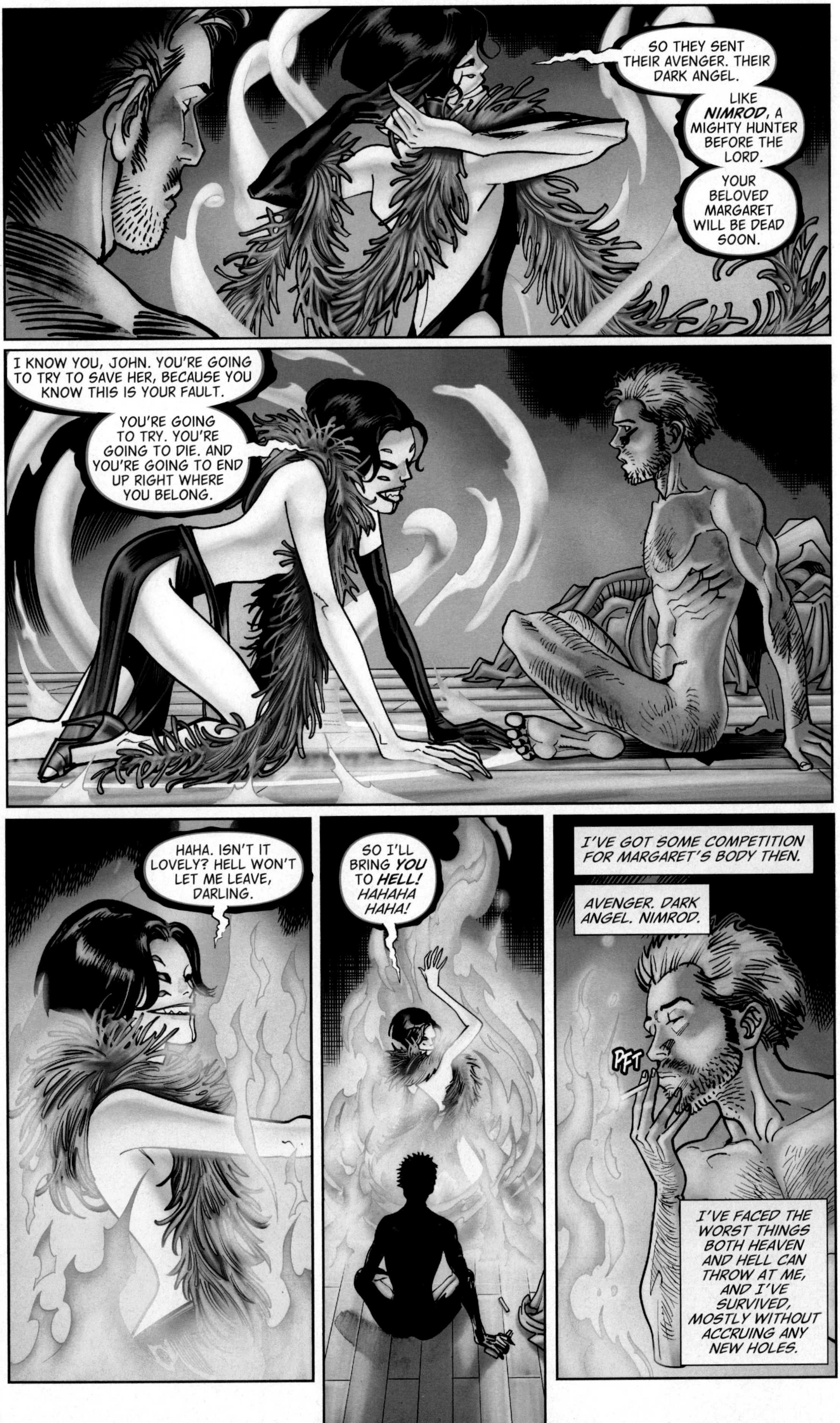
SO THEY SENT THEIR AVENGER. THEIR DARK ANGEL.
LIKE NIMROD, A MIGHTY HUNTER BEFORE THE LORD.
YOUR BELOVED MARGARET WILL BE DEAD SOON.
I KNOW YOU, JOHN. YOU'RE GOING TO TRY TO SAVE HER, BECAUSE YOU KNOW THIS IS YOUR FAULT.
YOU'RE GOING TO TRY. YOU'RE GOING TO DIE. AND YOU'RE GOING TO END UP RIGHT WHERE YOU BELONG.
HAHA. ISN'T IT LOVELY? HELL WON'T LET ME LEAVE, DARLING.
SO I'LL BRING YOU TO HELL! HAHAHA HAHA!
I'VE GOT SOME COMPETITION FOR MARGARET'S BODY THEN.
AVENGER. DARK ANGEL. NIMROD.
PFT
I'VE FACED THE WORST THINGS BOTH HEAVEN AND HELL CAN THROW AT ME, AND I'VE SURVIVED, MOSTLY WITHOUT ACCRUING ANY NEW HOLES.

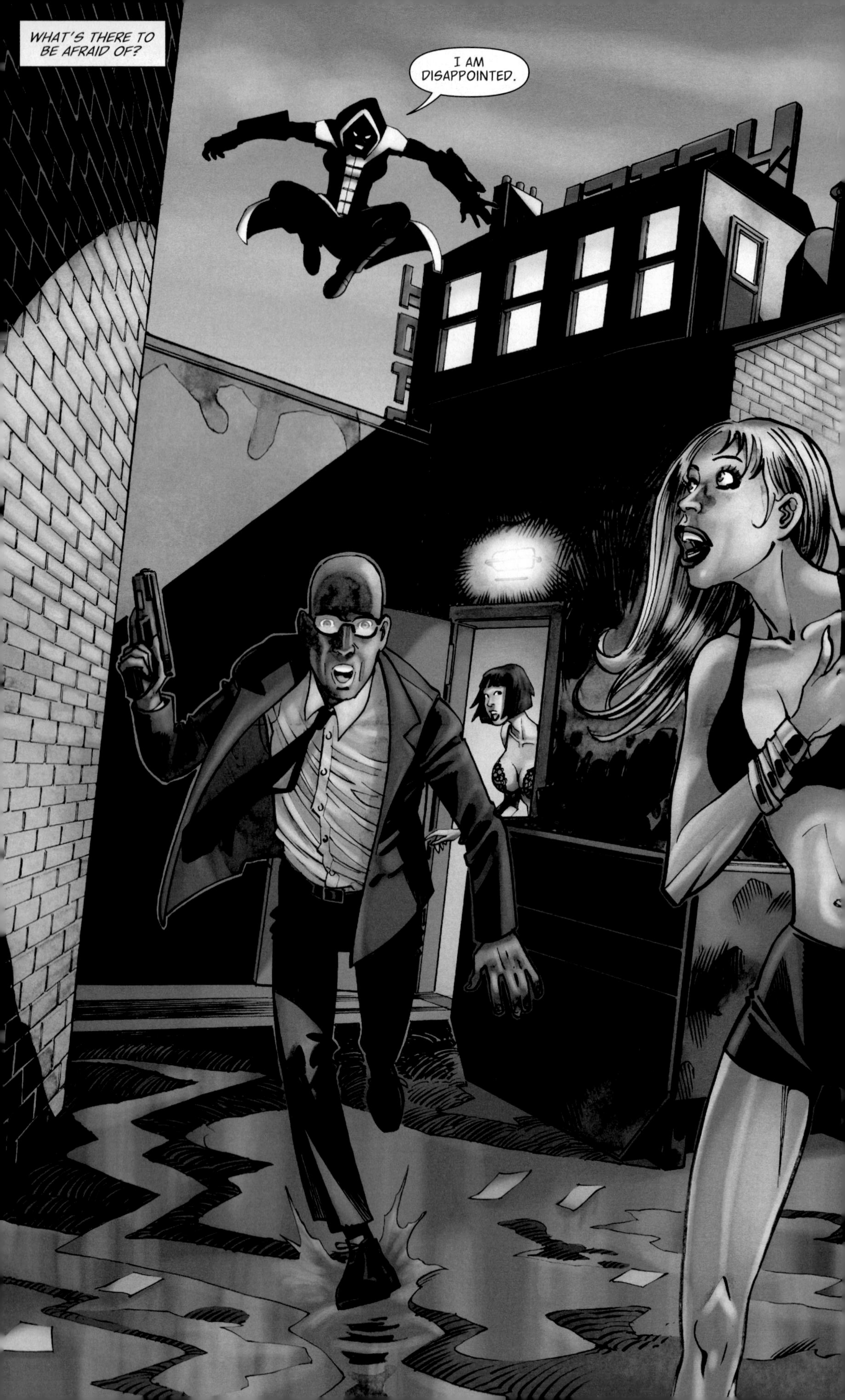
WHAT'S THERE TO BE AFRAID OF?
I AM DISAPPOINTED.

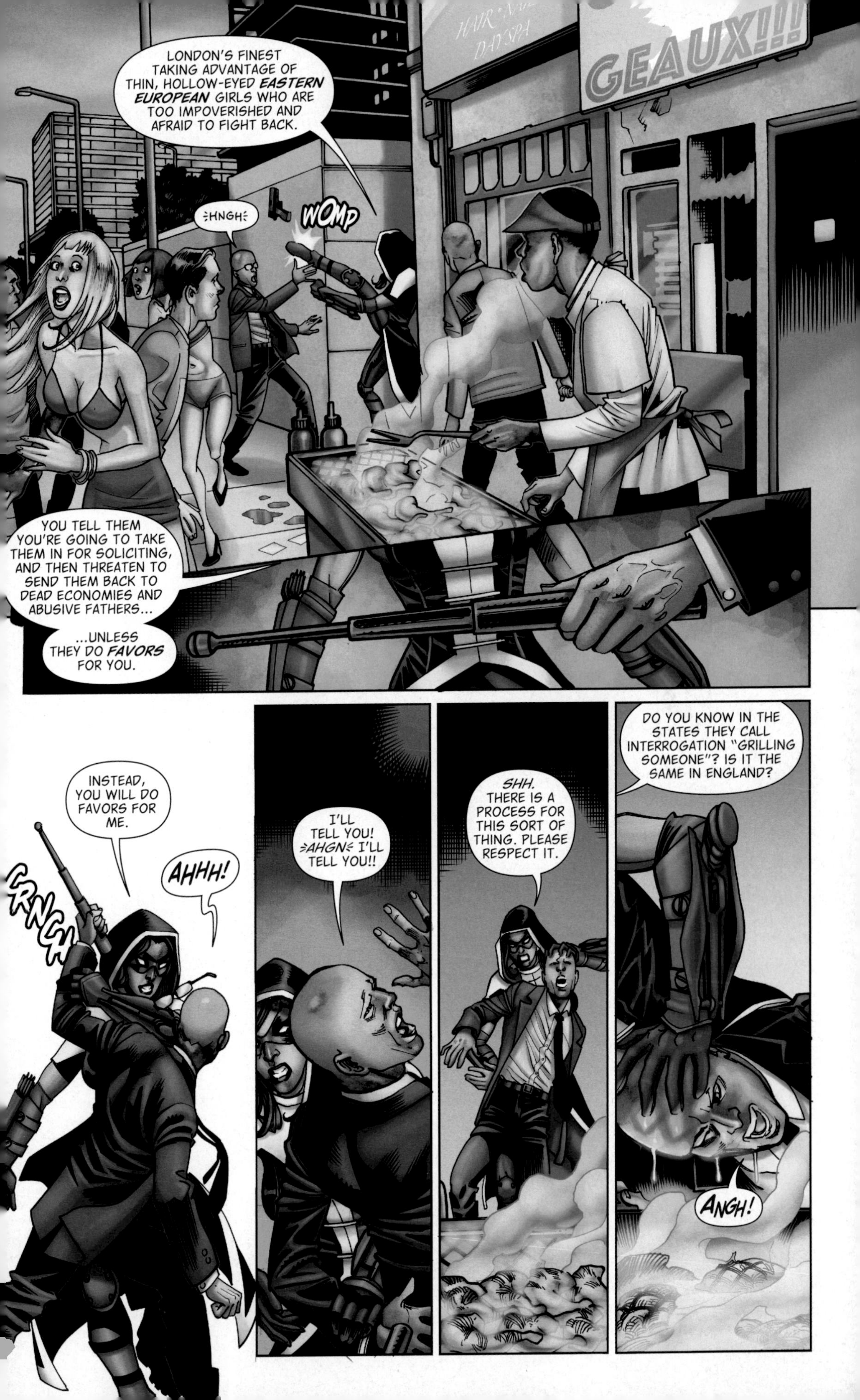
HAIR + NAIL DAY SPA
GEAUX!!!
LONDON'S FINEST TAKING ADVANTAGE OF THIN, HOLLOW-EYED **EASTERN EUROPEAN** GIRLS WHO ARE TOO IMPOVERISHED AND AFRAID TO FIGHT BACK.
HNGH
WOMP
YOU TELL THEM YOU'RE GOING TO TAKE THEM IN FOR SOLICITING, AND THEN THREATEN TO SEND THEM BACK TO DEAD ECONOMIES AND ABUSIVE FATHERS...
...UNLESS THEY DO **FAVORS** FOR YOU.
INSTEAD, YOU WILL DO FAVORS FOR ME.
CRNCH
AHHH!
I'LL TELL YOU! AHGN I'LL TELL YOU!!
SHH. THERE IS A PROCESS FOR THIS SORT OF THING. PLEASE RESPECT IT.
DO YOU KNOW IN THE STATES THEY CALL INTERROGATION "GRILLING SOMEONE"? IS IT THE SAME IN ENGLAND?
ANGH!

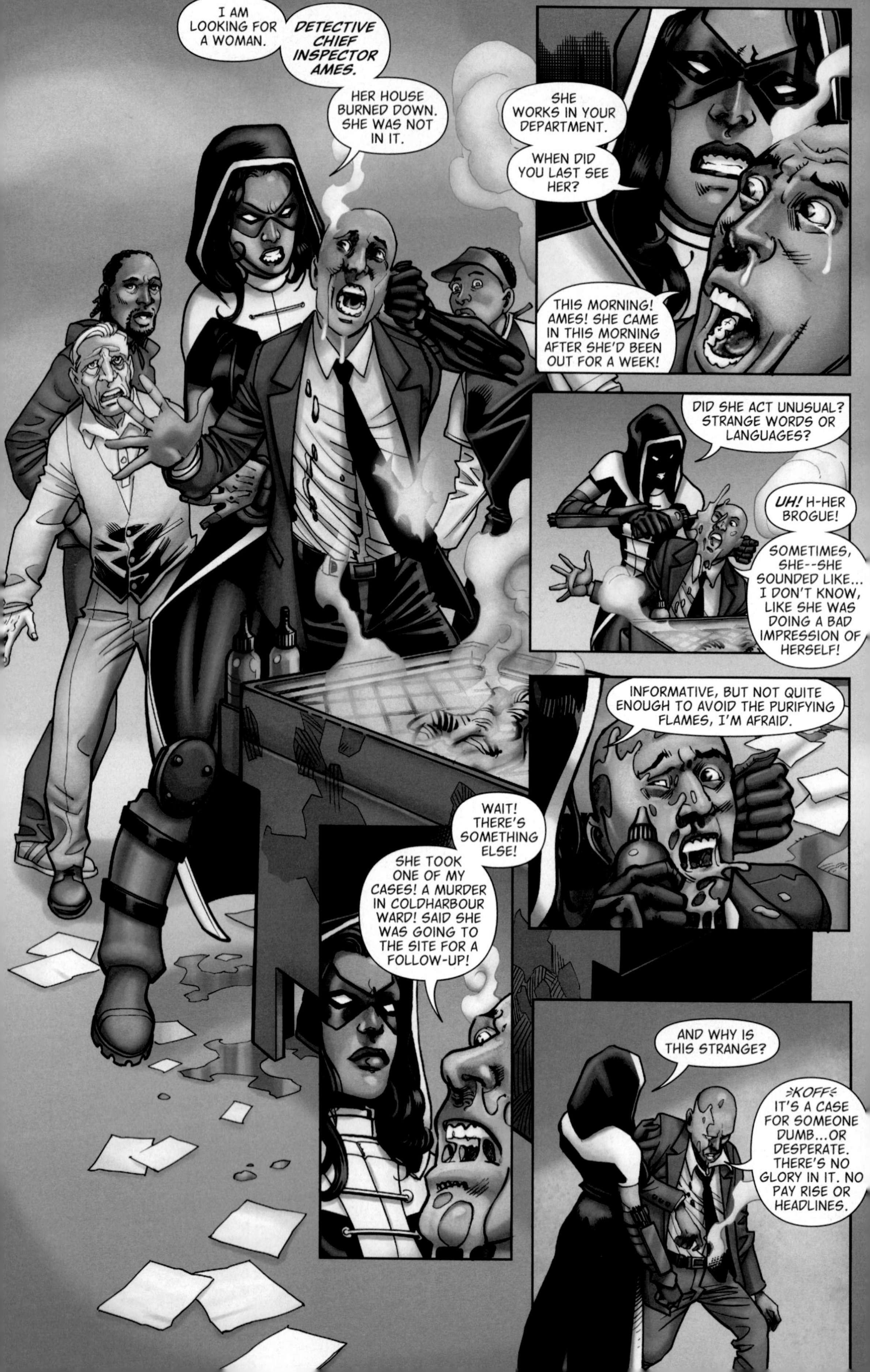
I AM LOOKING FOR A WOMAN.
DETECTIVE CHIEF INSPECTOR AMES.
HER HOUSE BURNED DOWN. SHE WAS NOT IN IT.
SHE WORKS IN YOUR DEPARTMENT.
WHEN DID YOU LAST SEE HER?
THIS MORNING! AMES! SHE CAME IN THIS MORNING AFTER SHE'D BEEN OUT FOR A WEEK!
DID SHE ACT UNUSUAL? STRANGE WORDS OR LANGUAGES?
UH! H-HER BROGUE!
SOMETIMES, SHE--SHE SOUNDED LIKE... I DON'T KNOW, LIKE SHE WAS DOING A BAD IMPRESSION OF HERSELF!
INFORMATIVE, BUT NOT QUITE ENOUGH TO AVOID THE PURIFYING FLAMES, I'M AFRAID.
WAIT! THERE'S SOMETHING ELSE!
SHE TOOK ONE OF MY CASES! A MURDER IN COLDHARBOUR WARD! SAID SHE WAS GOING TO THE SITE FOR A FOLLOW-UP!
AND WHY IS THIS STRANGE?
KOFF
IT'S A CASE FOR SOMEONE DUMB...OR DESPERATE. THERE'S NO GLORY IN IT. NO PAY RISE OR HEADLINES.

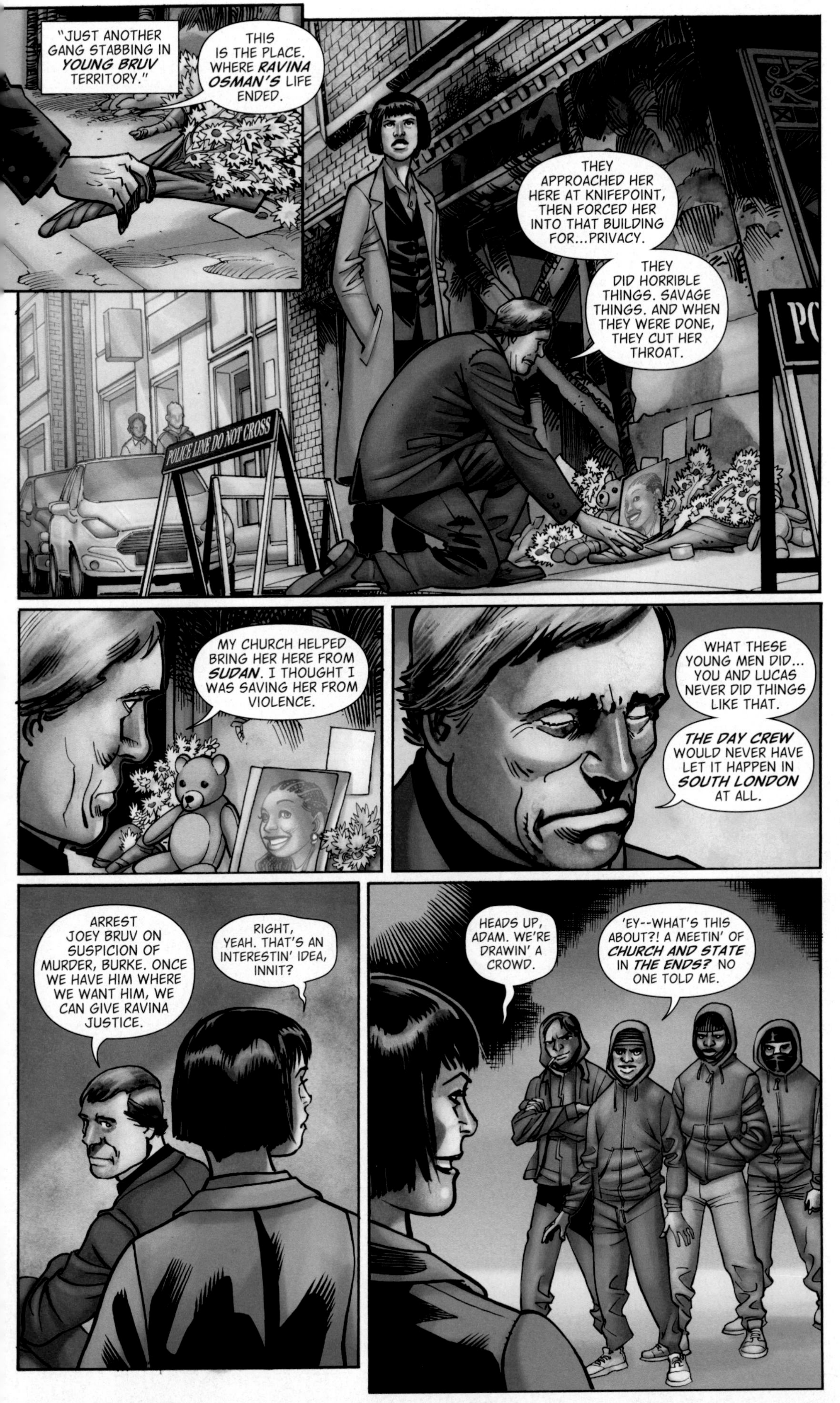
"JUST ANOTHER GANG STABBING IN YOUNG BRUV TERRITORY."
THIS IS THE PLACE. WHERE RAVINA OSMAN'S LIFE ENDED.
THEY APPROACHED HER HERE AT KNIFEPOINT, THEN FORCED HER INTO THAT BUILDING FOR...PRIVACY.
THEY DID HORRIBLE THINGS. SAVAGE THINGS. AND WHEN THEY WERE DONE, THEY CUT HER THROAT.
POLICE LINE DO NOT CROSS
MY CHURCH HELPED BRING HER HERE FROM SUDAN. I THOUGHT I WAS SAVING HER FROM VIOLENCE.
WHAT THESE YOUNG MEN DID... YOU AND LUCAS NEVER DID THINGS LIKE THAT.
THE DAY CREW WOULD NEVER HAVE LET IT HAPPEN IN SOUTH LONDON AT ALL.
ARREST JOEY BRUV ON SUSPICION OF MURDER, BURKE. ONCE WE HAVE HIM WHERE WE WANT HIM, WE CAN GIVE RAVINA JUSTICE.
RIGHT, YEAH. THAT'S AN INTERESTIN' IDEA, INNIT?
HEADS UP, ADAM. WE'RE DRAWIN' A CROWD.
'EY--WHAT'S THIS ABOUT?! A MEETIN' OF CHURCH AND STATE IN THE ENDS? NO ONE TOLD ME.

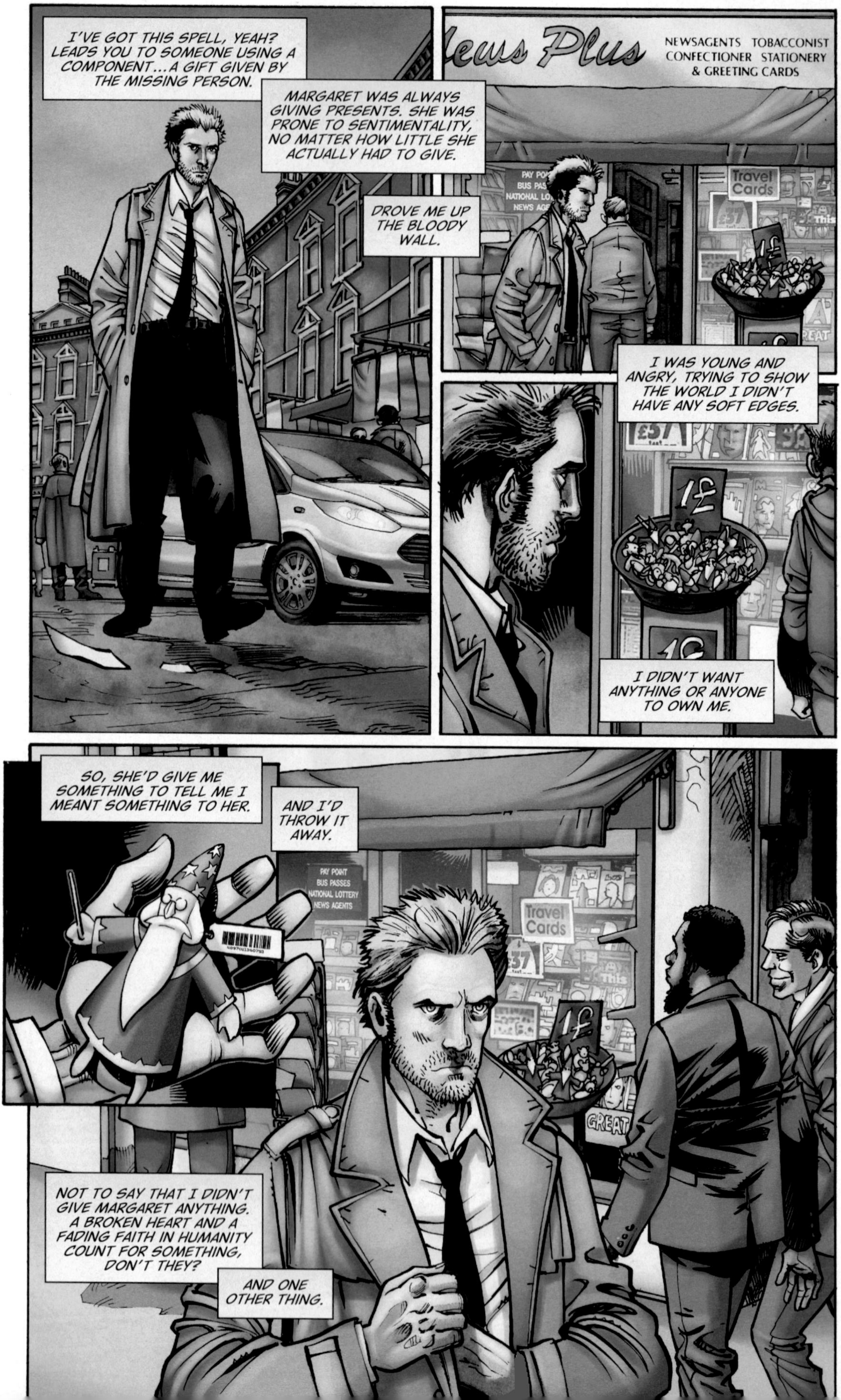
I'VE GOT THIS SPELL, YEAH? LEADS YOU TO SOMEONE USING A COMPONENT...A GIFT GIVEN BY THE MISSING PERSON.
MARGARET WAS ALWAYS GIVING PRESENTS. SHE WAS PRONE TO SENTIMENTALITY, NO MATTER HOW LITTLE SHE ACTUALLY HAD TO GIVE.
DROVE ME UP THE BLOODY WALL.
News Plus
NEWSAGENTS TOBACCONIST CONFECTIONER STATIONERY & GREETING CARDS
Travel Cards
I WAS YOUNG AND ANGRY, TRYING TO SHOW THE WORLD I DIDN'T HAVE ANY SOFT EDGES.
I DIDN'T WANT ANYTHING OR ANYONE TO OWN ME.
SO, SHE'D GIVE ME SOMETHING TO TELL ME I MEANT SOMETHING TO HER.
AND I'D THROW IT AWAY.
PAY POINT
BUS PASSES
NATIONAL LOTTERY
NEWS AGENTS
Travel Cards
GREAT
NOT TO SAY THAT I DIDN'T GIVE MARGARET ANYTHING. A BROKEN HEART AND A FADING FAITH IN HUMANITY COUNT FOR SOMETHING, DON'T THEY?
AND ONE OTHER THING.

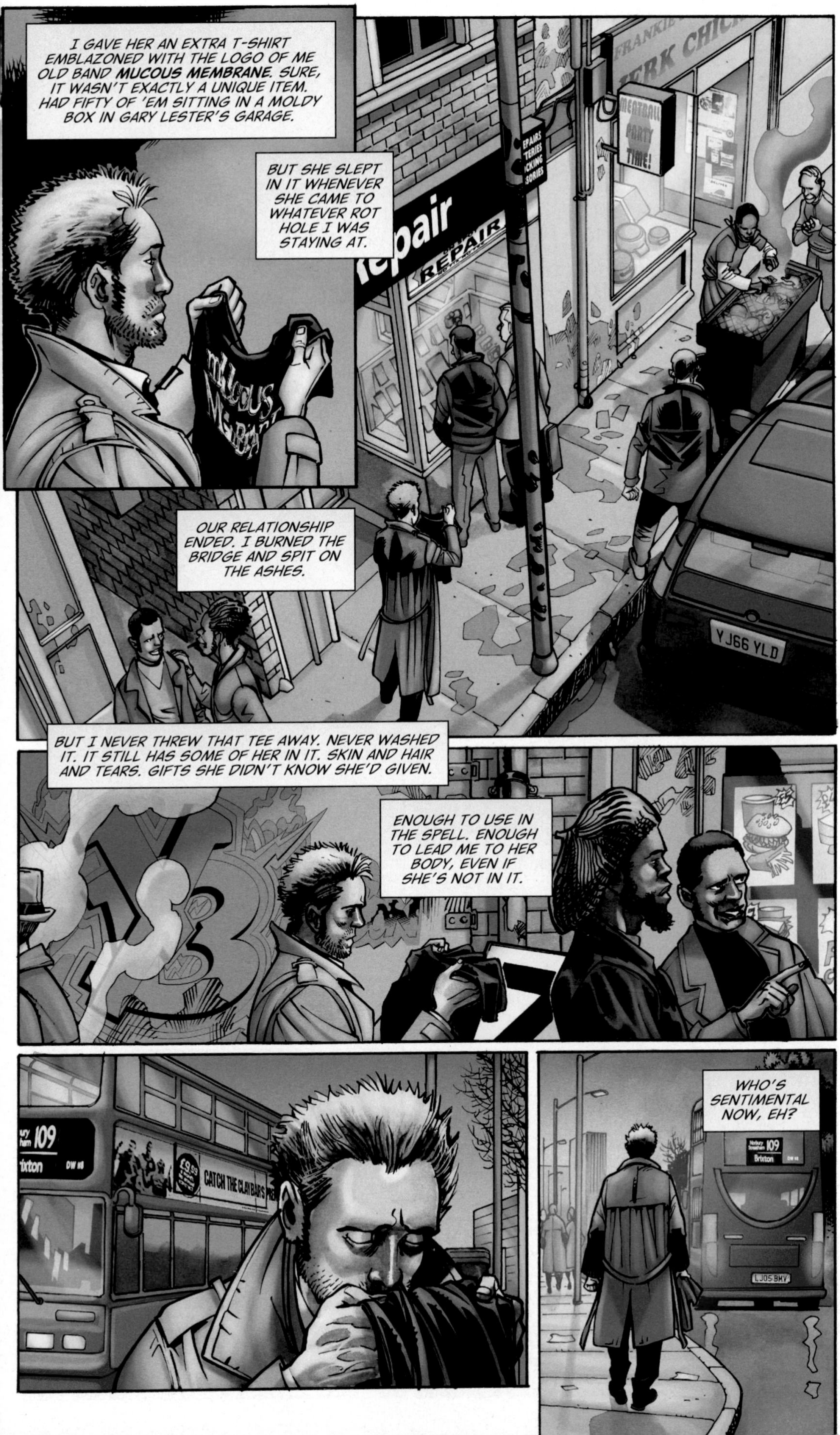
I GAVE HER AN EXTRA T-SHIRT EMBLAZONED WITH THE LOGO OF ME OLD BAND **MUCOUS MEMBRANE**. SURE, IT WASN'T EXACTLY A UNIQUE ITEM. HAD FIFTY OF 'EM SITTING IN A MOLDY BOX IN GARY LESTER'S GARAGE.
BUT SHE SLEPT IN IT WHENEVER SHE CAME TO WHATEVER ROT HOLE I WAS STAYING AT.
MEATBALL PARTY TIME!
REPAIR
OUR RELATIONSHIP ENDED. I BURNED THE BRIDGE AND SPIT ON THE ASHES.
YJ66 YLD
BUT I NEVER THREW THAT TEE AWAY. NEVER WASHED IT. IT STILL HAS SOME OF HER IN IT. SKIN AND HAIR AND TEARS. GIFTS SHE DIDN'T KNOW SHE'D GIVEN.
ENOUGH TO USE IN THE SPELL. ENOUGH TO LEAD ME TO HER BODY, EVEN IF SHE'S NOT IN IT.
109
CATCH THE CLAYBARS
WHO'S SENTIMENTAL NOW, EH?
109
Brixton
LJ05 BMV

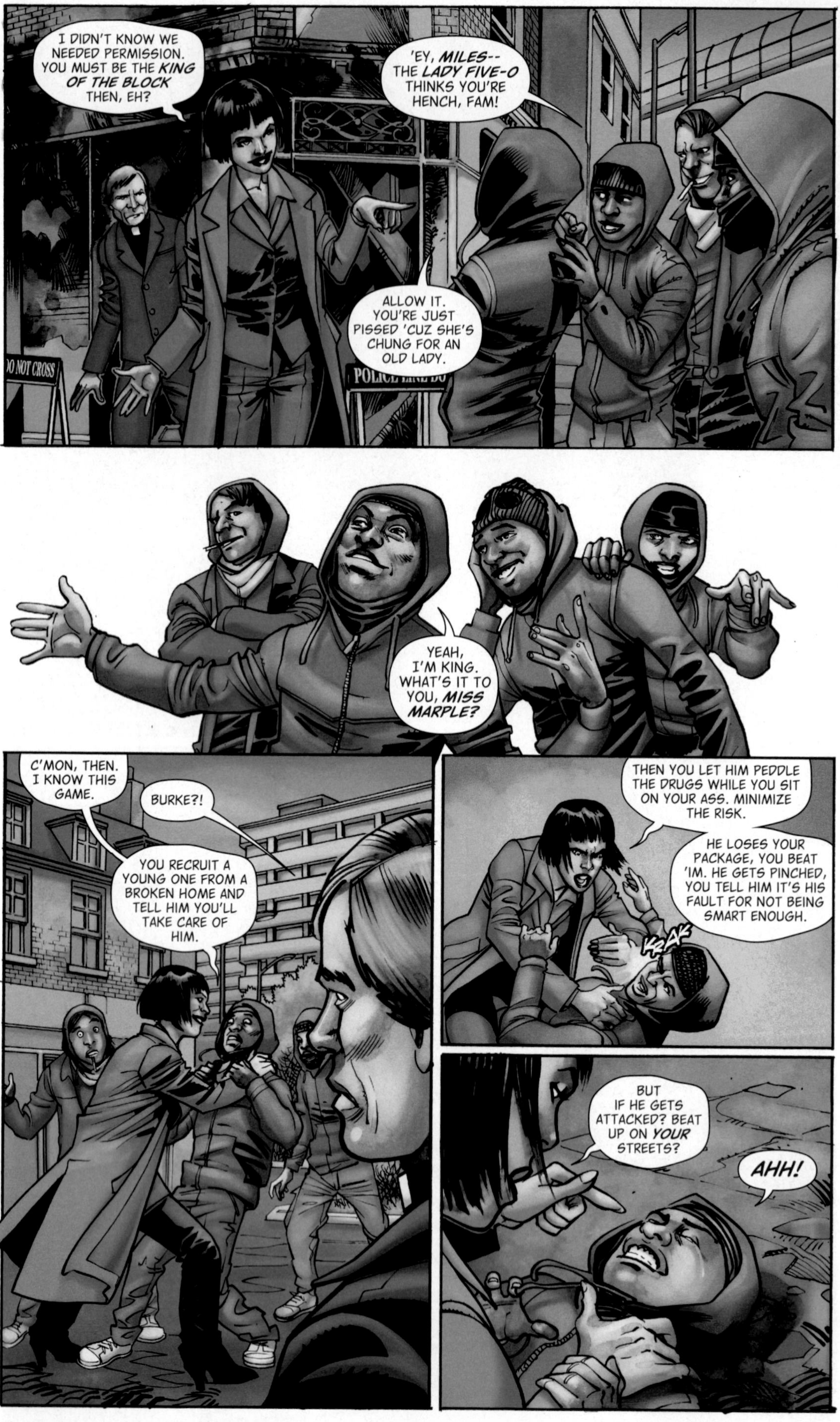
I DIDN'T KNOW WE NEEDED PERMISSION. YOU MUST BE THE *KING OF THE BLOCK* THEN, EH?
'EY, *MILES--* THE *LADY FIVE-O* THINKS YOU'RE HENCH, FAM!
ALLOW IT. YOU'RE JUST PISSED 'CUZ SHE'S CHUNG FOR AN OLD LADY.
YEAH, I'M KING. WHAT'S IT TO YOU, *MISS MARPLE?*
C'MON, THEN. I KNOW THIS GAME.
BURKE?!
YOU RECRUIT A YOUNG ONE FROM A BROKEN HOME AND TELL HIM YOU'LL TAKE CARE OF HIM.
THEN YOU LET HIM PEDDLE THE DRUGS WHILE YOU SIT ON YOUR ASS. MINIMIZE THE RISK.
HE LOSES YOUR PACKAGE, YOU BEAT 'IM. HE GETS PINCHED, YOU TELL HIM IT'S HIS FAULT FOR NOT BEING SMART ENOUGH.
KRAK
BUT IF HE GETS ATTACKED? BEAT UP ON *YOUR* STREETS?
AHH!

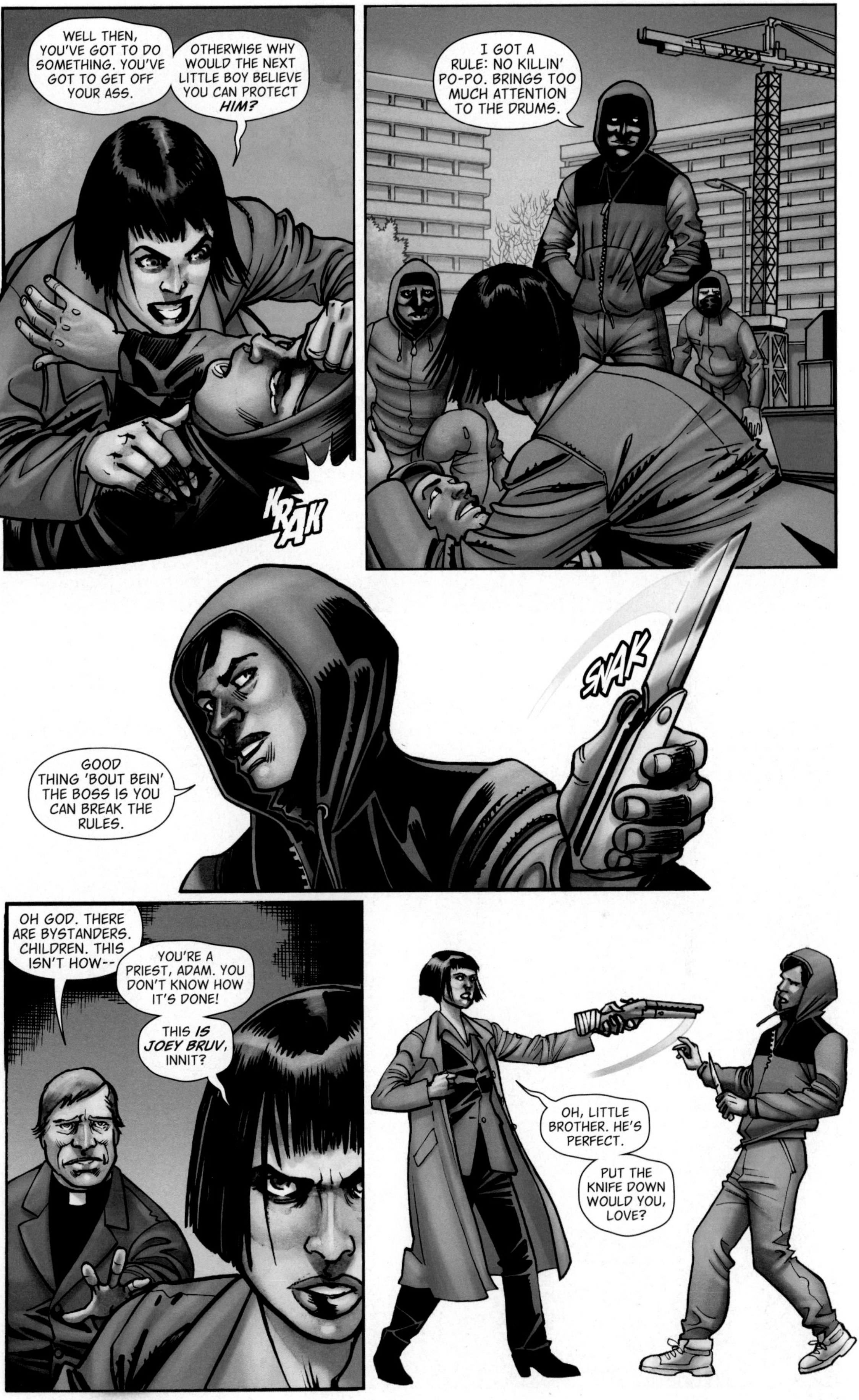
WELL THEN, YOU'VE GOT TO DO SOMETHING. YOU'VE GOT TO GET OFF YOUR ASS.
OTHERWISE WHY WOULD THE NEXT LITTLE BOY BELIEVE YOU CAN PROTECT HIM?
KRAK
I GOT A RULE: NO KILLIN' PO-PO. BRINGS TOO MUCH ATTENTION TO THE DRUMS.
SNAK
GOOD THING 'BOUT BEIN' THE BOSS IS YOU CAN BREAK THE RULES.
OH GOD. THERE ARE BYSTANDERS. CHILDREN. THIS ISN'T HOW--
YOU'RE A PRIEST, ADAM. YOU DON'T KNOW HOW IT'S DONE!
THIS IS JOEY BRUV, INNIT?
OH, LITTLE BROTHER. HE'S PERFECT.
PUT THE KNIFE DOWN WOULD YOU, LOVE?

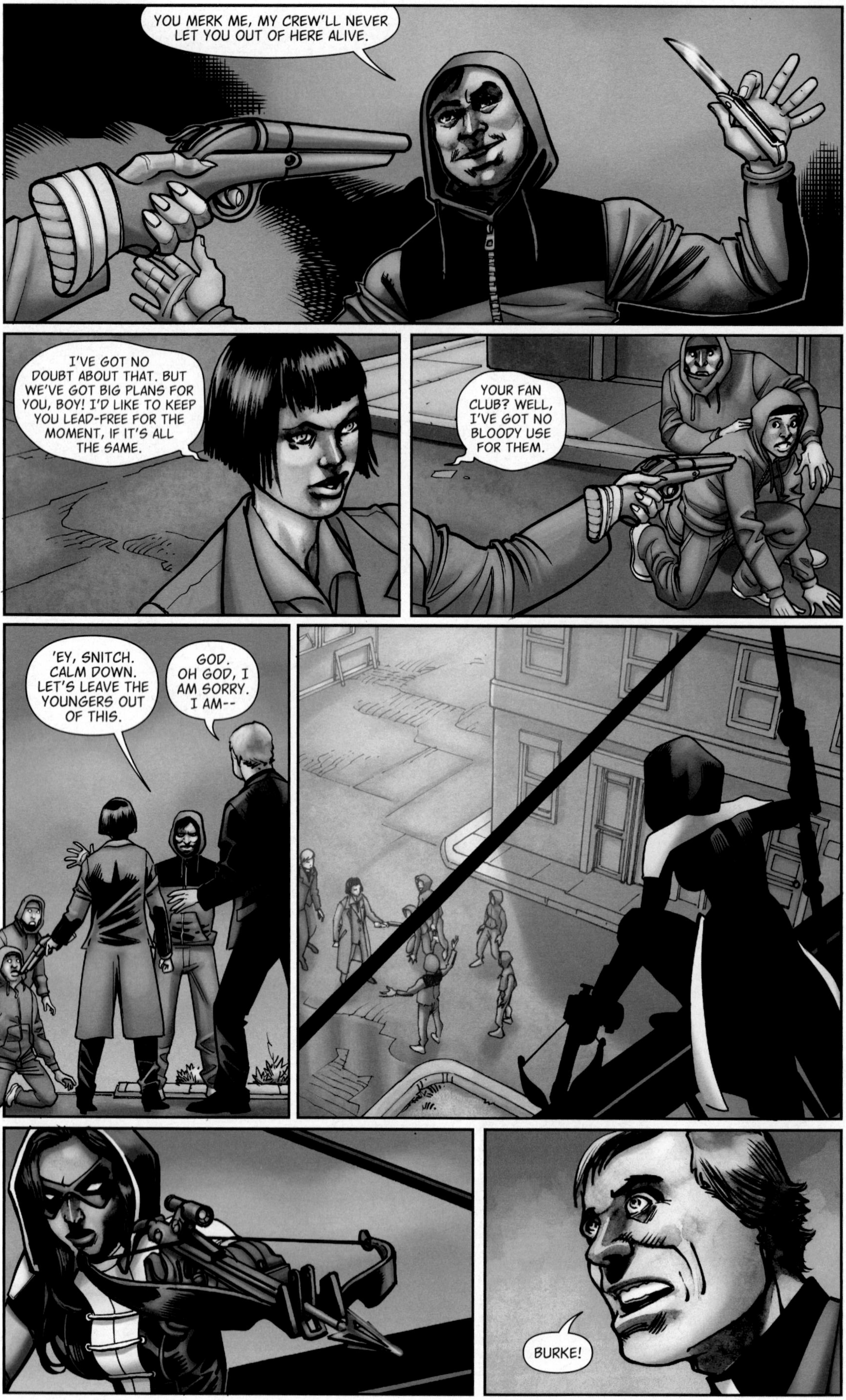
YOU MERK ME, MY CREW'LL NEVER LET YOU OUT OF HERE ALIVE.
I'VE GOT NO DOUBT ABOUT THAT. BUT WE'VE GOT BIG PLANS FOR YOU, BOY! I'D LIKE TO KEEP YOU LEAD-FREE FOR THE MOMENT, IF IT'S ALL THE SAME.
YOUR FAN CLUB? WELL, I'VE GOT NO BLOODY USE FOR THEM.
'EY, SNITCH. CALM DOWN. LET'S LEAVE THE YOUNGERS OUT OF THIS.
GOD. OH GOD, I AM SORRY. I AM--
BURKE!

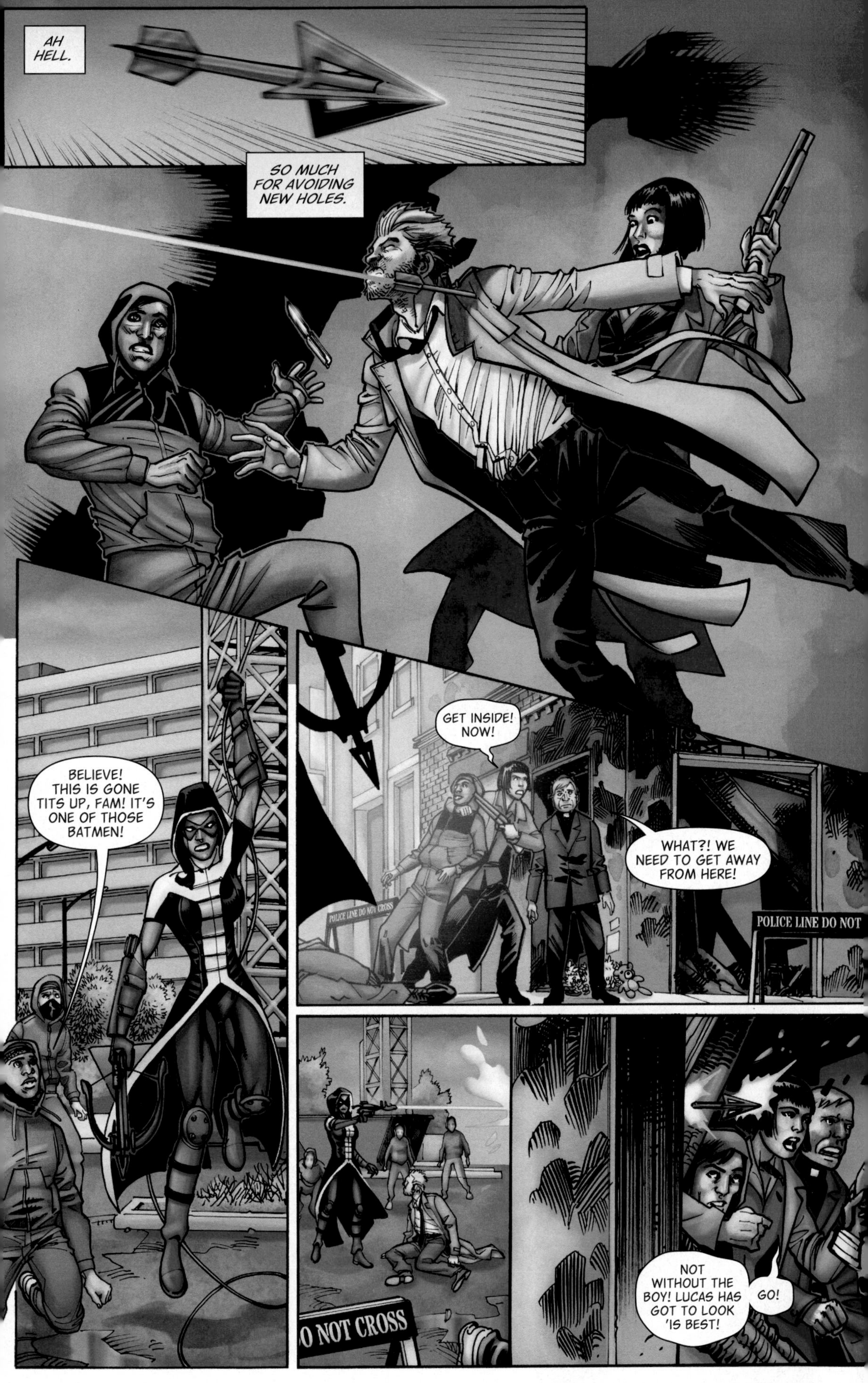
AH HELL.
SO MUCH FOR AVOIDING NEW HOLES.
BELIEVE! THIS IS GONE TITS UP, FAM! IT'S ONE OF THOSE BATMEN!
GET INSIDE! NOW!
WHAT?! WE NEED TO GET AWAY FROM HERE!
POLICE LINE DO NOT CROSS
POLICE LINE DO NOT
NOT WITHOUT THE BOY! LUCAS HAS GOT TO LOOK 'IS BEST!
GO!
O NOT CROSS

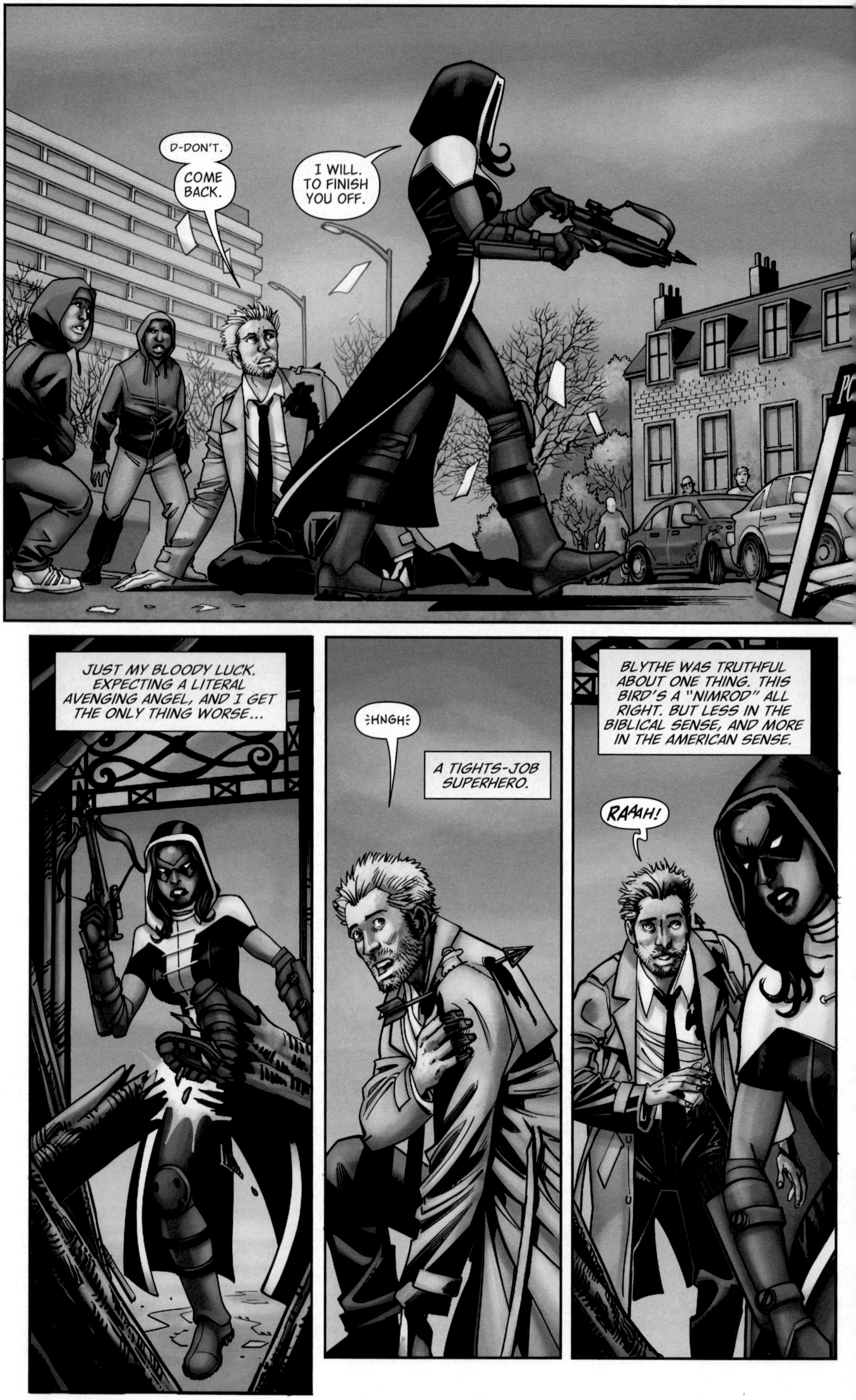
D-DON'T.
COME BACK.
I WILL. TO FINISH YOU OFF.
JUST MY BLOODY LUCK. EXPECTING A LITERAL AVENGING ANGEL, AND I GET THE ONLY THING WORSE...
HNGH
A TIGHTS-JOB SUPERHERO.
BLYTHE WAS TRUTHFUL ABOUT ONE THING. THIS BIRD'S A "NIMROD" ALL RIGHT. BUT LESS IN THE BIBLICAL SENSE, AND MORE IN THE AMERICAN SENSE.
RAAAH!

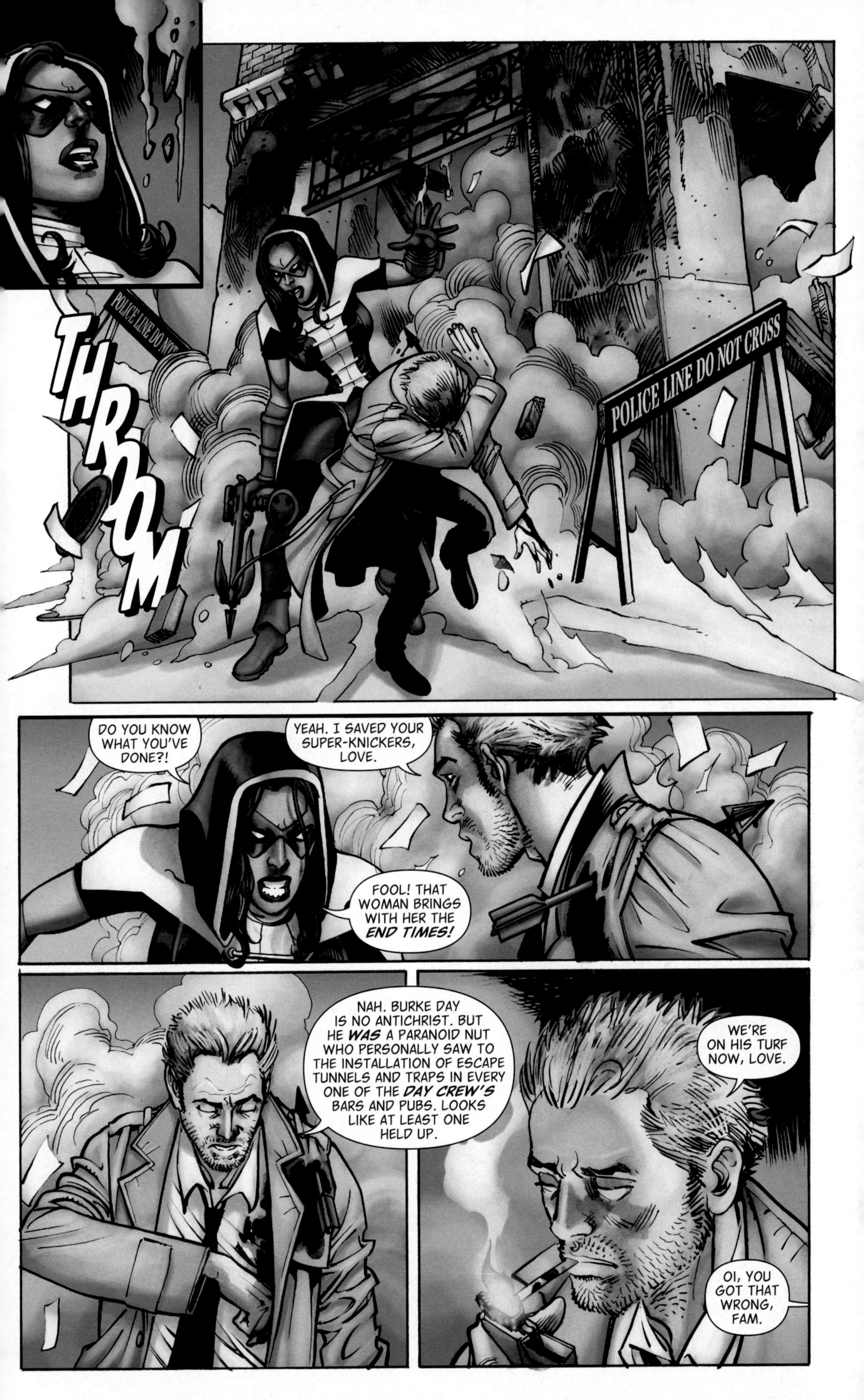
POLICE LINE DO NOT
THROOM!
POLICE LINE DO NOT CROSS
DO YOU KNOW WHAT YOU'VE DONE?!
YEAH. I SAVED YOUR SUPER-KNICKERS, LOVE.
FOOL! THAT WOMAN BRINGS WITH HER THE END TIMES!
NAH. BURKE DAY IS NO ANTICHRIST. BUT HE WAS A PARANOID NUT WHO PERSONALLY SAW TO THE INSTALLATION OF ESCAPE TUNNELS AND TRAPS IN EVERY ONE OF THE DAY CREW'S BARS AND PUBS. LOOKS LIKE AT LEAST ONE HELD UP.
WE'RE ON HIS TURF NOW, LOVE.
OI, YOU GOT THAT WRONG, FAM.

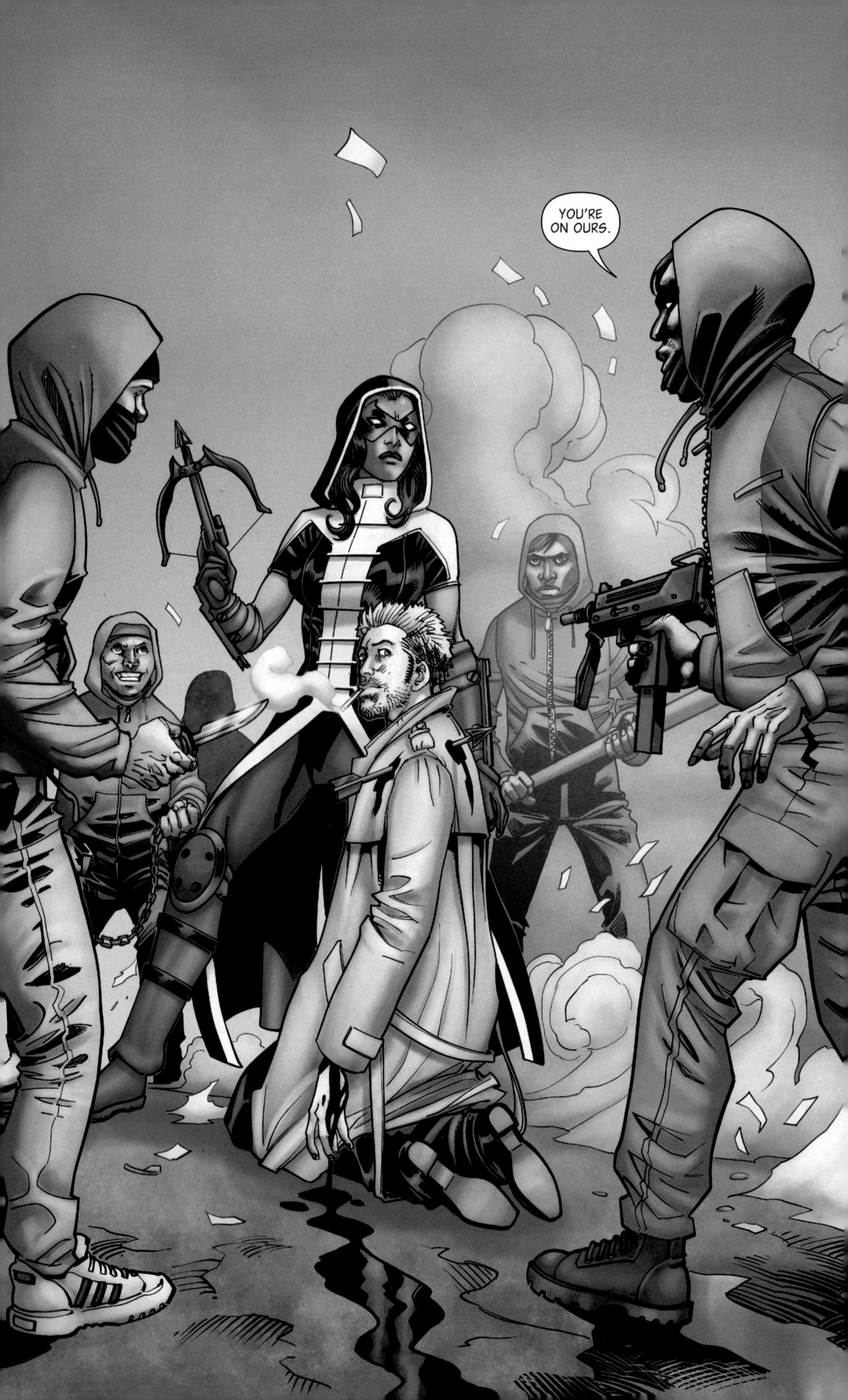
YOU'RE ON OURS.

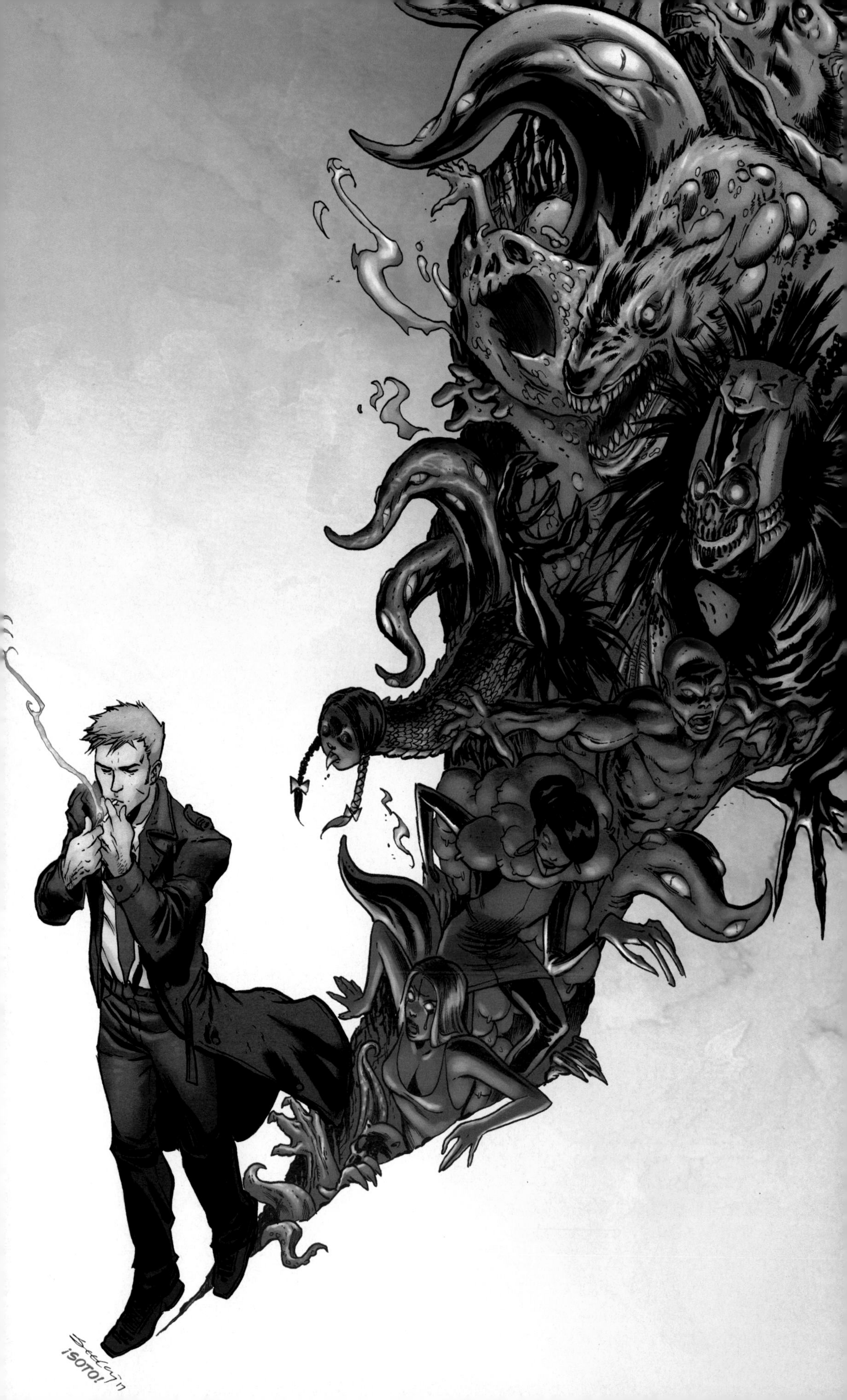
¡SOTO!

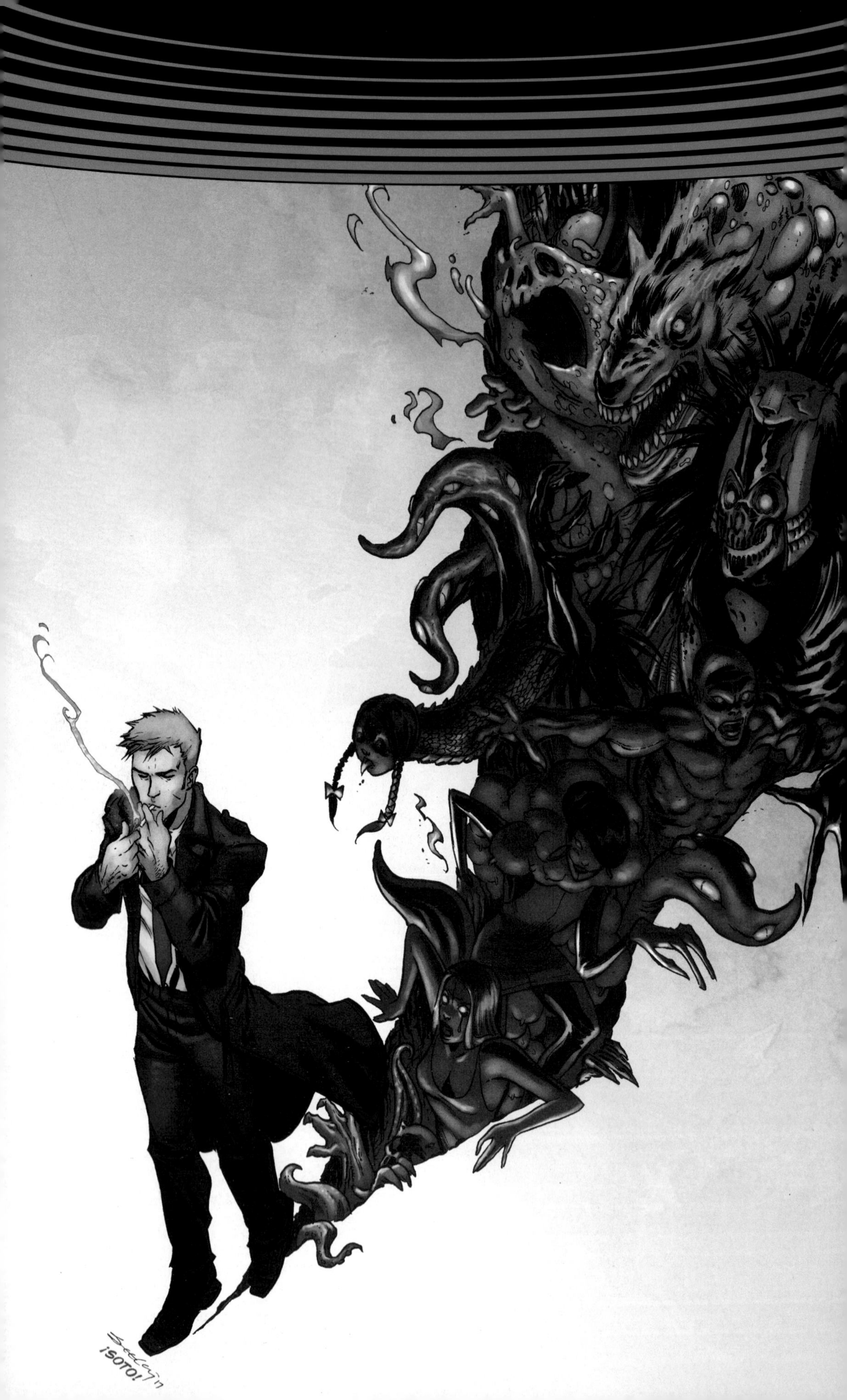
¡SOTO!

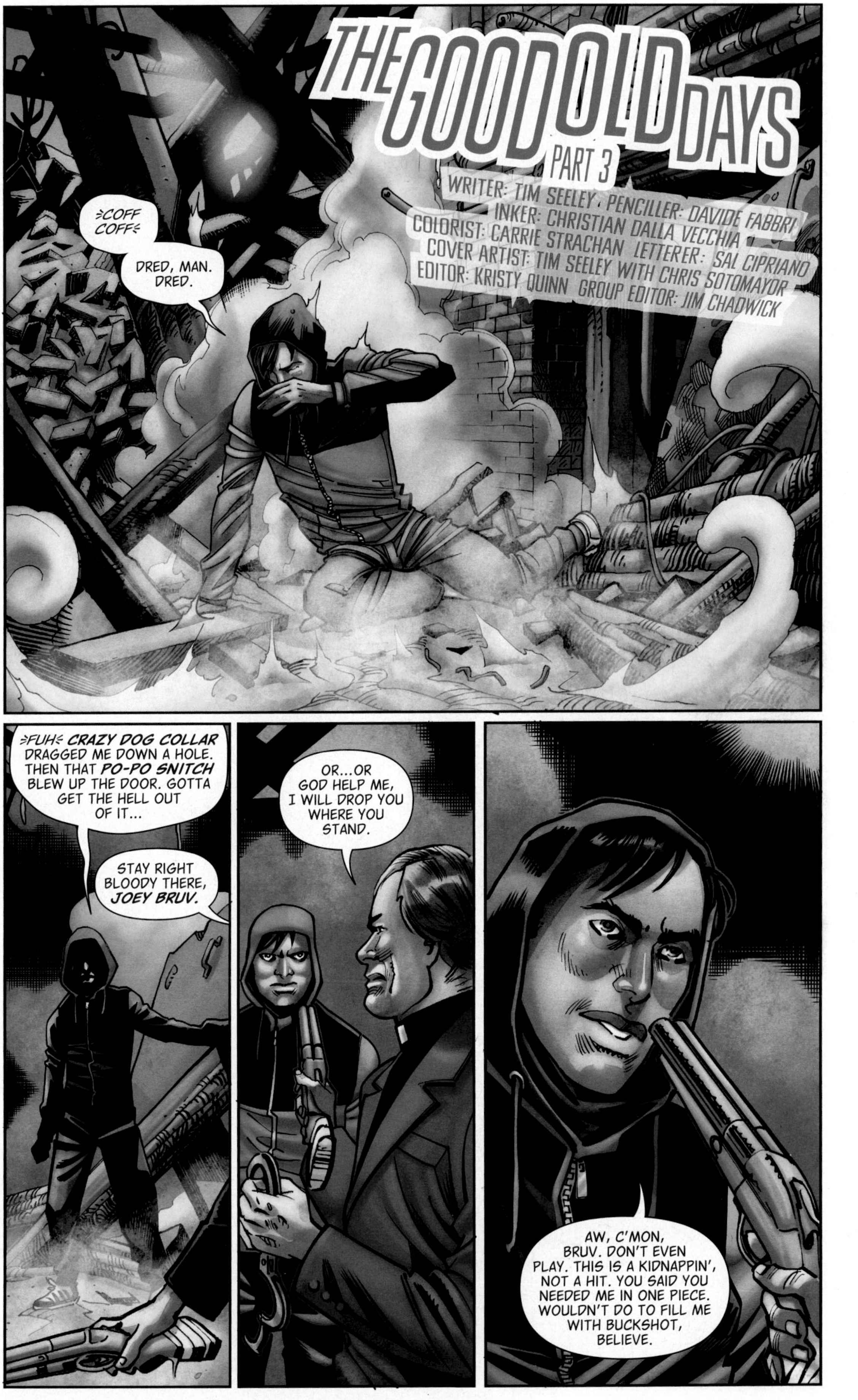
THE GOOD OLD DAYS
PART 3
WRITER: TIM SEELEY PENCILLER: DAVIDE FABBRI
INKER: CHRISTIAN DALLA VECCHIA
COLORIST: CARRIE STRACHAN LETTERER: SAL CIPRIANO
COVER ARTIST: TIM SEELEY WITH CHRIS SOTOMAYOR
EDITOR: KRISTY QUINN GROUP EDITOR: JIM CHADWICK
COFF COFF
DRED, MAN. DRED.
FUH CRAZY DOG COLLAR DRAGGED ME DOWN A HOLE. THEN THAT PO-PO SNITCH BLEW UP THE DOOR. GOTTA GET THE HELL OUT OF IT...
STAY RIGHT BLOODY THERE, JOEY BRUV.
OR...OR GOD HELP ME, I WILL DROP YOU WHERE YOU STAND.
AW, C'MON, BRUV. DON'T EVEN PLAY. THIS IS A KIDNAPPIN', NOT A HIT. YOU SAID YOU NEEDED ME IN ONE PIECE. WOULDN'T DO TO FILL ME WITH BUCKSHOT, BELIEVE.

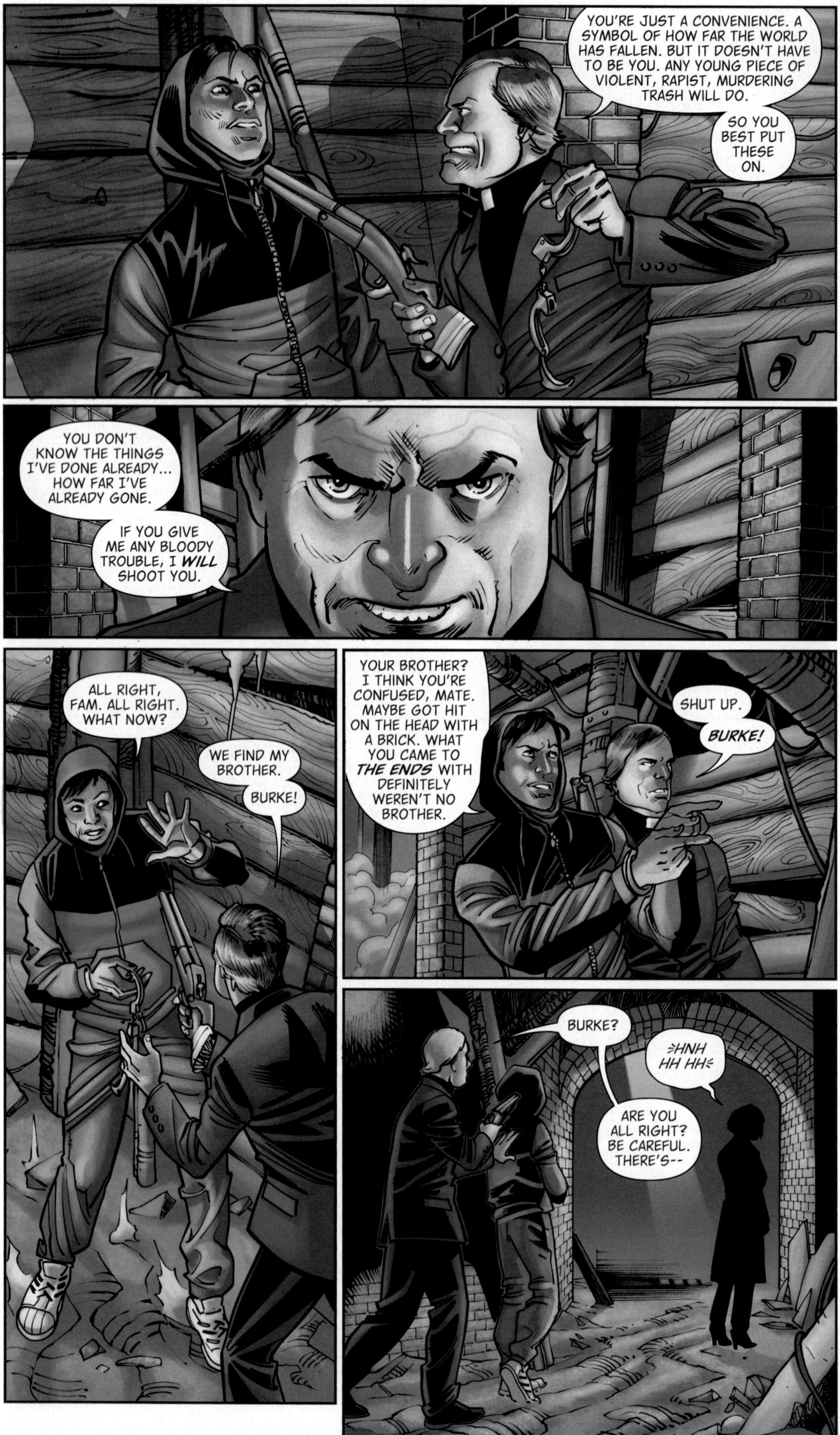
YOU'RE JUST A CONVENIENCE. A SYMBOL OF HOW FAR THE WORLD HAS FALLEN. BUT IT DOESN'T HAVE TO BE YOU. ANY YOUNG PIECE OF VIOLENT, RAPIST, MURDERING TRASH WILL DO.
SO YOU BEST PUT THESE ON.
YOU DON'T KNOW THE THINGS I'VE DONE ALREADY... HOW FAR I'VE ALREADY GONE.
IF YOU GIVE ME ANY BLOODY TROUBLE, I *WILL* SHOOT YOU.
ALL RIGHT, FAM. ALL RIGHT. WHAT NOW?
WE FIND MY BROTHER.
BURKE!
YOUR BROTHER? I THINK YOU'RE CONFUSED, MATE. MAYBE GOT HIT ON THE HEAD WITH A BRICK. WHAT YOU CAME TO *THE ENDS* WITH DEFINITELY WEREN'T NO BROTHER.
SHUT UP.
BURKE!
BURKE?
HNH HH HH
ARE YOU ALL RIGHT? BE CAREFUL. THERE'S--

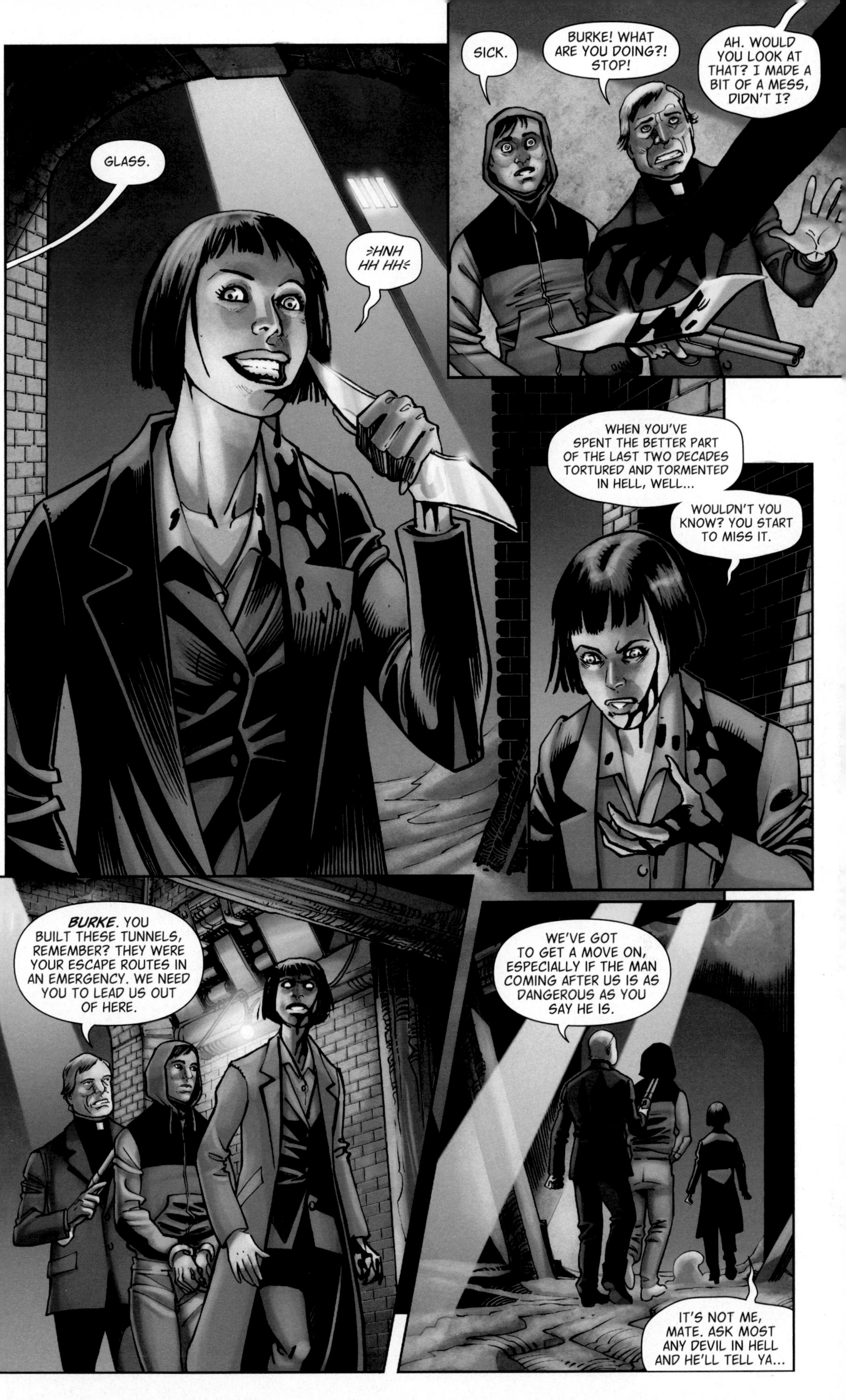
GLASS.
>HNH HH HH<
SICK.
BURKE! WHAT ARE YOU DOING?! STOP!
AH. WOULD YOU LOOK AT THAT? I MADE A BIT OF A MESS, DIDN'T I?
WHEN YOU'VE SPENT THE BETTER PART OF THE LAST TWO DECADES TORTURED AND TORMENTED IN HELL, WELL...
WOULDN'T YOU KNOW? YOU START TO MISS IT.
BURKE. YOU BUILT THESE TUNNELS, REMEMBER? THEY WERE YOUR ESCAPE ROUTES IN AN EMERGENCY. WE NEED YOU TO LEAD US OUT OF HERE.
WE'VE GOT TO GET A MOVE ON, ESPECIALLY IF THE MAN COMING AFTER US IS AS DANGEROUS AS YOU SAY HE IS.
IT'S NOT ME, MATE. ASK MOST ANY DEVIL IN HELL AND HE'LL TELL YA...

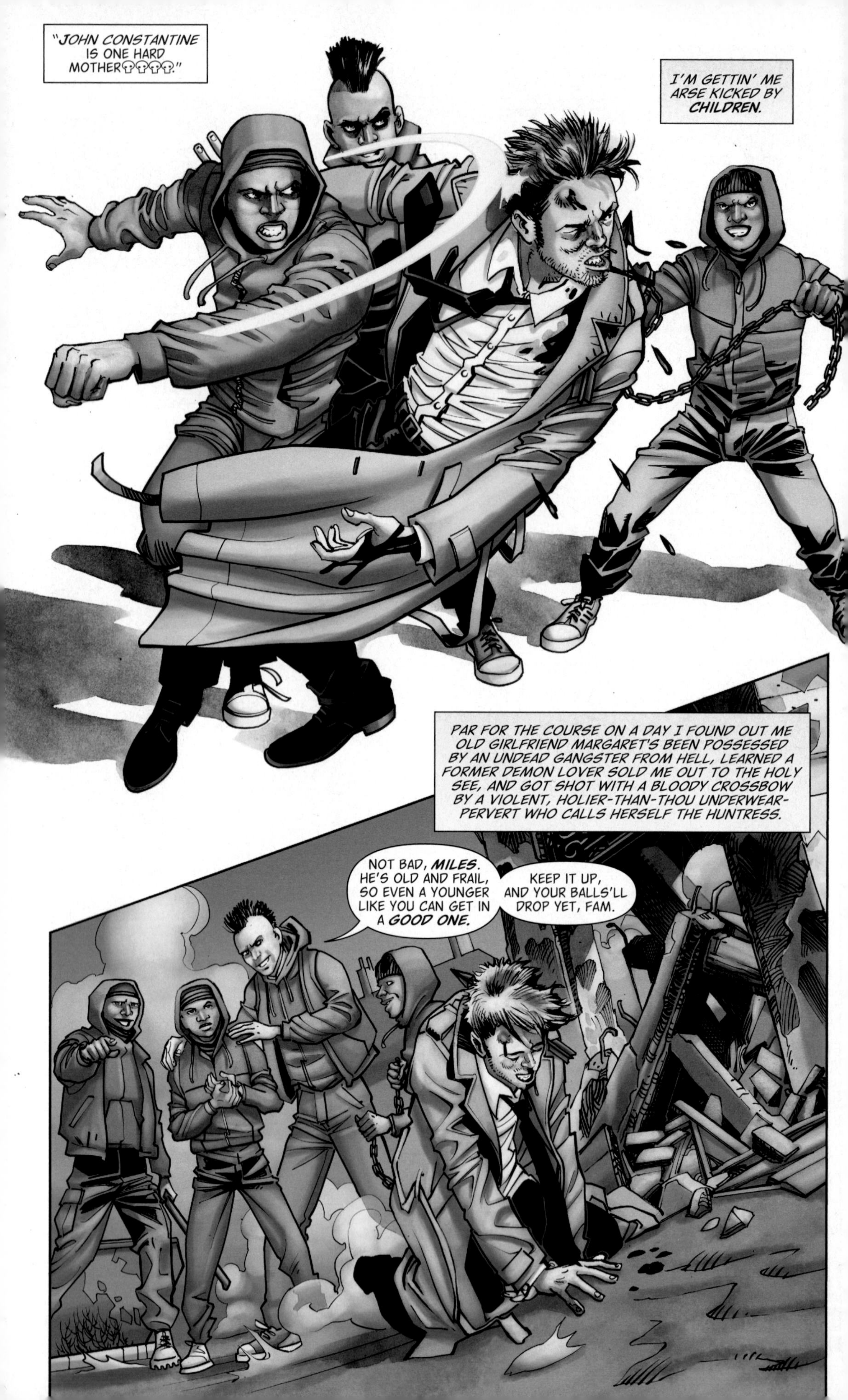
"JOHN CONSTANTINE IS ONE HARD MOTHER."
I'M GETTIN' ME ARSE KICKED BY CHILDREN.
PAR FOR THE COURSE ON A DAY I FOUND OUT ME OLD GIRLFRIEND MARGARET'S BEEN POSSESSED BY AN UNDEAD GANGSTER FROM HELL, LEARNED A FORMER DEMON LOVER SOLD ME OUT TO THE HOLY SEE, AND GOT SHOT WITH A BLOODY CROSSBOW BY A VIOLENT, HOLIER-THAN-THOU UNDERWEAR-PERVERT WHO CALLS HERSELF THE HUNTRESS.
NOT BAD, MILES. HE'S OLD AND FRAIL, SO EVEN A YOUNGER LIKE YOU CAN GET IN A GOOD ONE.
KEEP IT UP, AND YOUR BALLS'LL DROP YET, FAM.

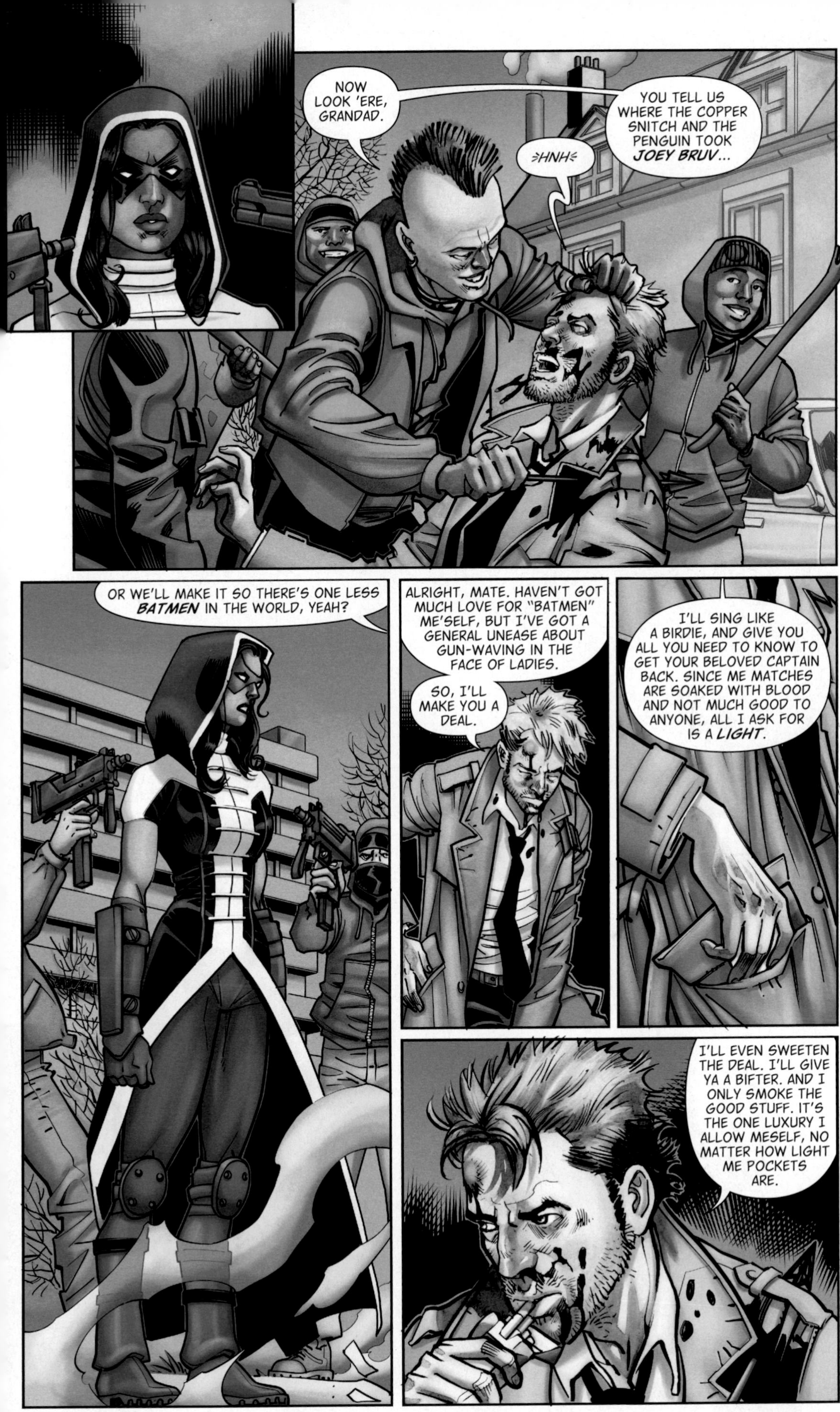
NOW LOOK 'ERE, GRANDAD.
YOU TELL US WHERE THE COPPER SNITCH AND THE PENGUIN TOOK JOEY BRUV...
HNH
OR WE'LL MAKE IT SO THERE'S ONE LESS BATMEN IN THE WORLD, YEAH?
ALRIGHT, MATE. HAVEN'T GOT MUCH LOVE FOR "BATMEN" ME'SELF, BUT I'VE GOT A GENERAL UNEASE ABOUT GUN-WAVING IN THE FACE OF LADIES.
SO, I'LL MAKE YOU A DEAL.
I'LL SING LIKE A BIRDIE, AND GIVE YOU ALL YOU NEED TO KNOW TO GET YOUR BELOVED CAPTAIN BACK. SINCE ME MATCHES ARE SOAKED WITH BLOOD AND NOT MUCH GOOD TO ANYONE, ALL I ASK FOR IS A LIGHT.
I'LL EVEN SWEETEN THE DEAL. I'LL GIVE YA A BIFTER. AND I ONLY SMOKE THE GOOD STUFF. IT'S THE ONE LUXURY I ALLOW MESELF, NO MATTER HOW LIGHT ME POCKETS ARE.

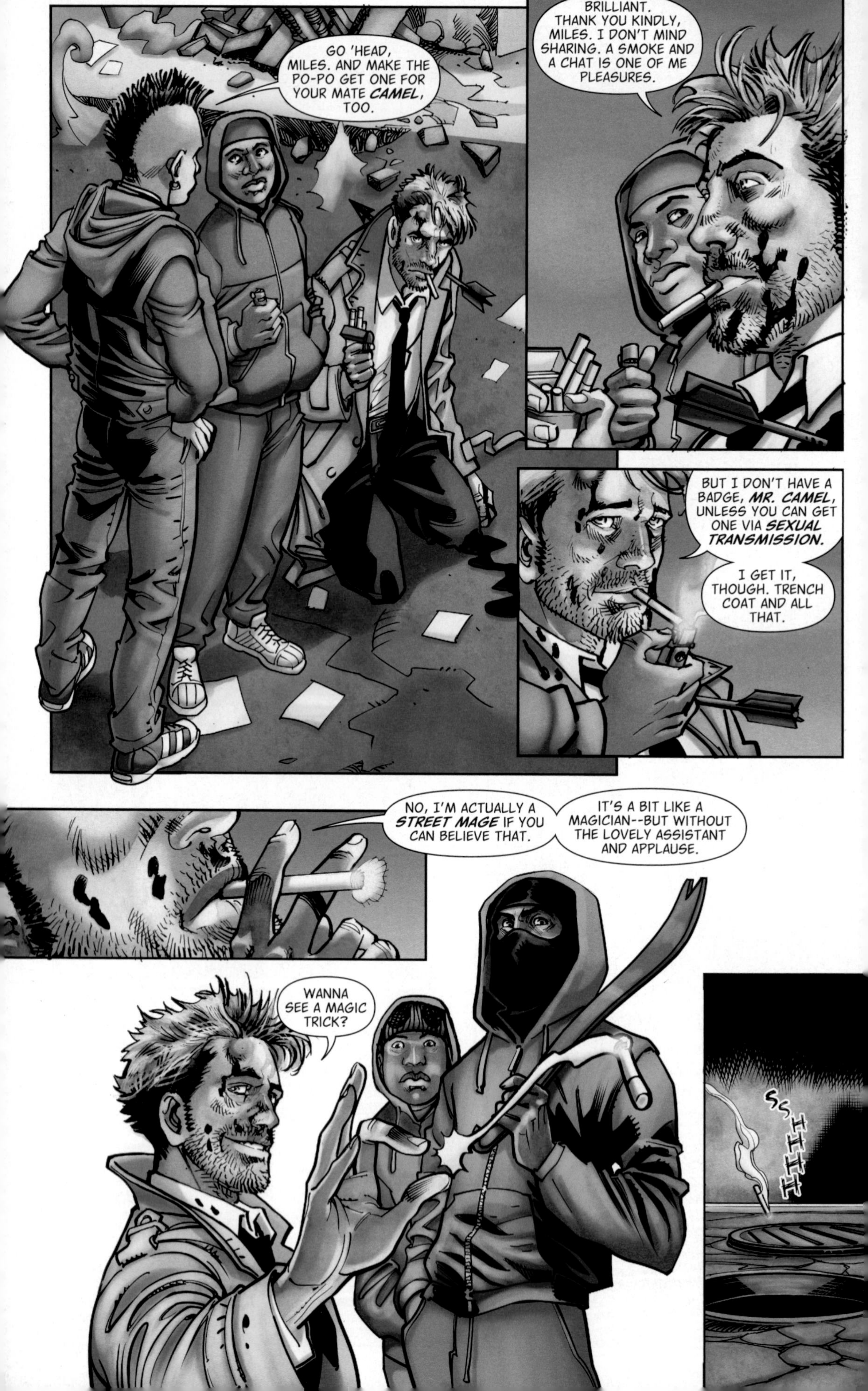
GO 'HEAD, MILES. AND MAKE THE PO-PO GET ONE FOR YOUR MATE CAMEL, TOO.
BRILLIANT. THANK YOU KINDLY, MILES. I DON'T MIND SHARING. A SMOKE AND A CHAT IS ONE OF ME PLEASURES.
BUT I DON'T HAVE A BADGE, MR. CAMEL, UNLESS YOU CAN GET ONE VIA SEXUAL TRANSMISSION.
I GET IT, THOUGH. TRENCH COAT AND ALL THAT.
NO, I'M ACTUALLY A STREET MAGE IF YOU CAN BELIEVE THAT.
IT'S A BIT LIKE A MAGICIAN--BUT WITHOUT THE LOVELY ASSISTANT AND APPLAUSE.
WANNA SEE A MAGIC TRICK?
SSHHHH

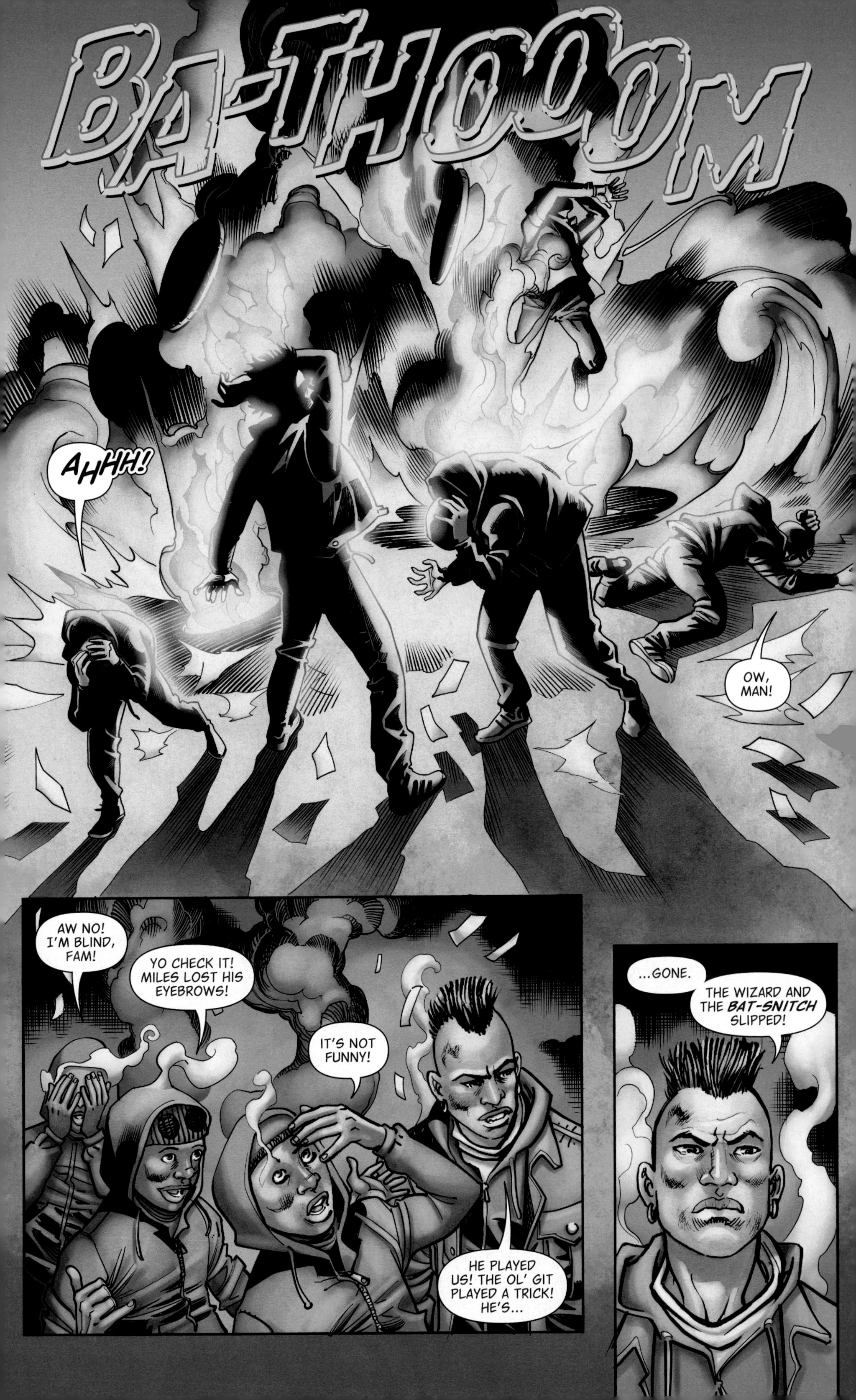
BA-THOOOOM
AHHH!
OW, MAN!
AW NO! I'M BLIND, FAM!
YO CHECK IT! MILES LOST HIS EYEBROWS!
IT'S NOT FUNNY!
HE PLAYED US! THE OL' GIT PLAYED A TRICK! HE'S...
...GONE.
THE WIZARD AND THE BAT-SNITCH SLIPPED!

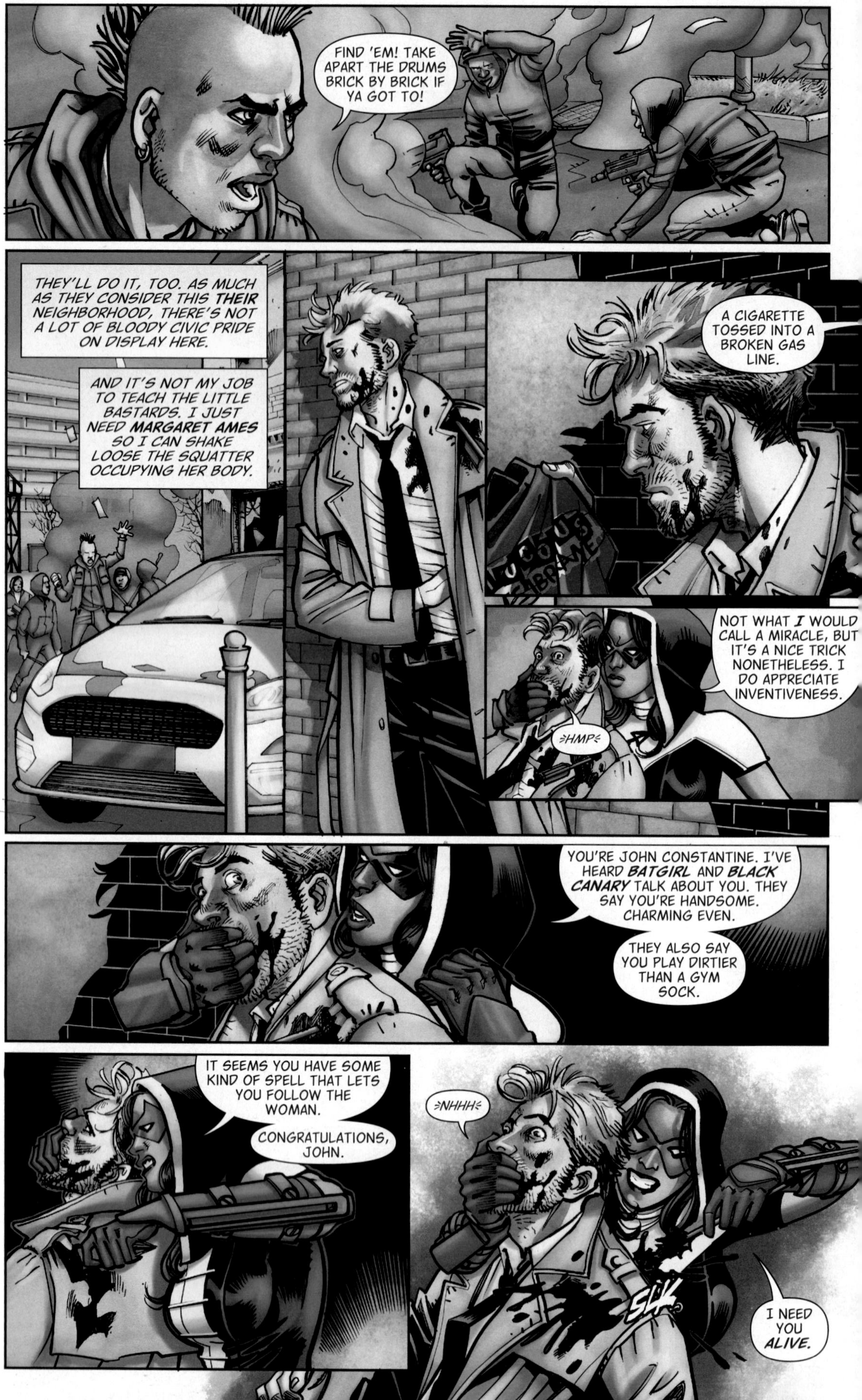
FIND 'EM! TAKE APART THE DRUMS BRICK BY BRICK IF YA GOT TO!
THEY'LL DO IT, TOO. AS MUCH AS THEY CONSIDER THIS THEIR NEIGHBORHOOD, THERE'S NOT A LOT OF BLOODY CIVIC PRIDE ON DISPLAY HERE.
AND IT'S NOT MY JOB TO TEACH THE LITTLE BASTARDS. I JUST NEED MARGARET AMES SO I CAN SHAKE LOOSE THE SQUATTER OCCUPYING HER BODY.
A CIGARETTE TOSSED INTO A BROKEN GAS LINE.
NOT WHAT I WOULD CALL A MIRACLE, BUT IT'S A NICE TRICK NONETHELESS. I DO APPRECIATE INVENTIVENESS.
HMP
YOU'RE JOHN CONSTANTINE. I'VE HEARD BATGIRL AND BLACK CANARY TALK ABOUT YOU. THEY SAY YOU'RE HANDSOME. CHARMING EVEN.
THEY ALSO SAY YOU PLAY DIRTIER THAN A GYM SOCK.
IT SEEMS YOU HAVE SOME KIND OF SPELL THAT LETS YOU FOLLOW THE WOMAN.
CONGRATULATIONS, JOHN.
NHHH
SCK
I NEED YOU ALIVE.

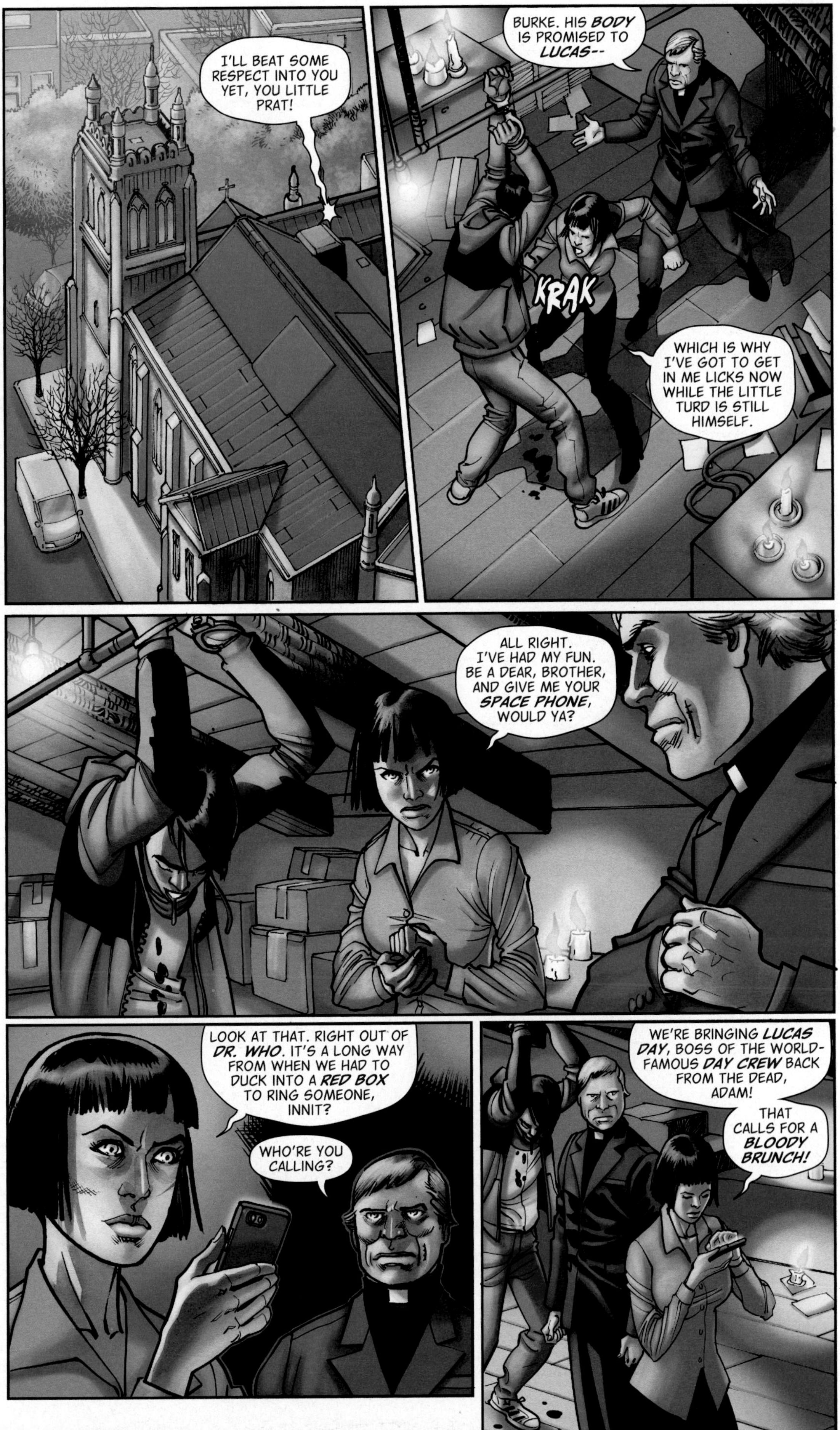

I'LL BEAT SOME RESPECT INTO YOU YET, YOU LITTLE PRAT!
BURKE. HIS BODY IS PROMISED TO LUCAS--
KRAK
WHICH IS WHY I'VE GOT TO GET IN ME LICKS NOW WHILE THE LITTLE TURD IS STILL HIMSELF.
ALL RIGHT. I'VE HAD MY FUN. BE A DEAR, BROTHER, AND GIVE ME YOUR SPACE PHONE, WOULD YA?
LOOK AT THAT. RIGHT OUT OF DR. WHO. IT'S A LONG WAY FROM WHEN WE HAD TO DUCK INTO A RED BOX TO RING SOMEONE, INNIT?
WHO'RE YOU CALLING?
WE'RE BRINGING LUCAS DAY, BOSS OF THE WORLD-FAMOUS DAY CREW BACK FROM THE DEAD, ADAM!
THAT CALLS FOR A BLOODY BRUNCH!

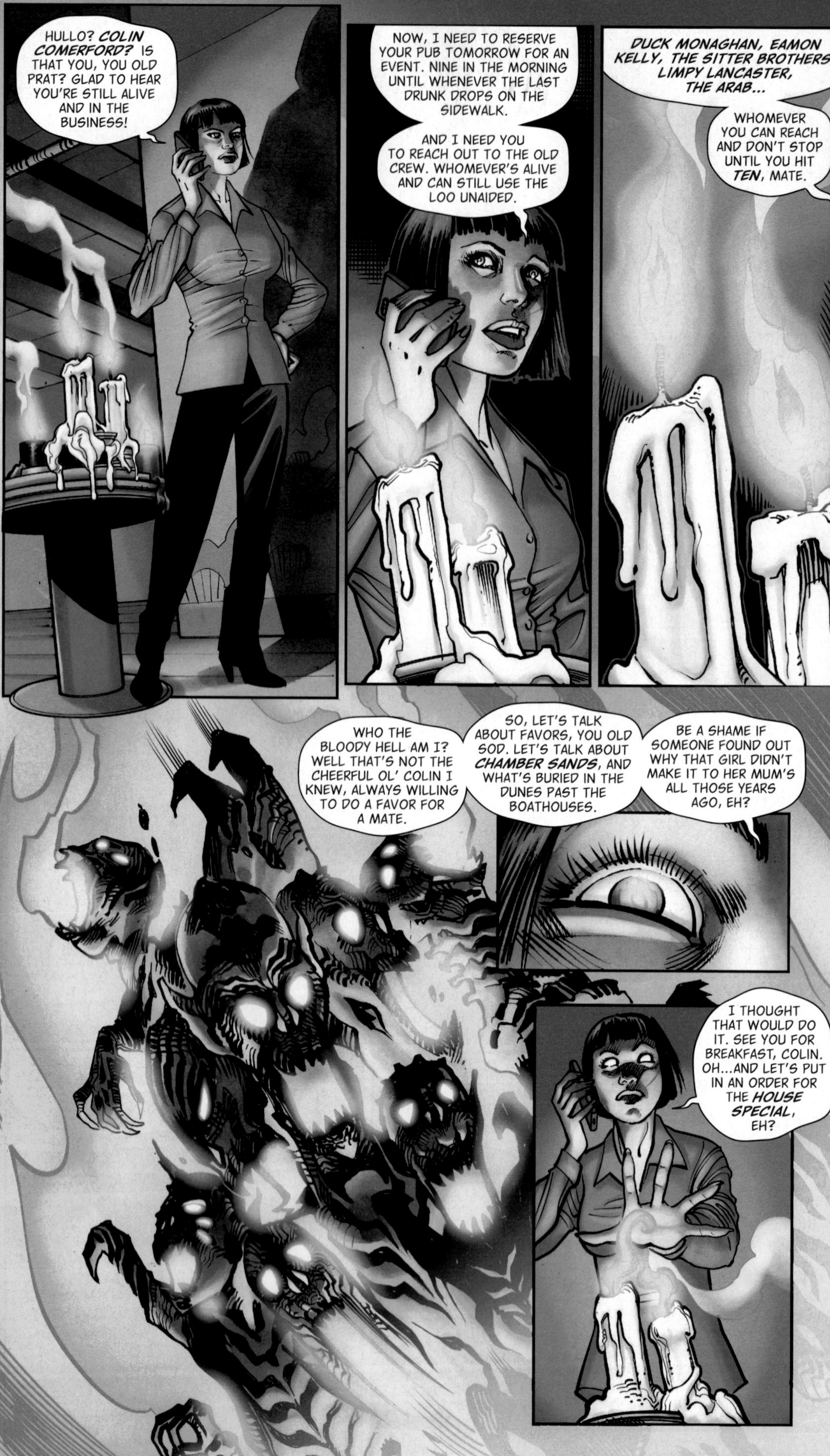
HULLO? *COLIN COMERFORD?* IS THAT YOU, YOU OLD PRAT? GLAD TO HEAR YOU'RE STILL ALIVE AND IN THE BUSINESS!
NOW, I NEED TO RESERVE YOUR PUB TOMORROW FOR AN EVENT. NINE IN THE MORNING UNTIL WHENEVER THE LAST DRUNK DROPS ON THE SIDEWALK.
AND I NEED YOU TO REACH OUT TO THE OLD CREW. WHOMEVER'S ALIVE AND CAN STILL USE THE LOO UNAIDED.
DUCK MONAGHAN, EAMON KELLY, THE SITTER BROTHERS, LIMPY LANCASTER, THE ARAB...
WHOMEVER YOU CAN REACH AND DON'T STOP UNTIL YOU HIT *TEN*, MATE.
WHO THE BLOODY HELL AM I? WELL THAT'S NOT THE CHEERFUL OL' COLIN I KNEW, ALWAYS WILLING TO DO A FAVOR FOR A MATE.
SO, LET'S TALK ABOUT FAVORS, YOU OLD SOD. LET'S TALK ABOUT *CHAMBER SANDS*, AND WHAT'S BURIED IN THE DUNES PAST THE BOATHOUSES.
BE A SHAME IF SOMEONE FOUND OUT WHY THAT GIRL DIDN'T MAKE IT TO HER MUM'S ALL THOSE YEARS AGO, EH?
I THOUGHT THAT WOULD DO IT. SEE YOU FOR BREAKFAST, COLIN. OH...AND LET'S PUT IN AN ORDER FOR THE *HOUSE SPECIAL*, EH?

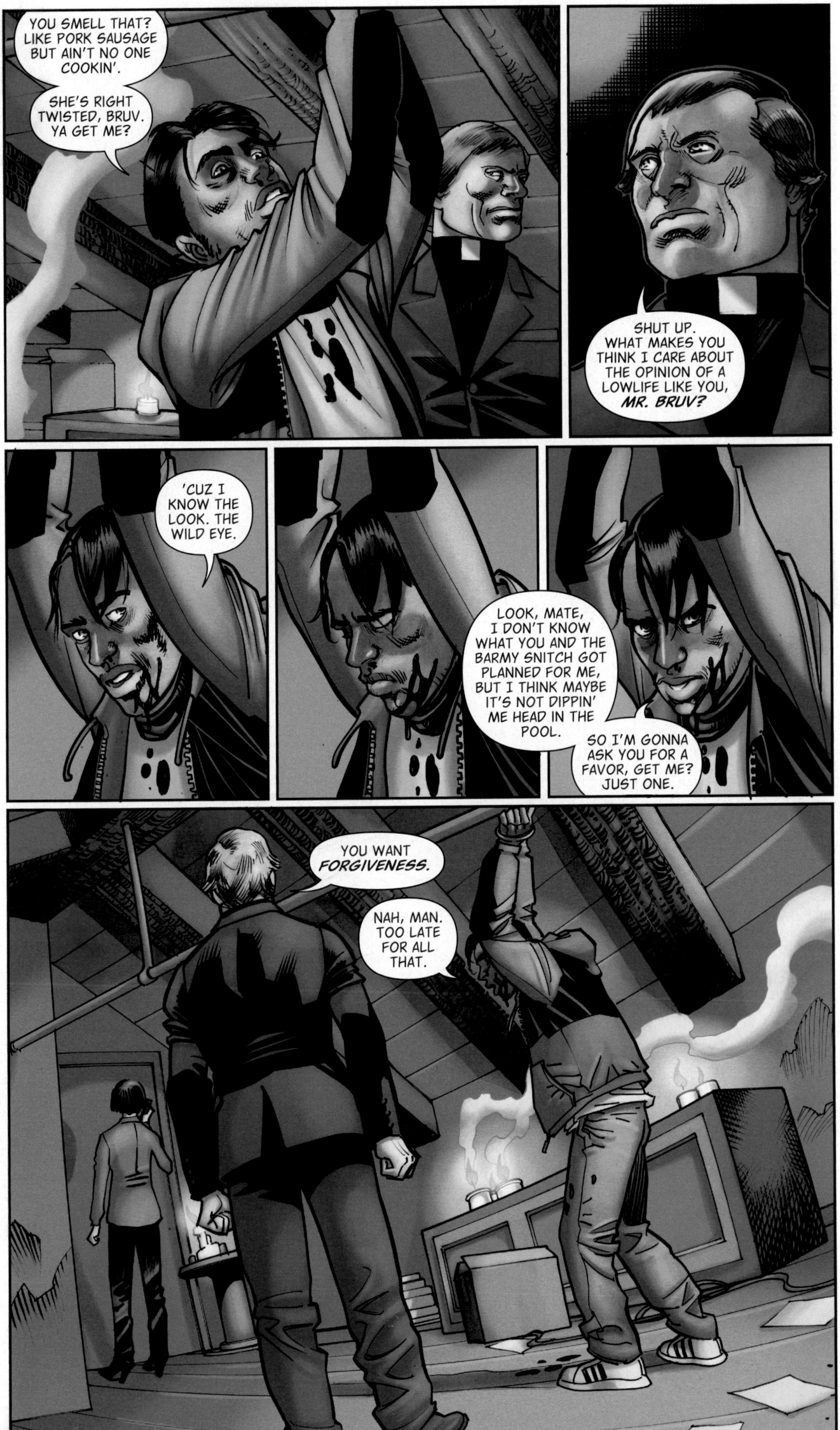
YOU SMELL THAT? LIKE PORK SAUSAGE BUT AIN'T NO ONE COOKIN'.
SHE'S RIGHT TWISTED, BRUV. YA GET ME?
SHUT UP. WHAT MAKES YOU THINK I CARE ABOUT THE OPINION OF A LOWLIFE LIKE YOU, MR. BRUV?
'CUZ I KNOW THE LOOK. THE WILD EYE.
LOOK, MATE, I DON'T KNOW WHAT YOU AND THE BARMY SNITCH GOT PLANNED FOR ME, BUT I THINK MAYBE IT'S NOT DIPPIN' ME HEAD IN THE POOL.
SO I'M GONNA ASK YOU FOR A FAVOR, GET ME? JUST ONE.
YOU WANT FORGIVENESS.
NAH, MAN. TOO LATE FOR ALL THAT.

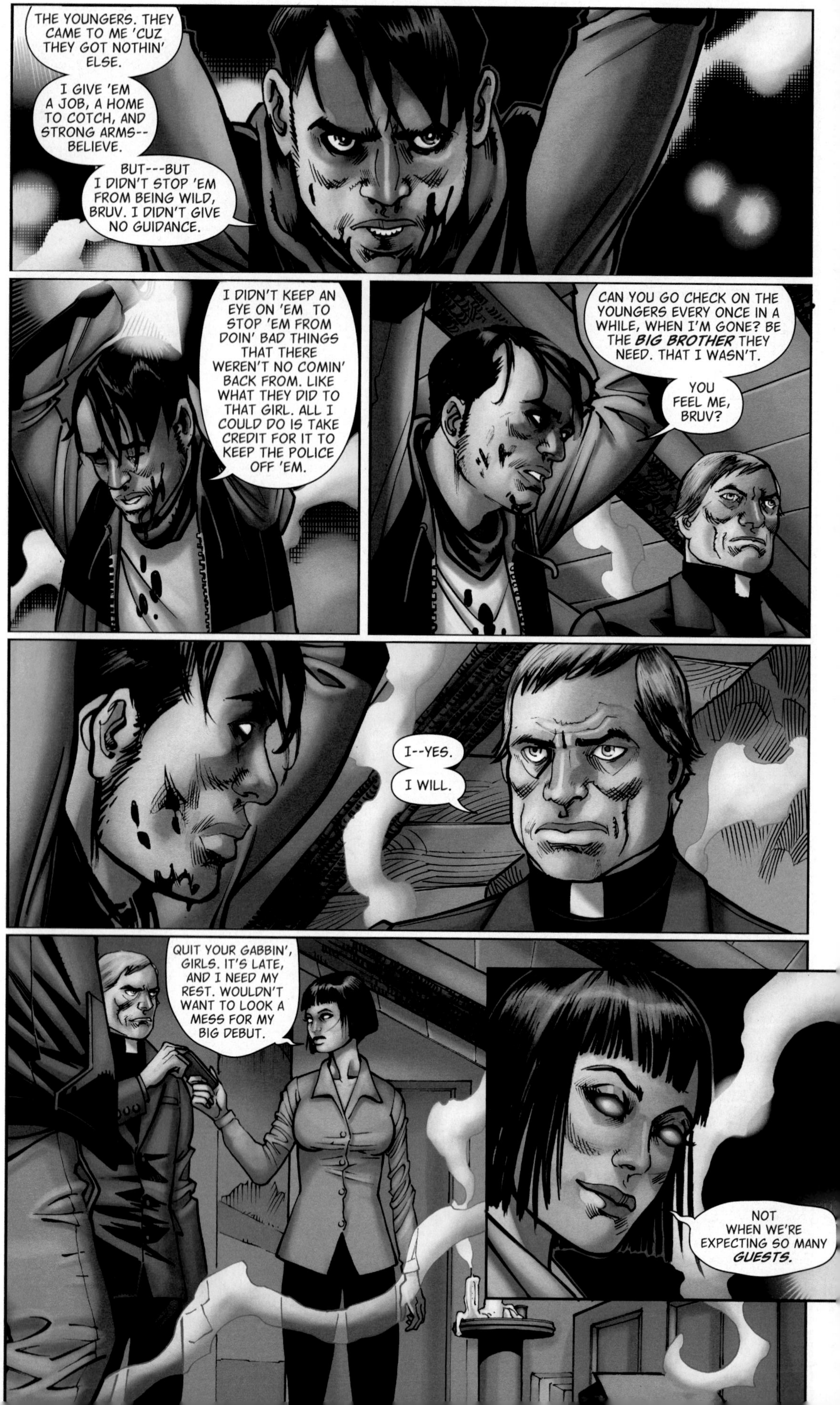
THE YOUNGERS. THEY CAME TO ME 'CUZ THEY GOT NOTHIN' ELSE.
I GIVE 'EM A JOB, A HOME TO COTCH, AND STRONG ARMS--BELIEVE.
BUT---BUT I DIDN'T STOP 'EM FROM BEING WILD, BRUV. I DIDN'T GIVE NO GUIDANCE.
I DIDN'T KEEP AN EYE ON 'EM TO STOP 'EM FROM DOIN' BAD THINGS THAT THERE WEREN'T NO COMIN' BACK FROM. LIKE WHAT THEY DID TO THAT GIRL. ALL I COULD DO IS TAKE CREDIT FOR IT TO KEEP THE POLICE OFF 'EM.
CAN YOU GO CHECK ON THE YOUNGERS EVERY ONCE IN A WHILE, WHEN I'M GONE? BE THE ***BIG BROTHER*** THEY NEED. THAT I WASN'T.
YOU FEEL ME, BRUV?
I--YES.
I WILL.
QUIT YOUR GABBIN', GIRLS. IT'S LATE, AND I NEED MY REST. WOULDN'T WANT TO LOOK A MESS FOR MY BIG DEBUT.
NOT WHEN WE'RE EXPECTING SO MANY ***GUESTS.***

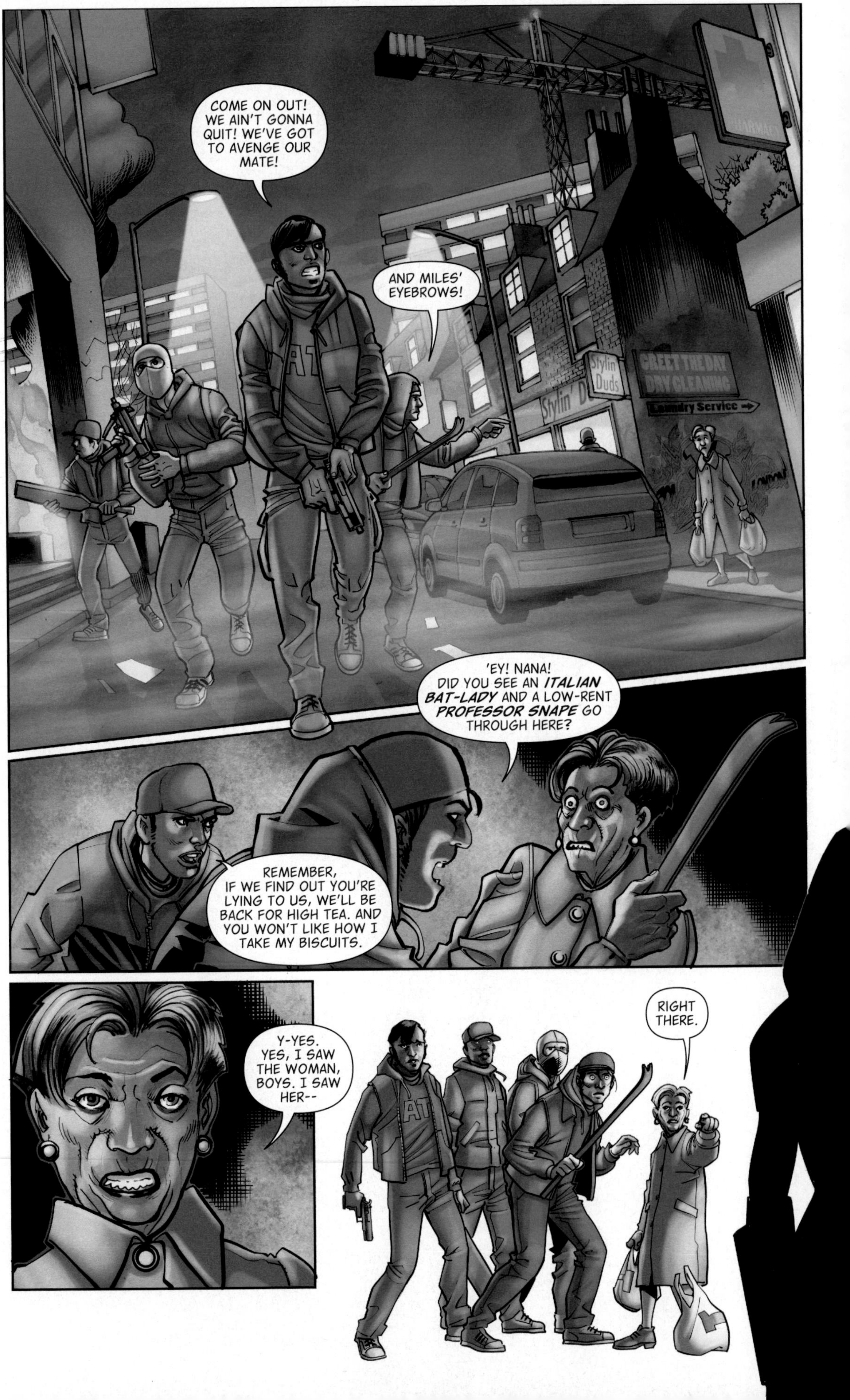
COME ON OUT! WE AIN'T GONNA QUIT! WE'VE GOT TO AVENGE OUR MATE!
AND MILES' EYEBROWS!
Stylin Duds
GREET THE DAY
DRY CLEANING
Laundry Service
'EY! NANA! DID YOU SEE AN *ITALIAN BAT-LADY* AND A LOW-RENT *PROFESSOR SNAPE* GO THROUGH HERE?
REMEMBER, IF WE FIND OUT YOU'RE LYING TO US, WE'LL BE BACK FOR HIGH TEA. AND YOU WON'T LIKE HOW I TAKE MY BISCUITS.
Y-YES. YES, I SAW THE WOMAN, BOYS. I SAW HER--
RIGHT THERE.

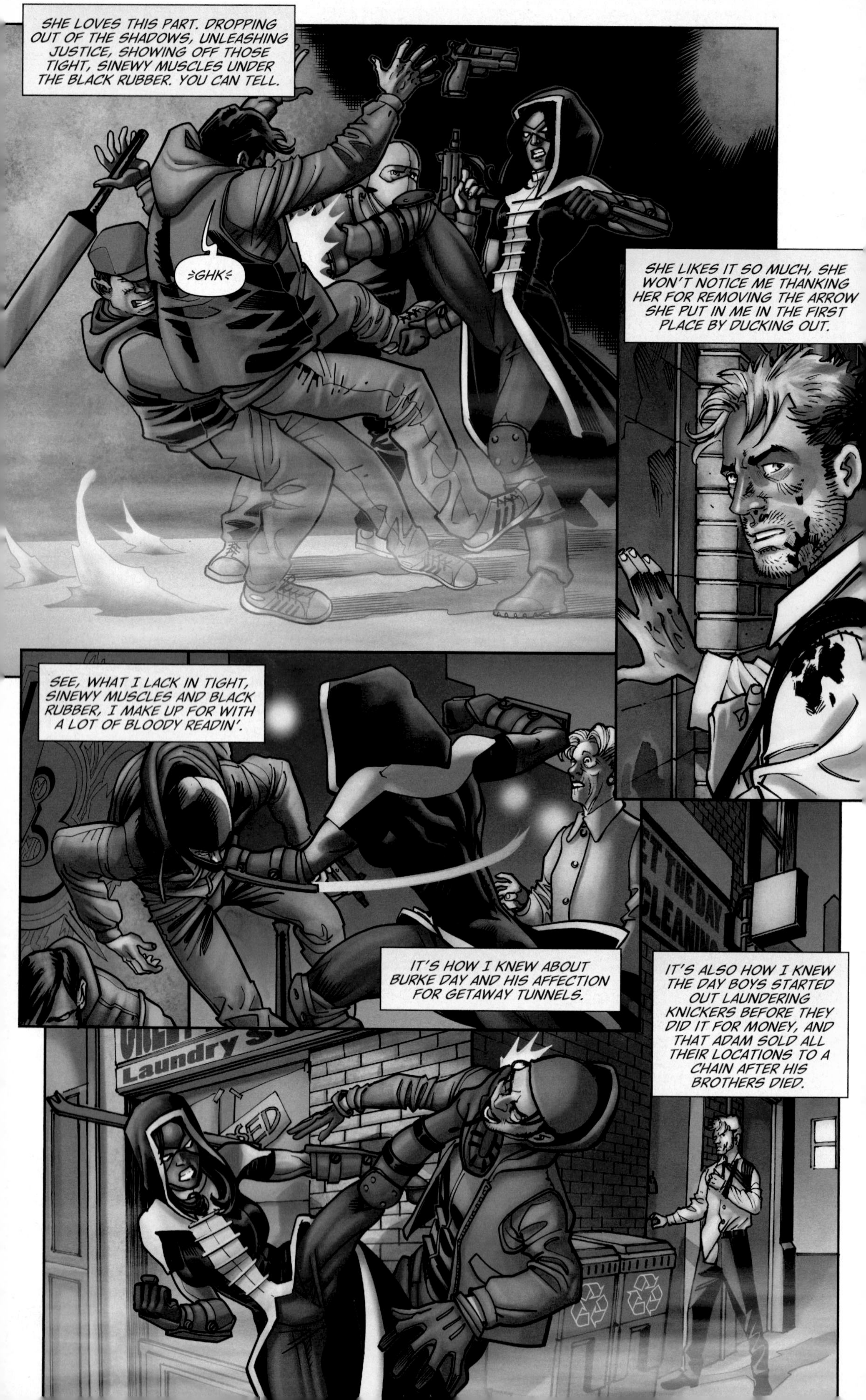
SHE LOVES THIS PART. DROPPING OUT OF THE SHADOWS, UNLEASHING JUSTICE, SHOWING OFF THOSE TIGHT, SINEWY MUSCLES UNDER THE BLACK RUBBER. YOU CAN TELL.
GHK
SHE LIKES IT SO MUCH, SHE WON'T NOTICE ME THANKING HER FOR REMOVING THE ARROW SHE PUT IN ME IN THE FIRST PLACE BY DUCKING OUT.
SEE, WHAT I LACK IN TIGHT, SINEWY MUSCLES AND BLACK RUBBER, I MAKE UP FOR WITH A LOT OF BLOODY READIN'.
IT'S HOW I KNEW ABOUT BURKE DAY AND HIS AFFECTION FOR GETAWAY TUNNELS.
IT'S ALSO HOW I KNEW THE DAY BOYS STARTED OUT LAUNDERING KNICKERS BEFORE THEY DID IT FOR MONEY, AND THAT ADAM SOLD ALL THEIR LOCATIONS TO A CHAIN AFTER HIS BROTHERS DIED.
Laundry

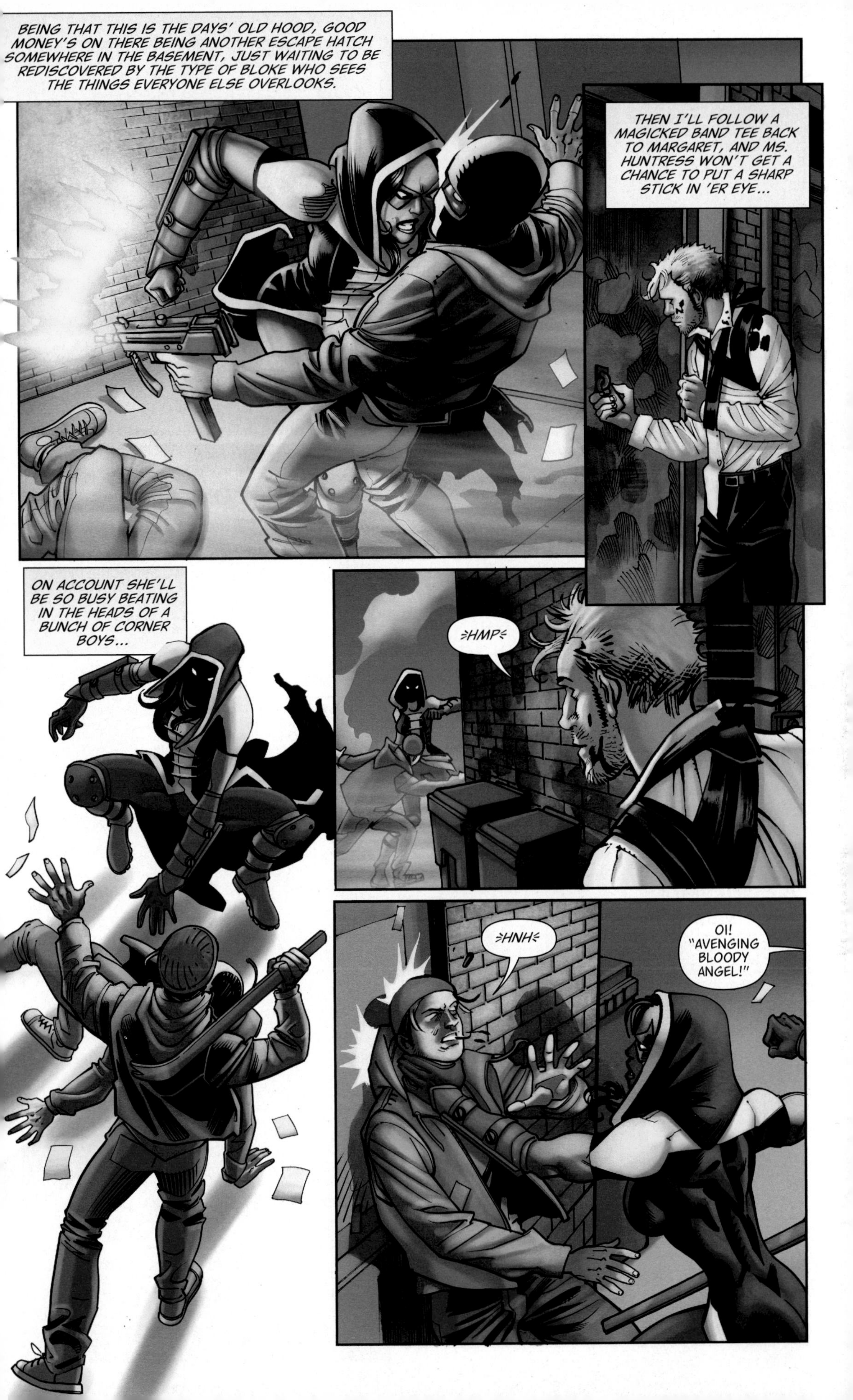
BEING THAT THIS IS THE DAYS' OLD HOOD, GOOD MONEY'S ON THERE BEING ANOTHER ESCAPE HATCH SOMEWHERE IN THE BASEMENT, JUST WAITING TO BE REDISCOVERED BY THE TYPE OF BLOKE WHO SEES THE THINGS EVERYONE ELSE OVERLOOKS.
THEN I'LL FOLLOW A MAGICKED BAND TEE BACK TO MARGARET, AND MS. HUNTRESS WON'T GET A CHANCE TO PUT A SHARP STICK IN 'ER EYE...
ON ACCOUNT SHE'LL BE SO BUSY BEATING IN THE HEADS OF A BUNCH OF CORNER BOYS...
HMP
HNH
OI! "AVENGING BLOODY ANGEL!"

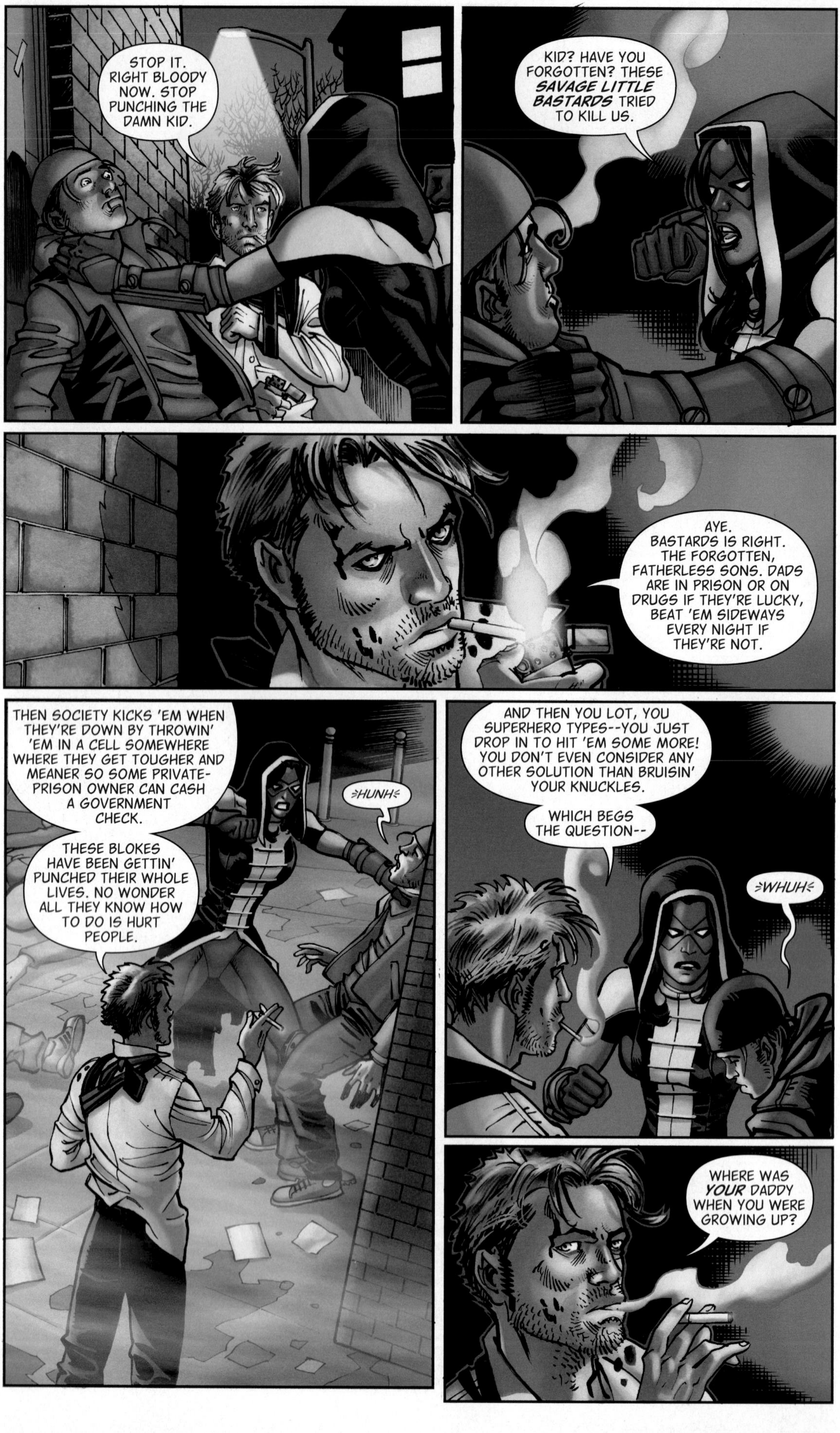
STOP IT. RIGHT BLOODY NOW. STOP PUNCHING THE DAMN KID.
KID? HAVE YOU FORGOTTEN? THESE SAVAGE LITTLE BASTARDS TRIED TO KILL US.
AYE. BASTARDS IS RIGHT. THE FORGOTTEN, FATHERLESS SONS. DADS ARE IN PRISON OR ON DRUGS IF THEY'RE LUCKY, BEAT 'EM SIDEWAYS EVERY NIGHT IF THEY'RE NOT.
THEN SOCIETY KICKS 'EM WHEN THEY'RE DOWN BY THROWIN' 'EM IN A CELL SOMEWHERE WHERE THEY GET TOUGHER AND MEANER SO SOME PRIVATE-PRISON OWNER CAN CASH A GOVERNMENT CHECK.
THESE BLOKES HAVE BEEN GETTIN' PUNCHED THEIR WHOLE LIVES. NO WONDER ALL THEY KNOW HOW TO DO IS HURT PEOPLE.
HUNH
AND THEN YOU LOT, YOU SUPERHERO TYPES--YOU JUST DROP IN TO HIT 'EM SOME MORE! YOU DON'T EVEN CONSIDER ANY OTHER SOLUTION THAN BRUISIN' YOUR KNUCKLES.
WHICH BEGS THE QUESTION--
WHUH
WHERE WAS YOUR DADDY WHEN YOU WERE GROWING UP?

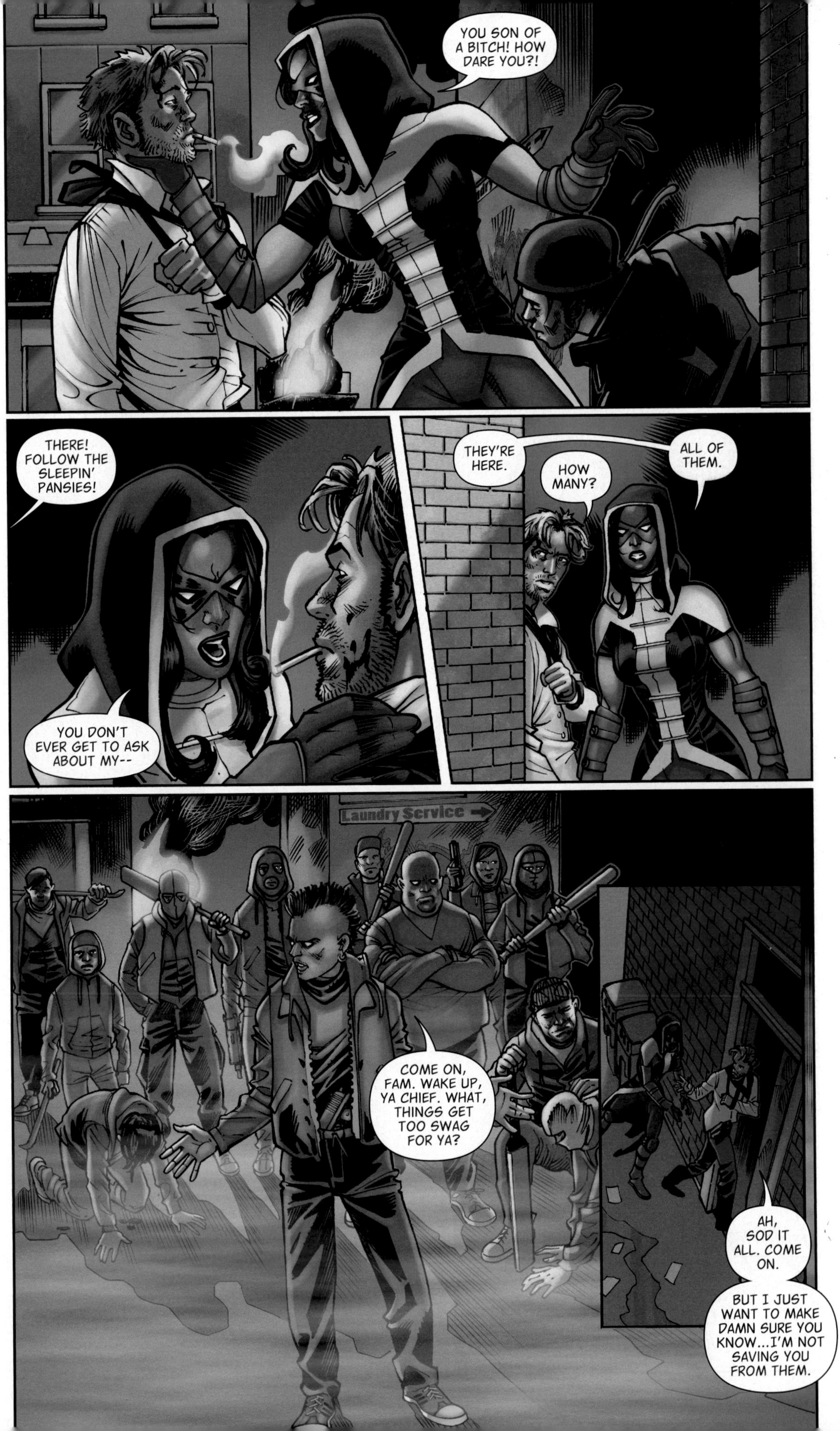
YOU SON OF A BITCH! HOW DARE YOU?!
THERE! FOLLOW THE SLEEPIN' PANSIES!
YOU DON'T EVER GET TO ASK ABOUT MY--
THEY'RE HERE.
HOW MANY?
ALL OF THEM.
Laundry Service
COME ON, FAM. WAKE UP, YA CHIEF. WHAT, THINGS GET TOO SWAG FOR YA?
AH, SOD IT ALL. COME ON.
BUT I JUST WANT TO MAKE DAMN SURE YOU KNOW...I'M NOT SAVING YOU FROM THEM.

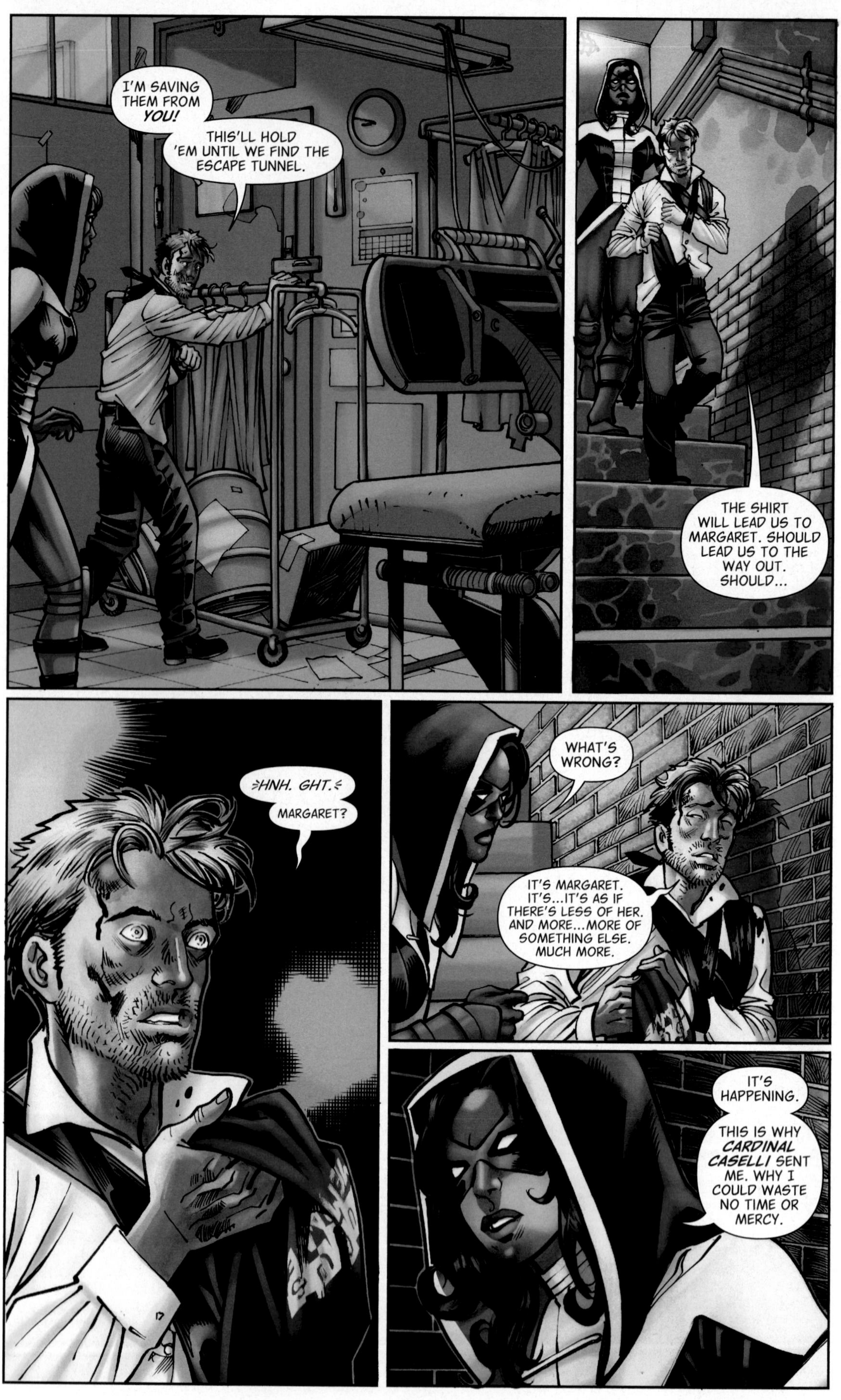
I'M SAVING THEM FROM YOU!
THIS'LL HOLD 'EM UNTIL WE FIND THE ESCAPE TUNNEL.
THE SHIRT WILL LEAD US TO MARGARET. SHOULD LEAD US TO THE WAY OUT. SHOULD...
HNH. GHT.
MARGARET?
WHAT'S WRONG?
IT'S MARGARET. IT'S...IT'S AS IF THERE'S LESS OF HER. AND MORE...MORE OF SOMETHING ELSE. MUCH MORE.
IT'S HAPPENING.
THIS IS WHY CARDINAL CASELLI SENT ME. WHY I COULD WASTE NO TIME OR MERCY.

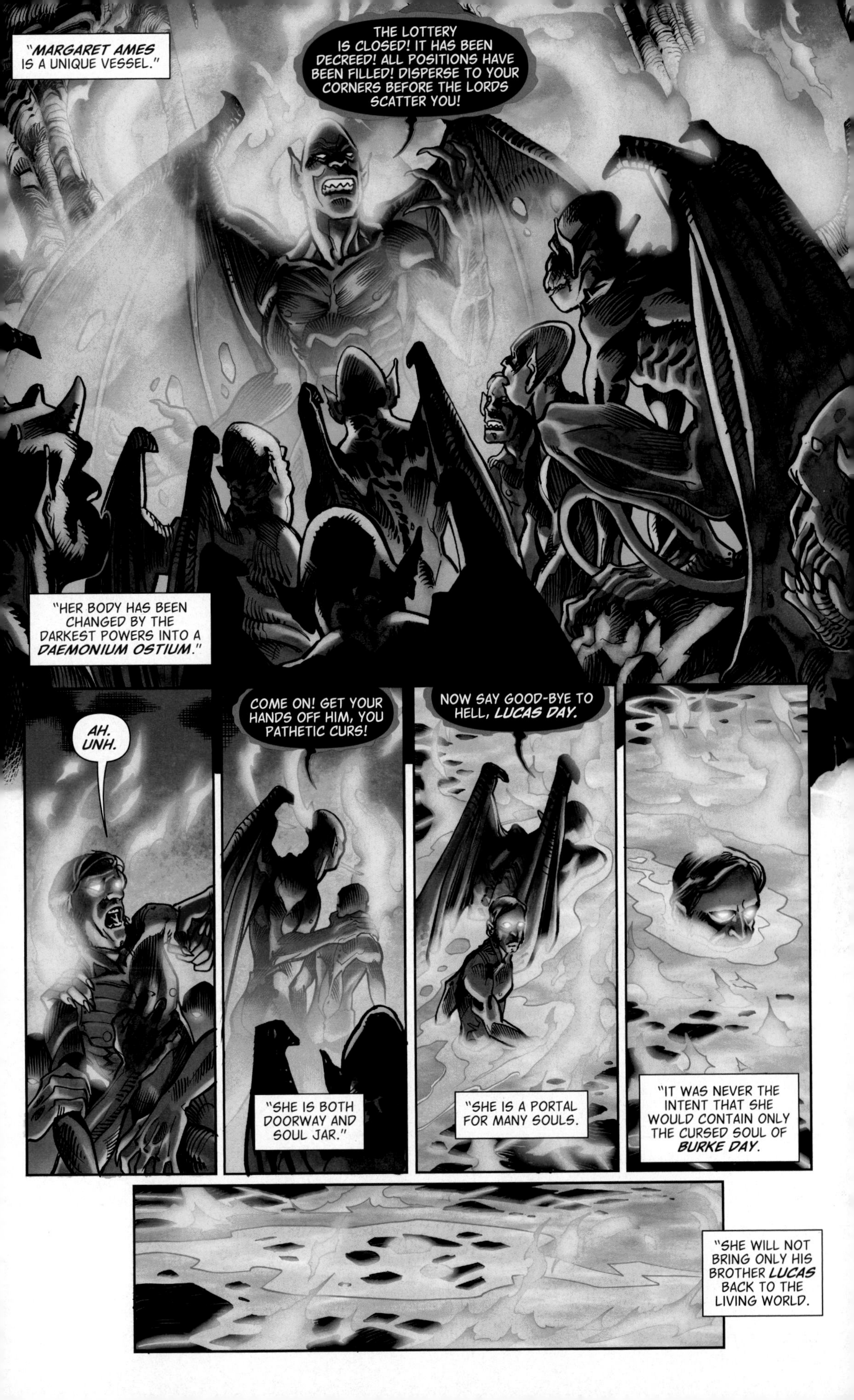
"MARGARET AMES IS A UNIQUE VESSEL."
THE LOTTERY IS CLOSED! IT HAS BEEN DECREED! ALL POSITIONS HAVE BEEN FILLED! DISPERSE TO YOUR CORNERS BEFORE THE LORDS SCATTER YOU!
"HER BODY HAS BEEN CHANGED BY THE DARKEST POWERS INTO A DAEMONIUM OSTIUM."
AH. UNH.
COME ON! GET YOUR HANDS OFF HIM, YOU PATHETIC CURS!
"SHE IS BOTH DOORWAY AND SOUL JAR."
NOW SAY GOOD-BYE TO HELL, LUCAS DAY.
"SHE IS A PORTAL FOR MANY SOULS.
"IT WAS NEVER THE INTENT THAT SHE WOULD CONTAIN ONLY THE CURSED SOUL OF BURKE DAY.
"SHE WILL NOT BRING ONLY HIS BROTHER LUCAS BACK TO THE LIVING WORLD.

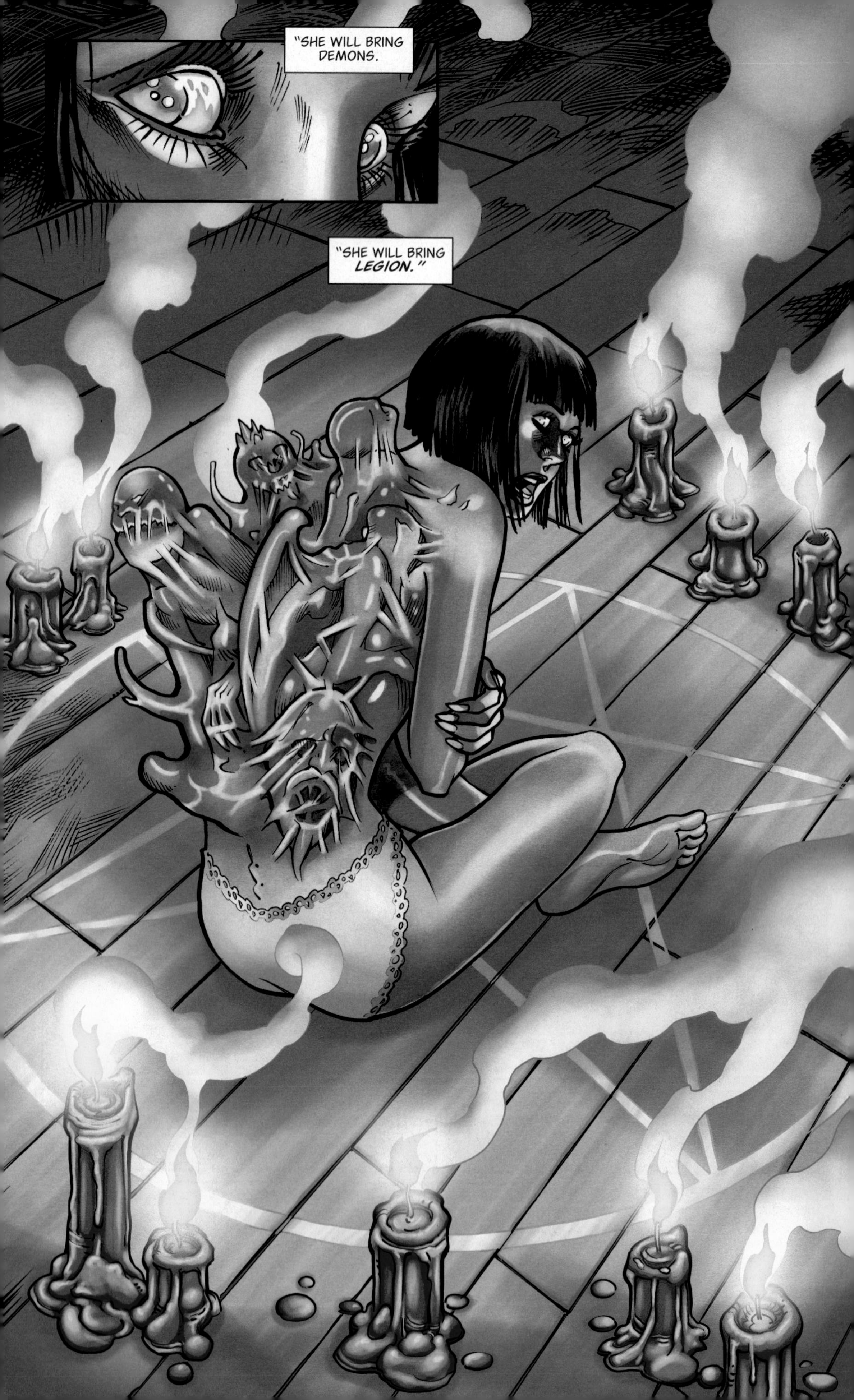
"SHE WILL BRING DEMONS.
"SHE WILL BRING LEGION."

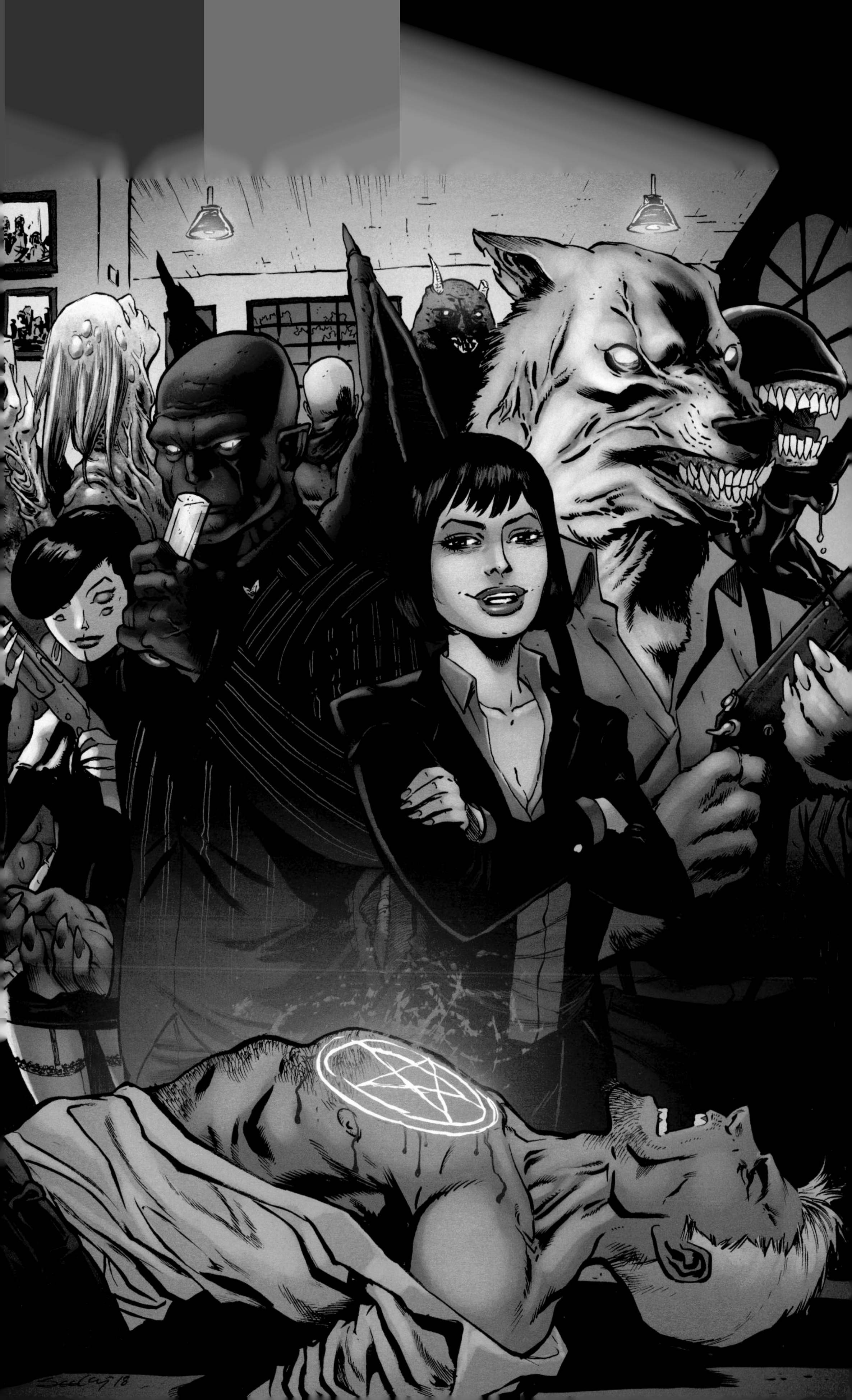

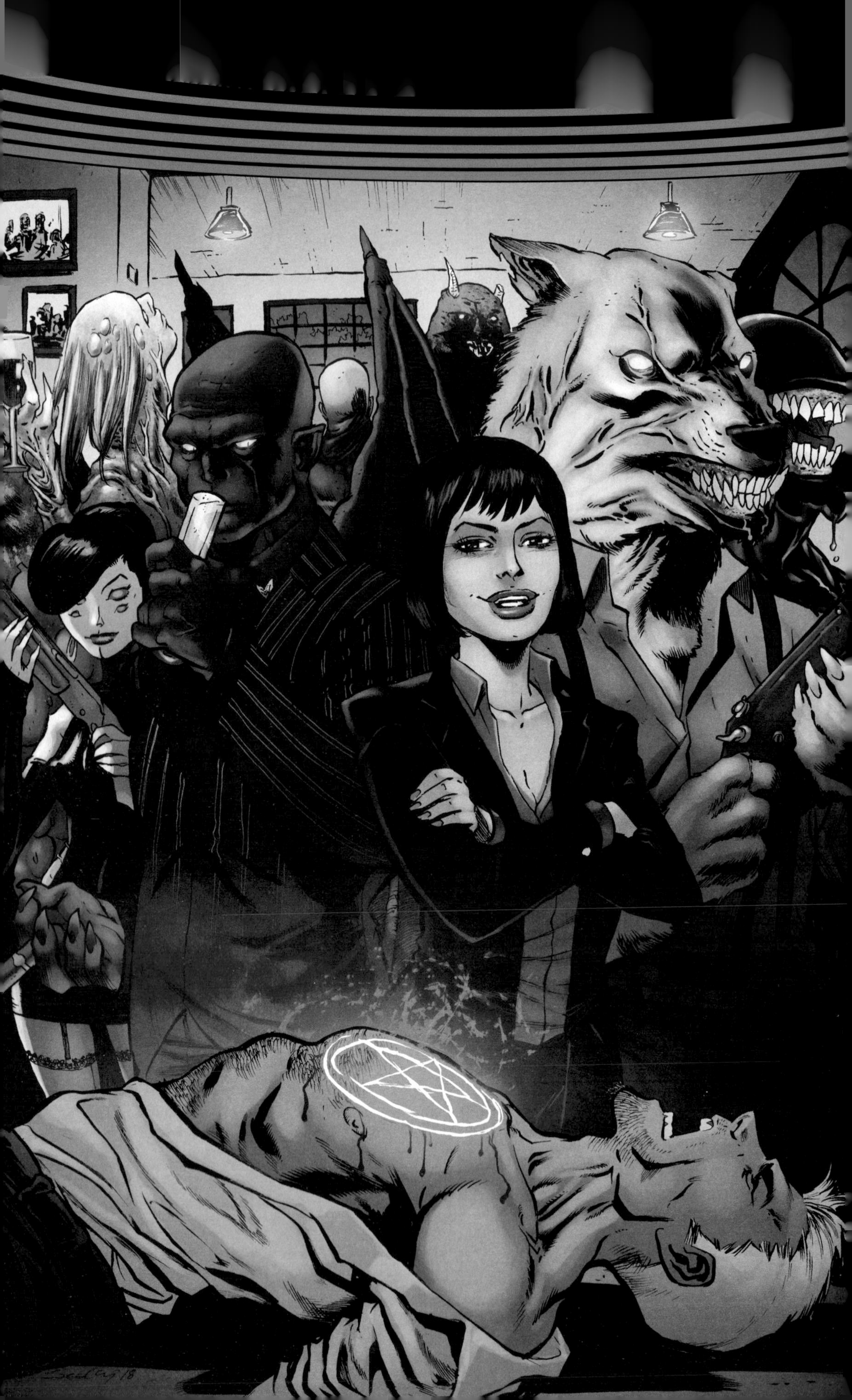

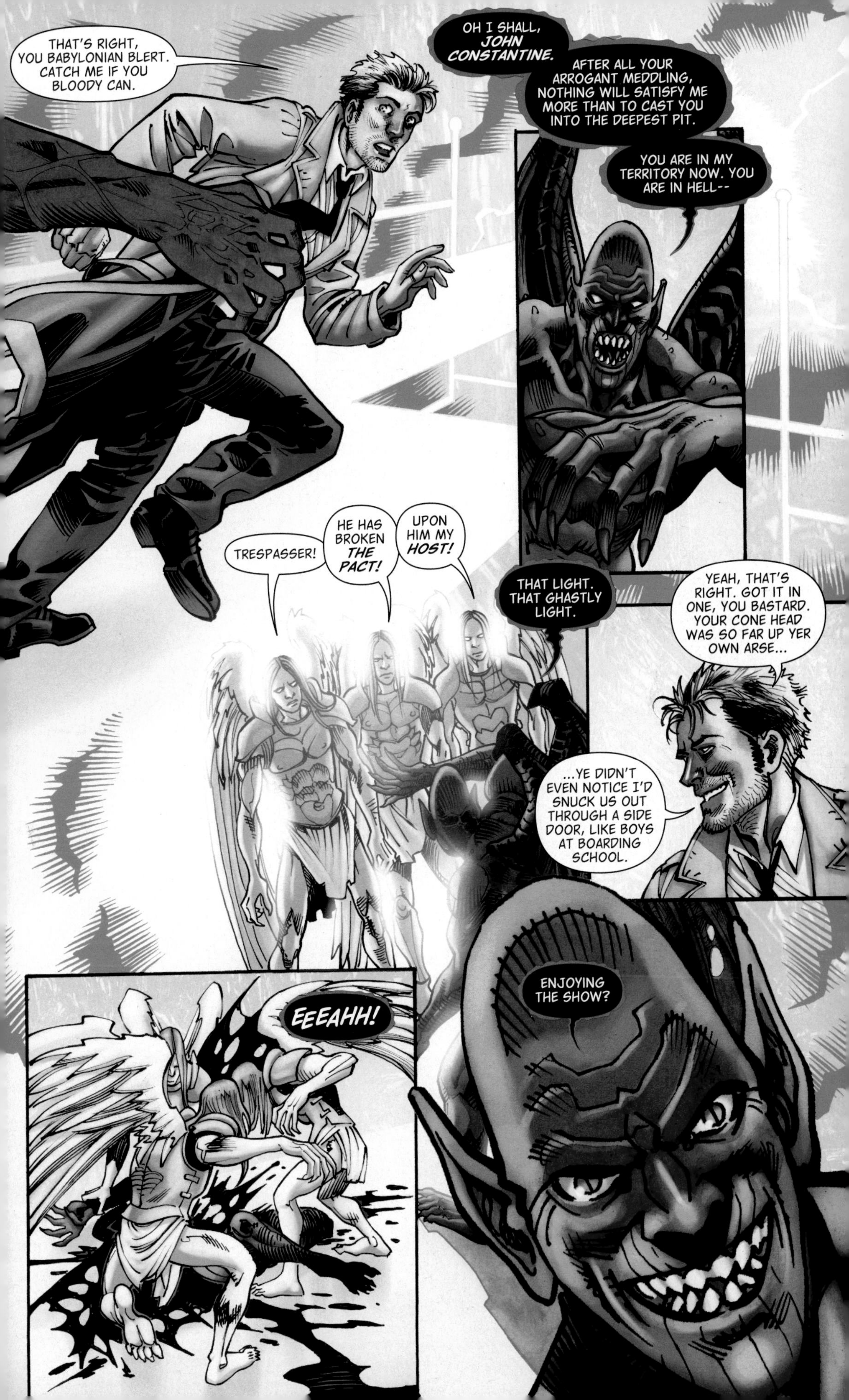
THAT'S RIGHT, YOU BABYLONIAN BLERT. CATCH ME IF YOU BLOODY CAN.
OH I SHALL, *JOHN CONSTANTINE.*
AFTER ALL YOUR ARROGANT MEDDLING, NOTHING WILL SATISFY ME MORE THAN TO CAST YOU INTO THE DEEPEST PIT.
YOU ARE IN MY TERRITORY NOW. YOU ARE IN HELL--
TRESPASSER!
HE HAS BROKEN *THE PACT!*
UPON HIM MY *HOST!*
THAT LIGHT. THAT GHASTLY LIGHT.
YEAH, THAT'S RIGHT. GOT IT IN ONE, YOU BASTARD. YOUR CONE HEAD WAS SO FAR UP YER OWN ARSE...
...YE DIDN'T EVEN NOTICE I'D SNUCK US OUT THROUGH A SIDE DOOR, LIKE BOYS AT BOARDING SCHOOL.
EEEAHH!
ENJOYING THE SHOW?

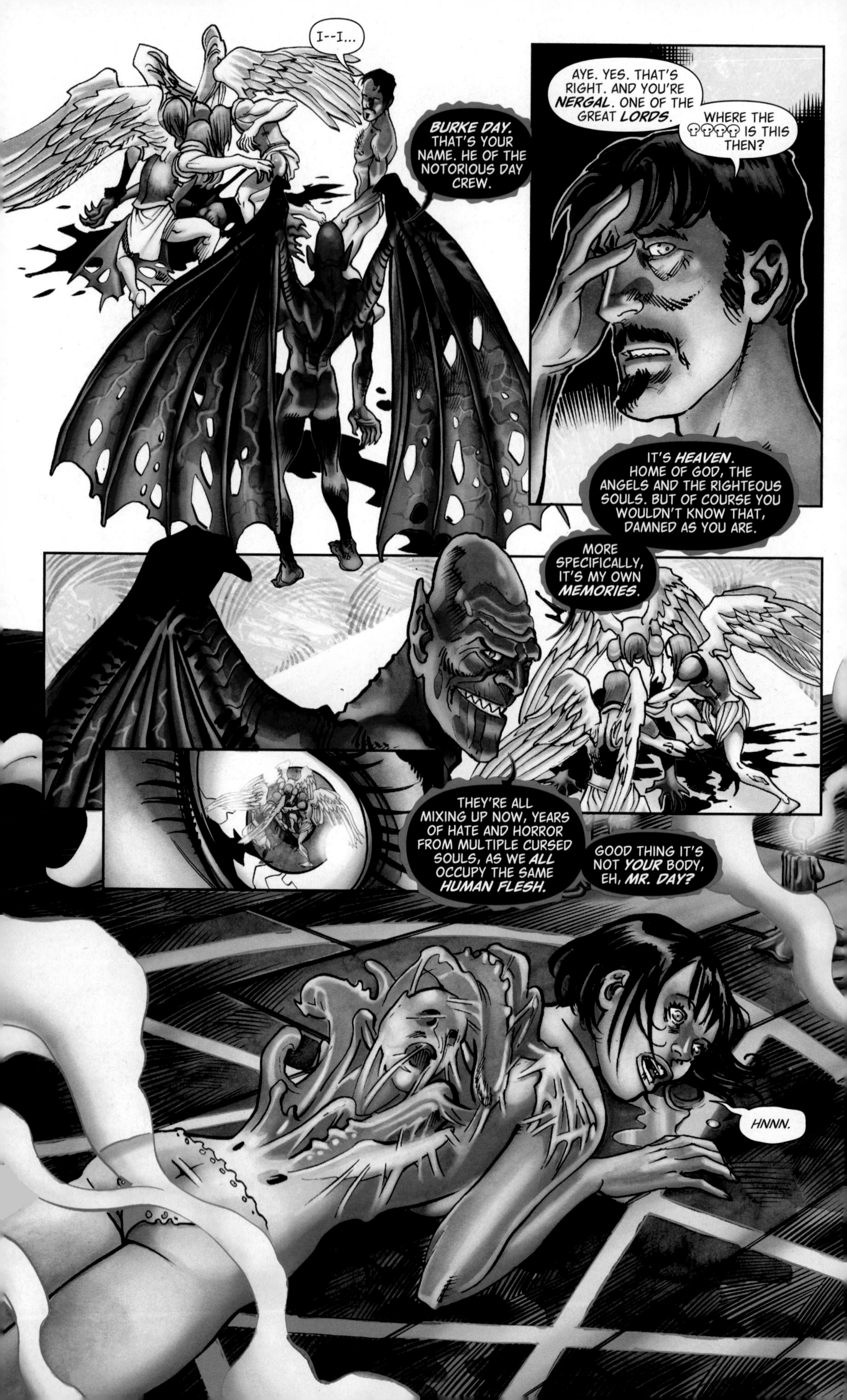
I--I...
BURKE DAY. THAT'S YOUR NAME. HE OF THE NOTORIOUS DAY CREW.
AYE. YES. THAT'S RIGHT. AND YOU'RE NERGAL. ONE OF THE GREAT LORDS.
WHERE THE ☠☠☠☠ IS THIS THEN?
IT'S HEAVEN. HOME OF GOD, THE ANGELS AND THE RIGHTEOUS SOULS. BUT OF COURSE YOU WOULDN'T KNOW THAT, DAMNED AS YOU ARE.
MORE SPECIFICALLY, IT'S MY OWN MEMORIES.
THEY'RE ALL MIXING UP NOW, YEARS OF HATE AND HORROR FROM MULTIPLE CURSED SOULS, AS WE ALL OCCUPY THE SAME HUMAN FLESH.
GOOD THING IT'S NOT YOUR BODY, EH, MR. DAY?
HNNN.

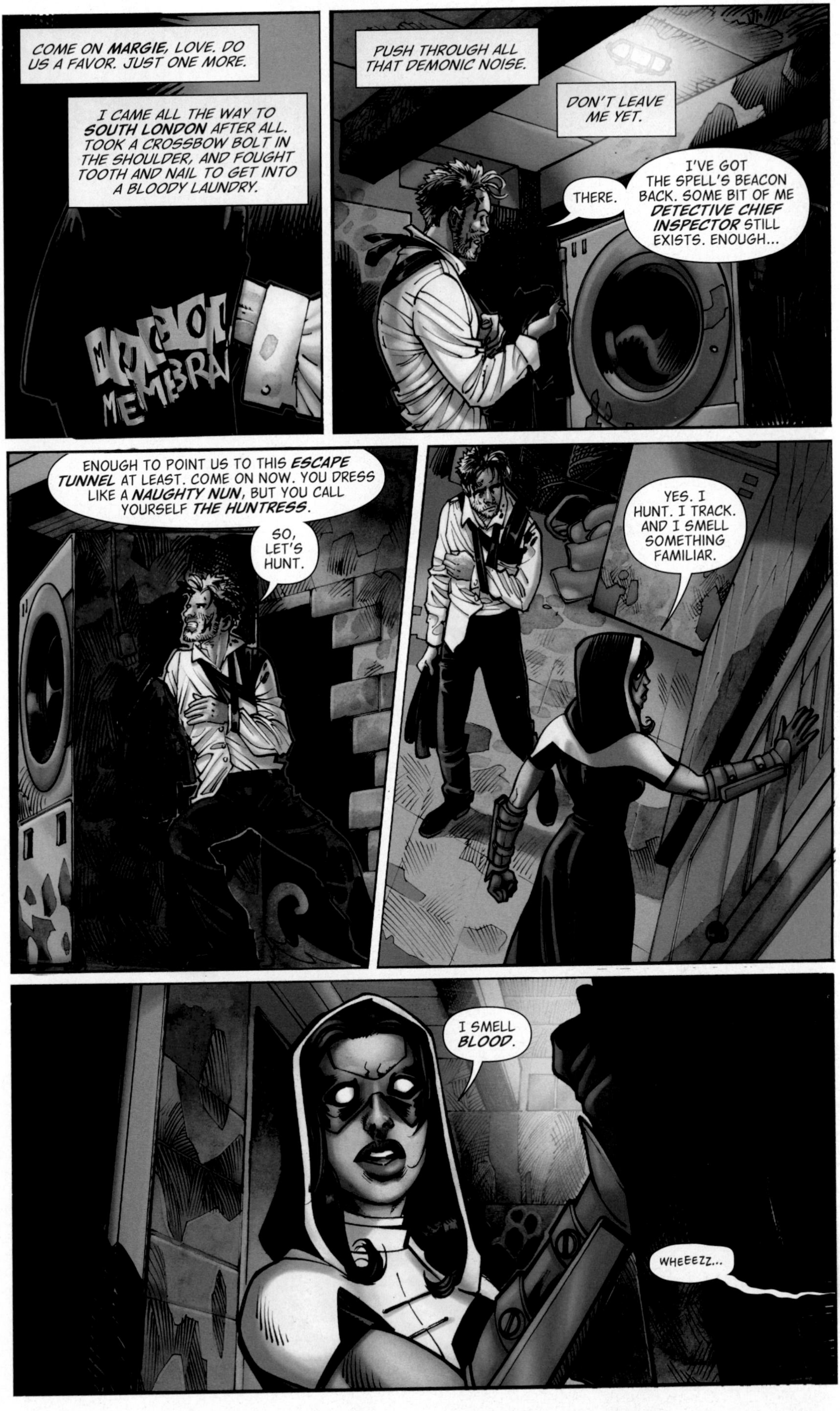

COME ON MARGIE, LOVE. DO US A FAVOR. JUST ONE MORE.
I CAME ALL THE WAY TO SOUTH LONDON AFTER ALL. TOOK A CROSSBOW BOLT IN THE SHOULDER, AND FOUGHT TOOTH AND NAIL TO GET INTO A BLOODY LAUNDRY.
PUSH THROUGH ALL THAT DEMONIC NOISE.
DON'T LEAVE ME YET.
THERE.
I'VE GOT THE SPELL'S BEACON BACK. SOME BIT OF ME DETECTIVE CHIEF INSPECTOR STILL EXISTS. ENOUGH...
ENOUGH TO POINT US TO THIS ESCAPE TUNNEL AT LEAST. COME ON NOW. YOU DRESS LIKE A NAUGHTY NUN, BUT YOU CALL YOURSELF THE HUNTRESS.
SO, LET'S HUNT.
YES. I HUNT. I TRACK. AND I SMELL SOMETHING FAMILIAR.
I SMELL BLOOD.
WHEEEZZ...

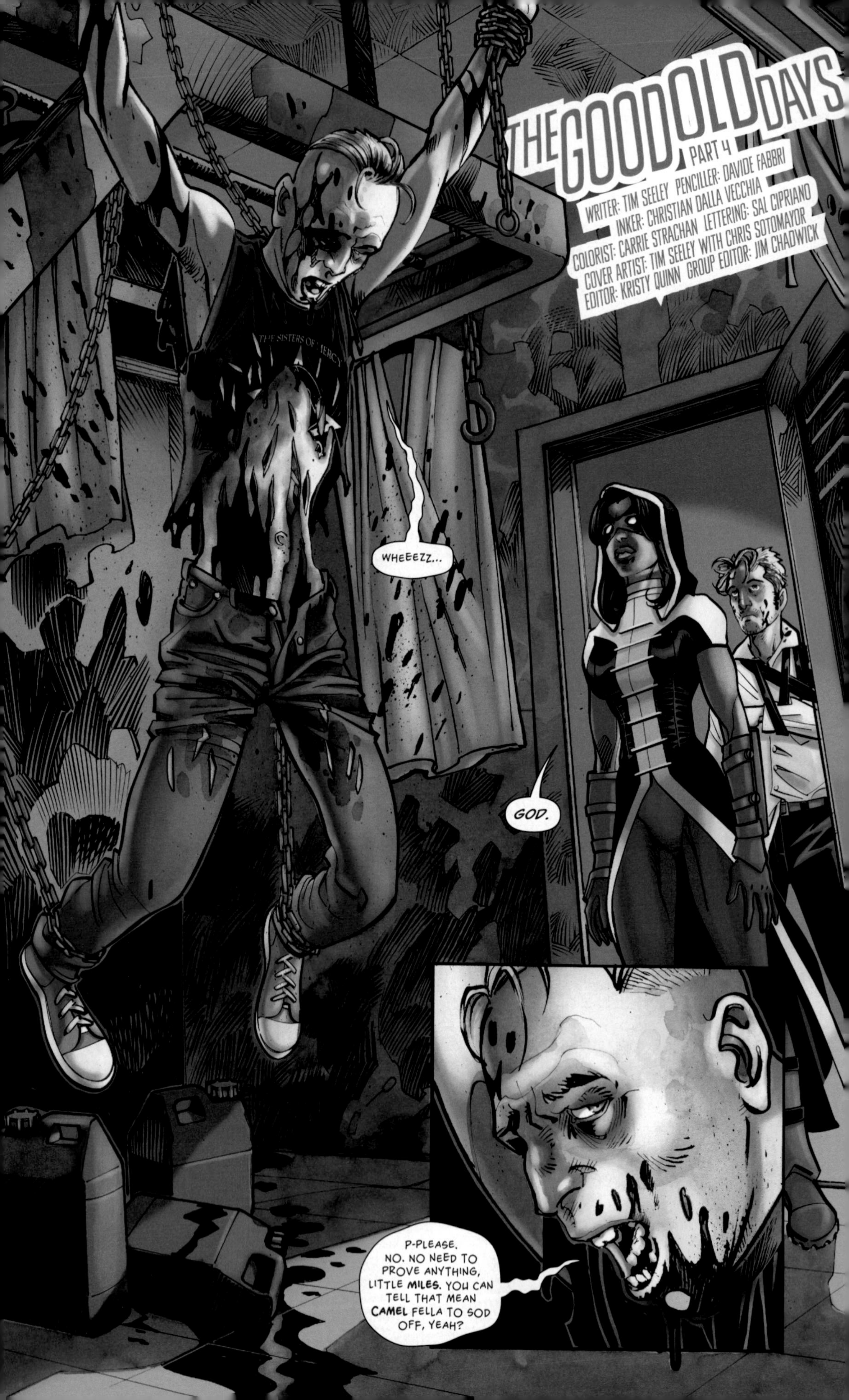
THE GOOD OLD DAYS
PART 4
WRITER: TIM SEELEY PENCILLER: DAVIDE FABBRI
INKER: CHRISTIAN DALLA VECCHIA
COLORIST: CARRIE STRACHAN LETTERING: SAL CIPRIANO
COVER ARTIST: TIM SEELEY WITH CHRIS SOTOMAYOR
EDITOR: KRISTY QUINN GROUP EDITOR: JIM CHADWICK
THE SISTERS OF MERCY
WHEEEZZ...
GOD.
P-PLEASE. NO. NO NEED TO PROVE ANYTHING, LITTLE MILES. YOU CAN TELL THAT MEAN CAMEL FELLA TO SOD OFF, YEAH?

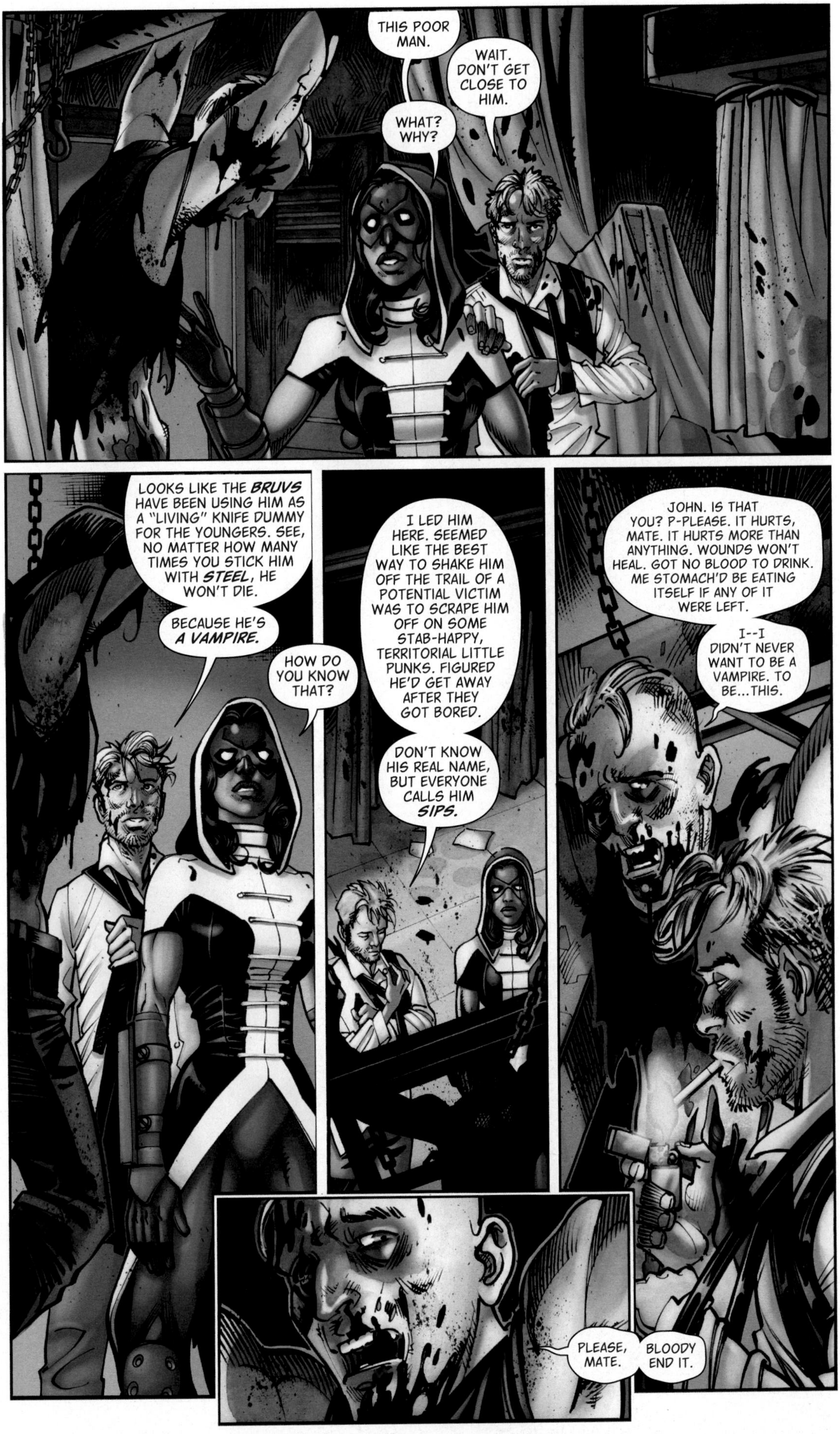
THIS POOR MAN.
WAIT. DON'T GET CLOSE TO HIM.
WHAT? WHY?
LOOKS LIKE THE BRUVS HAVE BEEN USING HIM AS A "LIVING" KNIFE DUMMY FOR THE YOUNGERS. SEE, NO MATTER HOW MANY TIMES YOU STICK HIM WITH STEEL, HE WON'T DIE.
BECAUSE HE'S A VAMPIRE.
HOW DO YOU KNOW THAT?
I LED HIM HERE. SEEMED LIKE THE BEST WAY TO SHAKE HIM OFF THE TRAIL OF A POTENTIAL VICTIM WAS TO SCRAPE HIM OFF ON SOME STAB-HAPPY, TERRITORIAL LITTLE PUNKS. FIGURED HE'D GET AWAY AFTER THEY GOT BORED.
DON'T KNOW HIS REAL NAME, BUT EVERYONE CALLS HIM SIPS.
JOHN. IS THAT YOU? P-PLEASE. IT HURTS, MATE. IT HURTS MORE THAN ANYTHING. WOUNDS WON'T HEAL. GOT NO BLOOD TO DRINK. ME STOMACH'D BE EATING ITSELF IF ANY OF IT WERE LEFT.
I--I DIDN'T NEVER WANT TO BE A VAMPIRE. TO BE...THIS.
PLEASE, MATE.
BLOODY END IT.

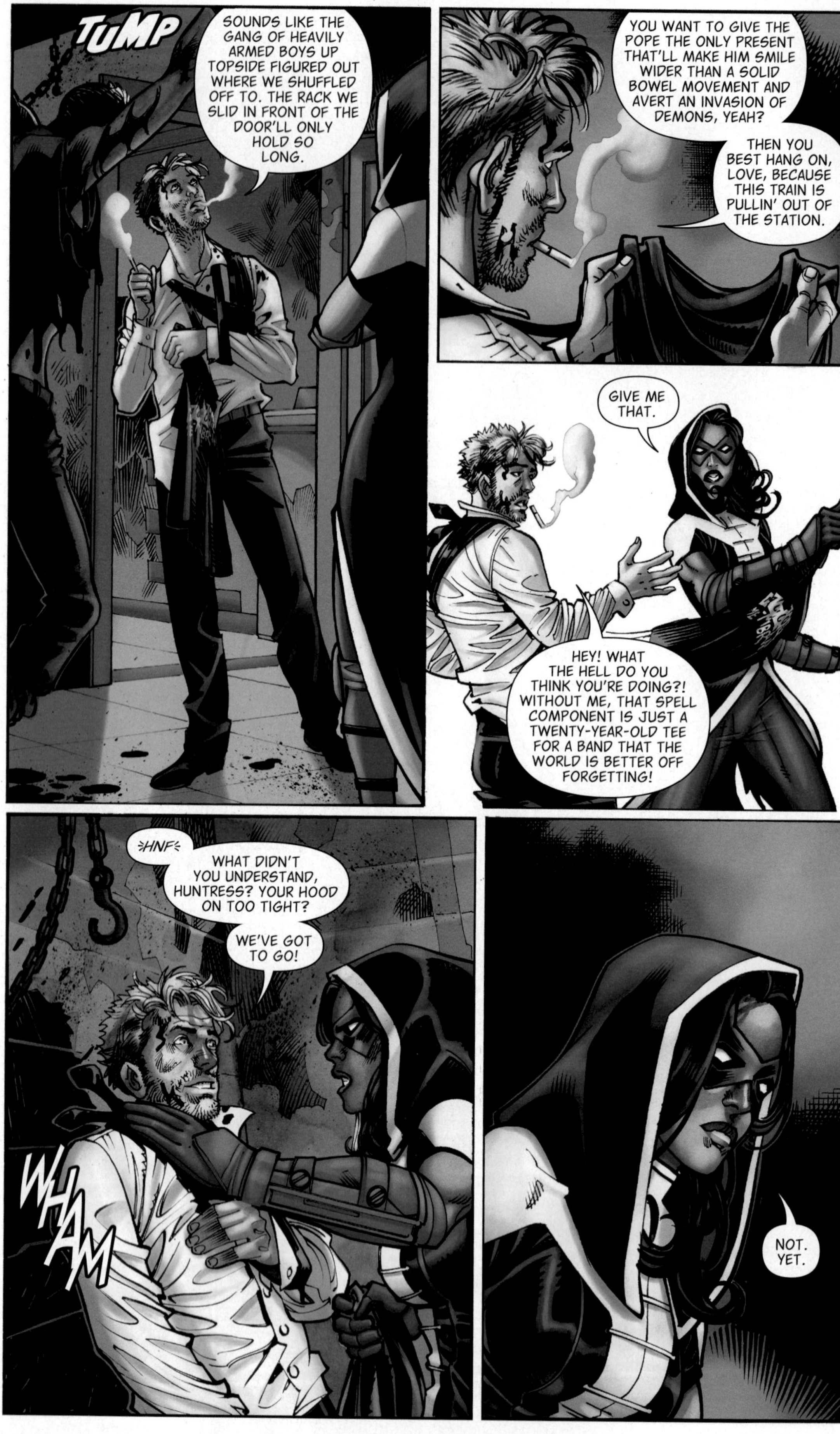
TUMP
SOUNDS LIKE THE GANG OF HEAVILY ARMED BOYS UP TOPSIDE FIGURED OUT WHERE WE SHUFFLED OFF TO. THE RACK WE SLID IN FRONT OF THE DOOR'LL ONLY HOLD SO LONG.
YOU WANT TO GIVE THE POPE THE ONLY PRESENT THAT'LL MAKE HIM SMILE WIDER THAN A SOLID BOWEL MOVEMENT AND AVERT AN INVASION OF DEMONS, YEAH?
THEN YOU BEST HANG ON, LOVE, BECAUSE THIS TRAIN IS PULLIN' OUT OF THE STATION.
GIVE ME THAT.
HEY! WHAT THE HELL DO YOU THINK YOU'RE DOING?! WITHOUT ME, THAT SPELL COMPONENT IS JUST A TWENTY-YEAR-OLD TEE FOR A BAND THAT THE WORLD IS BETTER OFF FORGETTING!
HNF
WHAT DIDN'T YOU UNDERSTAND, HUNTRESS? YOUR HOOD ON TOO TIGHT?
WE'VE GOT TO GO!
WHAM
NOT. YET.

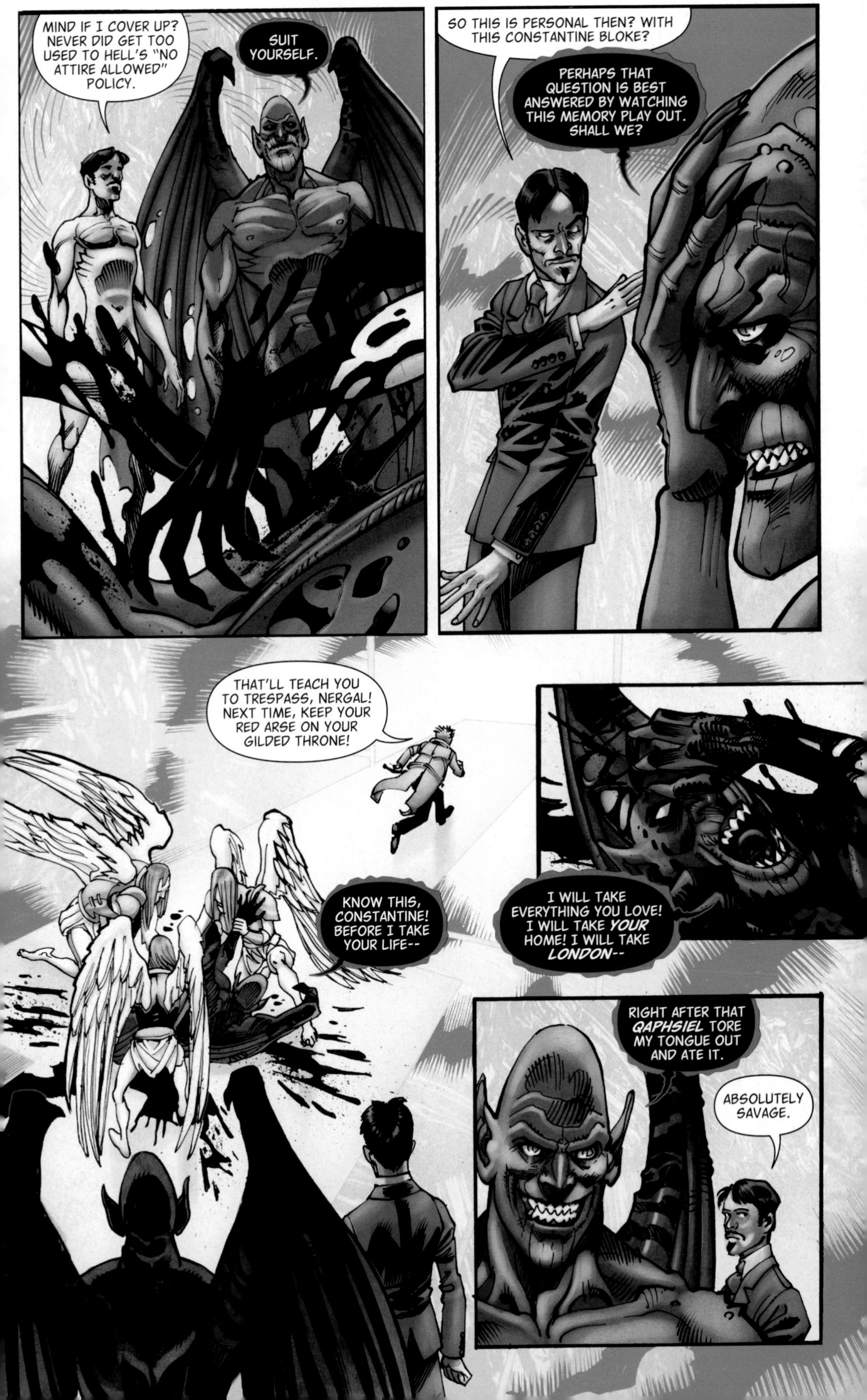

MIND IF I COVER UP? NEVER DID GET TOO USED TO HELL'S "NO ATTIRE ALLOWED" POLICY.
SUIT YOURSELF.
SO THIS IS PERSONAL THEN? WITH THIS CONSTANTINE BLOKE?
PERHAPS THAT QUESTION IS BEST ANSWERED BY WATCHING THIS MEMORY PLAY OUT. SHALL WE?
THAT'LL TEACH YOU TO TRESPASS, NERGAL! NEXT TIME, KEEP YOUR RED ARSE ON YOUR GILDED THRONE!
KNOW THIS, CONSTANTINE! BEFORE I TAKE YOUR LIFE--
I WILL TAKE EVERYTHING YOU LOVE! I WILL TAKE *YOUR* HOME! I WILL TAKE *LONDON*--
RIGHT AFTER THAT *QAPHSIEL* TORE MY TONGUE OUT AND ATE IT.
ABSOLUTELY SAVAGE.

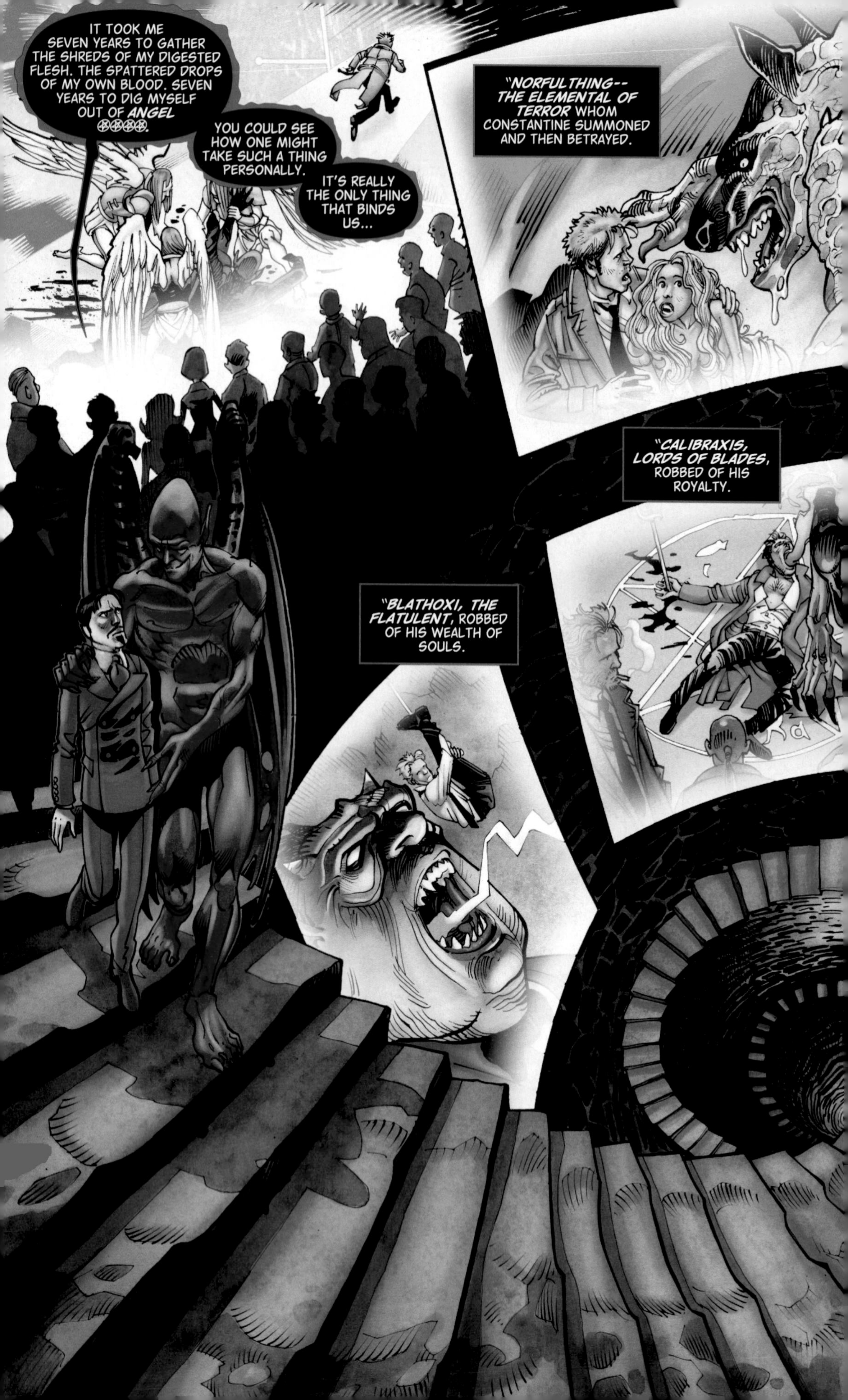
IT TOOK ME SEVEN YEARS TO GATHER THE SHREDS OF MY DIGESTED FLESH. THE SPATTERED DROPS OF MY OWN BLOOD. SEVEN YEARS TO DIG MYSELF OUT OF *ANGEL* ✪✪✪✪.
YOU COULD SEE HOW ONE MIGHT TAKE SUCH A THING PERSONALLY.
IT'S REALLY THE ONLY THING THAT BINDS US...
"*NORFULTHING-- THE ELEMENTAL OF TERROR* WHOM CONSTANTINE SUMMONED AND THEN BETRAYED.
"*CALIBRAXIS, LORDS OF BLADES*, ROBBED OF HIS ROYALTY.
"*BLATHOXI, THE FLATULENT*, ROBBED OF HIS WEALTH OF SOULS.

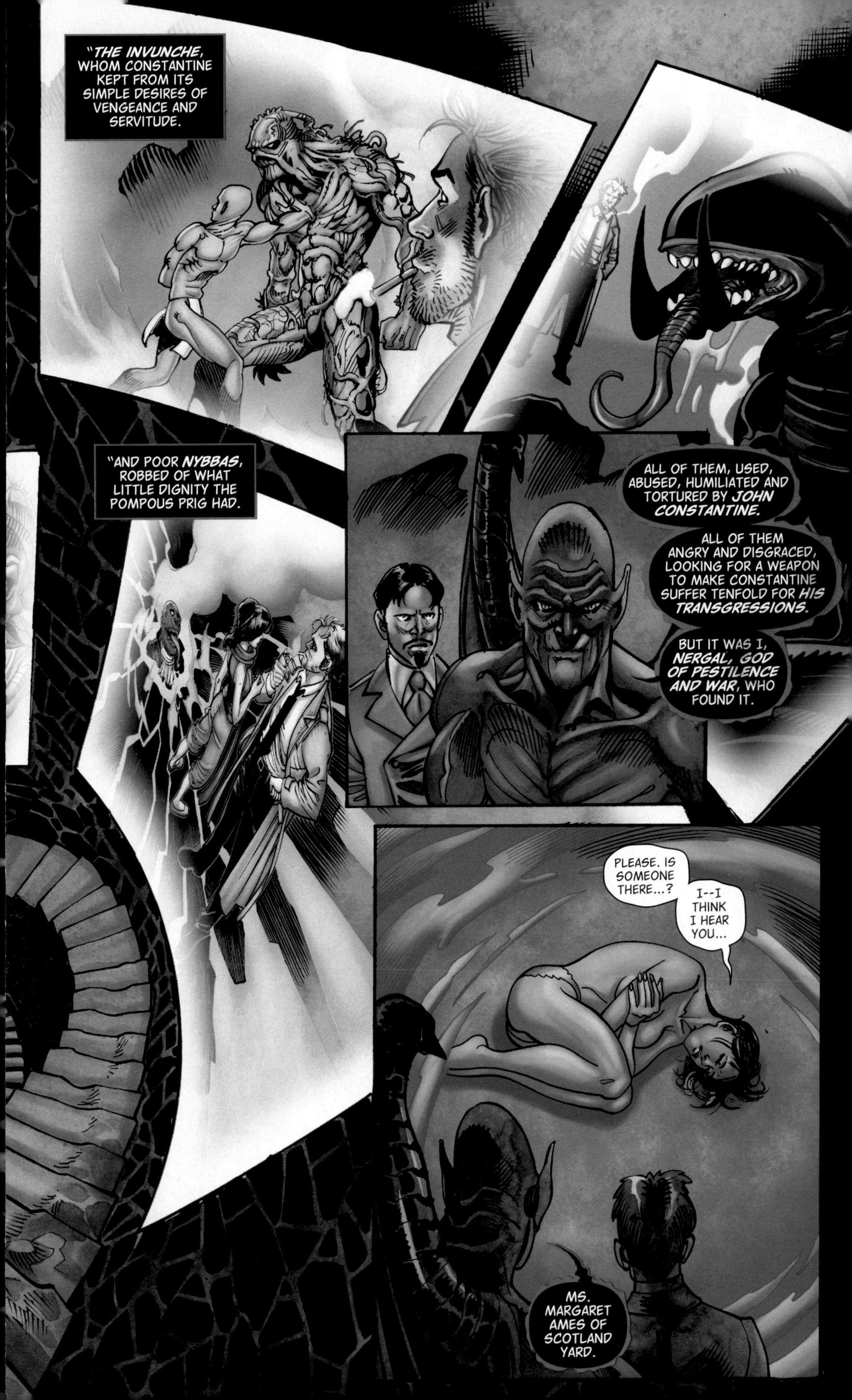
"THE INVUNCHE, WHOM CONSTANTINE KEPT FROM ITS SIMPLE DESIRES OF VENGEANCE AND SERVITUDE.
"AND POOR NYBBAS, ROBBED OF WHAT LITTLE DIGNITY THE POMPOUS PRIG HAD.
ALL OF THEM, USED, ABUSED, HUMILIATED AND TORTURED BY JOHN CONSTANTINE.
ALL OF THEM ANGRY AND DISGRACED, LOOKING FOR A WEAPON TO MAKE CONSTANTINE SUFFER TENFOLD FOR HIS TRANSGRESSIONS.
BUT IT WAS I, NERGAL, GOD OF PESTILENCE AND WAR, WHO FOUND IT.
PLEASE. IS SOMEONE THERE...?
I--I THINK I HEAR YOU...
MS. MARGARET AMES OF SCOTLAND YARD.

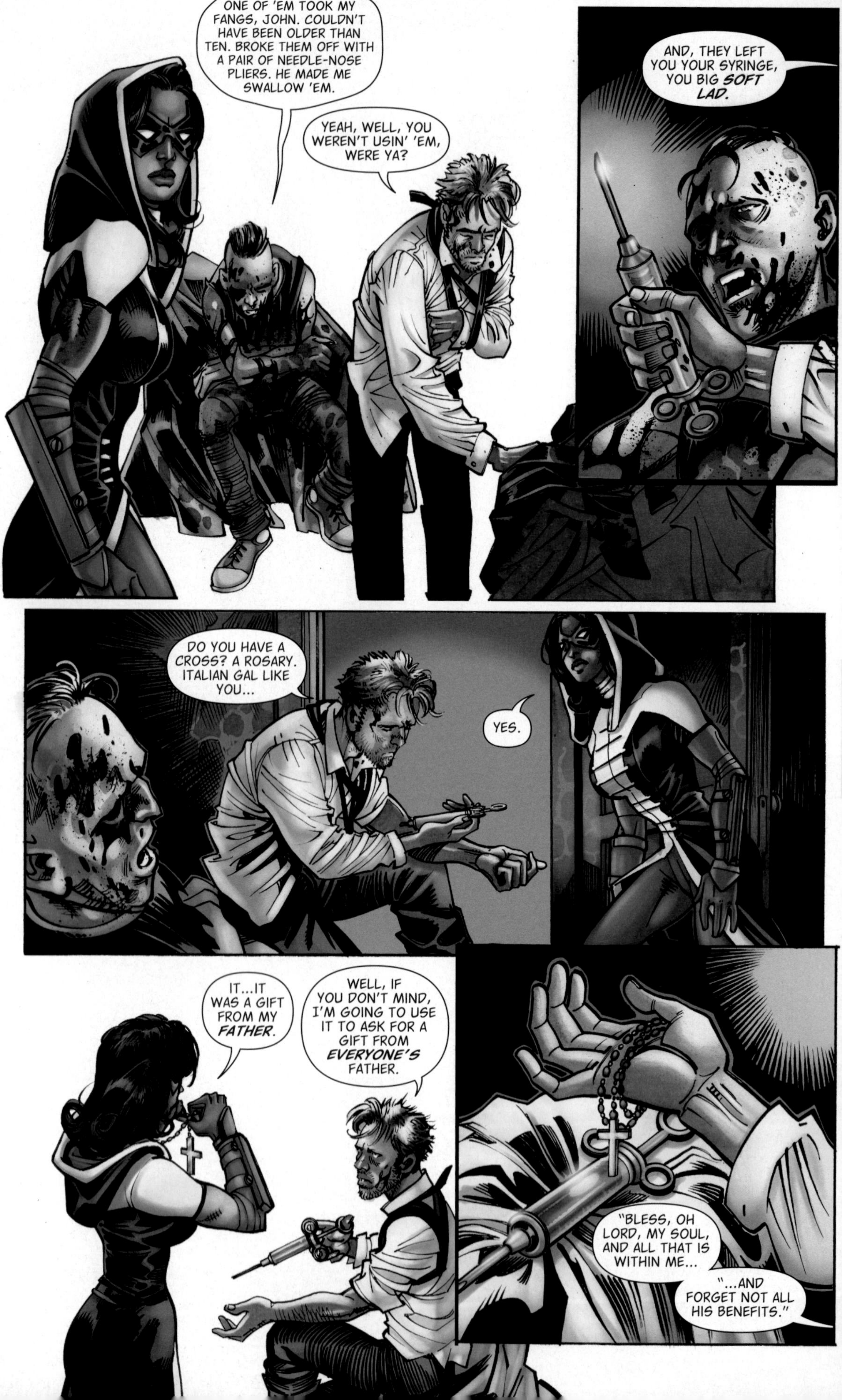
ONE OF 'EM TOOK MY FANGS, JOHN. COULDN'T HAVE BEEN OLDER THAN TEN. BROKE THEM OFF WITH A PAIR OF NEEDLE-NOSE PLIERS. HE MADE ME SWALLOW 'EM.
YEAH, WELL, YOU WEREN'T USIN' 'EM, WERE YA?
AND, THEY LEFT YOU YOUR SYRINGE, YOU BIG SOFT LAD.
DO YOU HAVE A CROSS? A ROSARY. ITALIAN GAL LIKE YOU...
YES.
IT...IT WAS A GIFT FROM MY FATHER.
WELL, IF YOU DON'T MIND, I'M GOING TO USE IT TO ASK FOR A GIFT FROM EVERYONE'S FATHER.
"BLESS, OH LORD, MY SOUL, AND ALL THAT IS WITHIN ME...
"...AND FORGET NOT ALL HIS BENEFITS."

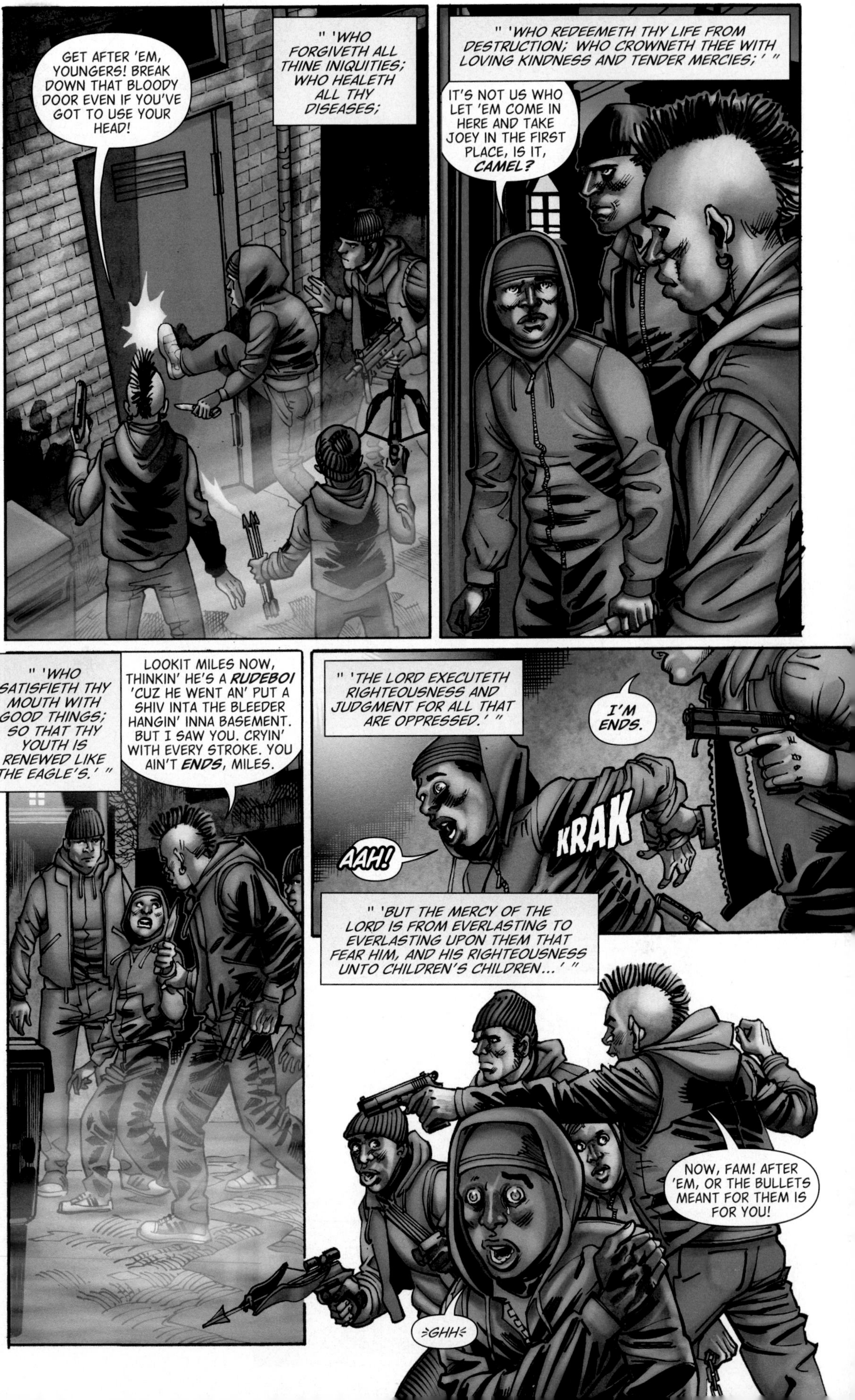
GET AFTER 'EM, YOUNGERS! BREAK DOWN THAT BLOODY DOOR EVEN IF YOU'VE GOT TO USE YOUR HEAD!
" 'WHO FORGIVETH ALL THINE INIQUITIES; WHO HEALETH ALL THY DISEASES;
" 'WHO REDEEMETH THY LIFE FROM DESTRUCTION; WHO CROWNETH THEE WITH LOVING KINDNESS AND TENDER MERCIES;' "
IT'S NOT US WHO LET 'EM COME IN HERE AND TAKE JOEY IN THE FIRST PLACE, IS IT, CAMEL?
" 'WHO SATISFIETH THY MOUTH WITH GOOD THINGS; SO THAT THY YOUTH IS RENEWED LIKE THE EAGLE'S.' "
LOOKIT MILES NOW, THINKIN' HE'S A RUDEBOI 'CUZ HE WENT AN' PUT A SHIV INTA THE BLEEDER HANGIN' INNA BASEMENT. BUT I SAW YOU. CRYIN' WITH EVERY STROKE. YOU AIN'T ENDS, MILES.
" 'THE LORD EXECUTETH RIGHTEOUSNESS AND JUDGMENT FOR ALL THAT ARE OPPRESSED.' "
I'M ENDS.
KRAK
AAH!
" 'BUT THE MERCY OF THE LORD IS FROM EVERLASTING TO EVERLASTING UPON THEM THAT FEAR HIM, AND HIS RIGHTEOUSNESS UNTO CHILDREN'S CHILDREN...' "
NOW, FAM! AFTER 'EM, OR THE BULLETS MEANT FOR THEM IS FOR YOU!
GHH

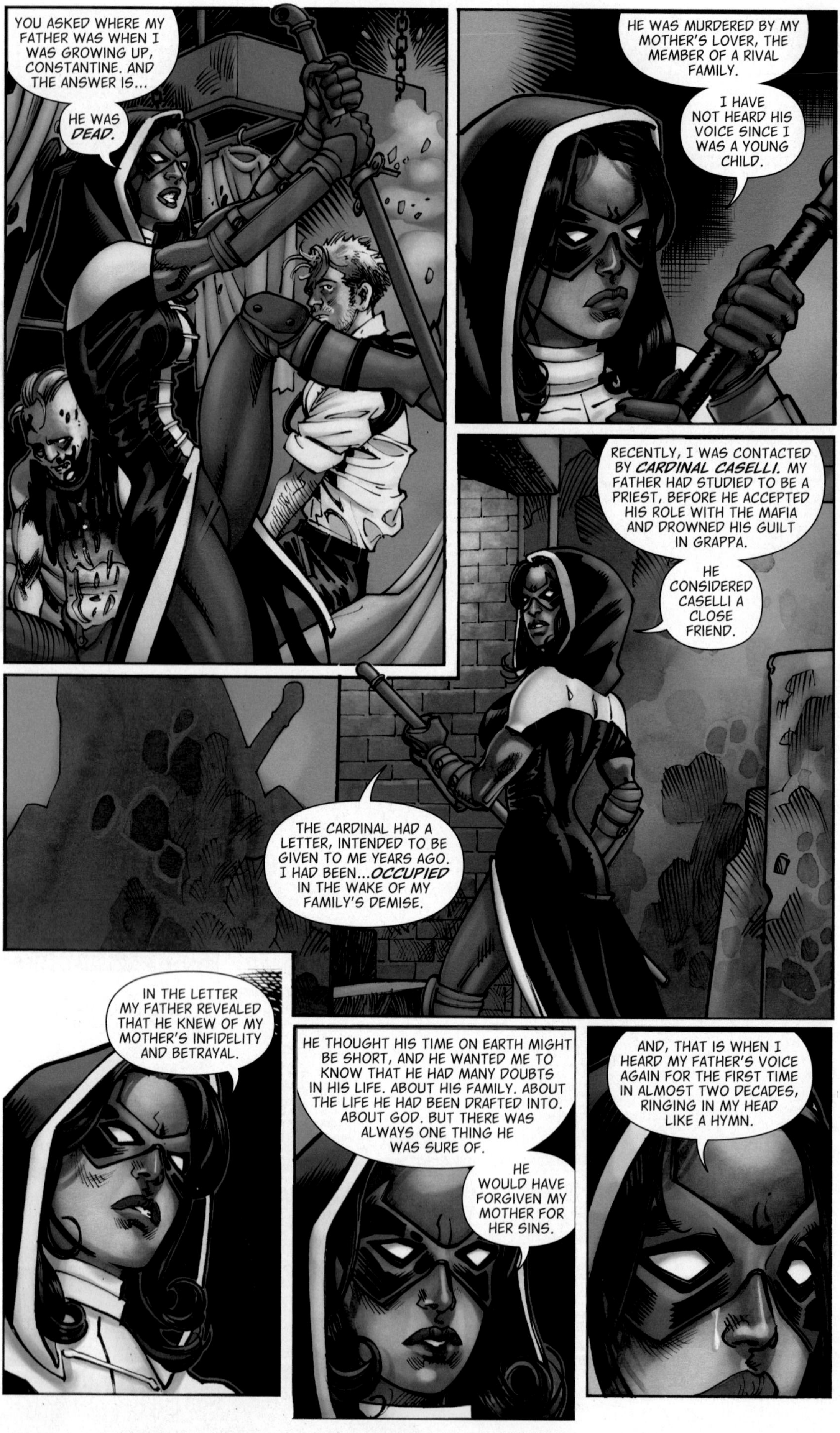
YOU ASKED WHERE MY FATHER WAS WHEN I WAS GROWING UP, CONSTANTINE. AND THE ANSWER IS...
HE WAS *DEAD.*
HE WAS MURDERED BY MY MOTHER'S LOVER, THE MEMBER OF A RIVAL FAMILY.
I HAVE NOT HEARD HIS VOICE SINCE I WAS A YOUNG CHILD.
RECENTLY, I WAS CONTACTED BY *CARDINAL CASELLI.* MY FATHER HAD STUDIED TO BE A PRIEST, BEFORE HE ACCEPTED HIS ROLE WITH THE MAFIA AND DROWNED HIS GUILT IN GRAPPA.
HE CONSIDERED CASELLI A CLOSE FRIEND.
THE CARDINAL HAD A LETTER, INTENDED TO BE GIVEN TO ME YEARS AGO. I HAD BEEN...*OCCUPIED* IN THE WAKE OF MY FAMILY'S DEMISE.
IN THE LETTER MY FATHER REVEALED THAT HE KNEW OF MY MOTHER'S INFIDELITY AND BETRAYAL.
HE THOUGHT HIS TIME ON EARTH MIGHT BE SHORT, AND HE WANTED ME TO KNOW THAT HE HAD MANY DOUBTS IN HIS LIFE. ABOUT HIS FAMILY. ABOUT THE LIFE HE HAD BEEN DRAFTED INTO. ABOUT GOD. BUT THERE WAS ALWAYS ONE THING HE WAS SURE OF.
HE WOULD HAVE FORGIVEN MY MOTHER FOR HER SINS.
AND, THAT IS WHEN I HEARD MY FATHER'S VOICE AGAIN FOR THE FIRST TIME IN ALMOST TWO DECADES, RINGING IN MY HEAD LIKE A HYMN.

"REMEMBER, MY HELENA. THERE IS A PLACE FOR ANGER. BUT WE MUST BE AS THE ANGEL MICHAEL, AND GIVE *MERCY* TO THOSE WHO ASK FOR IT."

CONSECRATED BLOOD.

BY ACCEPTING IT INTO YOUR BODY YOU ARE *FORGIVEN* OF THE *CURSE OF AMBROGIO,* WHICH HAS MADE YOU A SINNER.

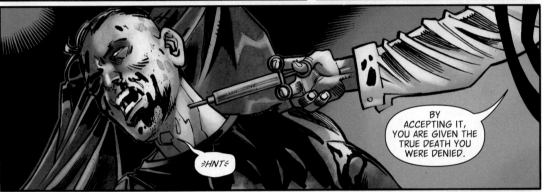

≥HNT≤

BY ACCEPTING IT, YOU ARE GIVEN THE TRUE DEATH YOU WERE DENIED.

YOUR *DAD.* HE SOUNDS LIKE A GOOD MAN, MISS. WHAT...WHAT WAS HIS NAME?

HIS NAME WAS BERTINELLI. *FRANK BERTINELLI.*

FRANK. NICE NAME. DAD NAME.

MAYBE... ≥HNT≤...MAYBE I'LL SAY HULLO IF I SEE HIM IN *HEAVEN.*

CONSTANTINE MADE MS. AMES DRINK THE *MEAD OF POETRY*, CONTAINING THE OLD BLOOD OF *AESIR AND VANIR*. WITH ITS POWER SHE CHANGED REALITY.*

IN ORDER FOR HER SOUL TO CONTAIN SUCH A POWER, IT HAD TO BECOME SOMETHING NEW.

*SEE HELLBLAZER VOL. 3: THE INSPIRATION GAME. -- MEAD OF KRISTY

I SENSED THIS CHANGE. FELT THE SHUDDERS THROUGHOUT MY REALM OF KUR. WITNESSED HER REBIRTH AS AN *ANNUNAKI*. AVATAR OF THE FIRST DRAGON, *TIAMAT*, WHO WILL SPIT DEMONS UPON THE EARTH.

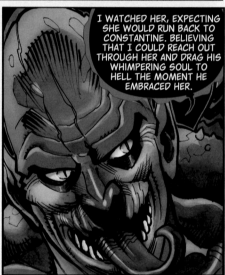

I WATCHED HER, EXPECTING SHE WOULD RUN BACK TO CONSTANTINE. BELIEVING THAT I COULD REACH OUT THROUGH HER AND DRAG HIS WHIMPERING SOUL TO HELL THE MOMENT HE EMBRACED HER.

BUT SHE TURNED INSTEAD TO A BROKEN PRIEST. YOUR BROTHER ADAM, LOOKING FOR A SIGN.

AND IN *ADAM* I SAW AN OPPORTUNITY THAT WOULD BENEFIT MANY OF THE DAMNED.

A PRIEST? CAN YOU BELIEVE IT?

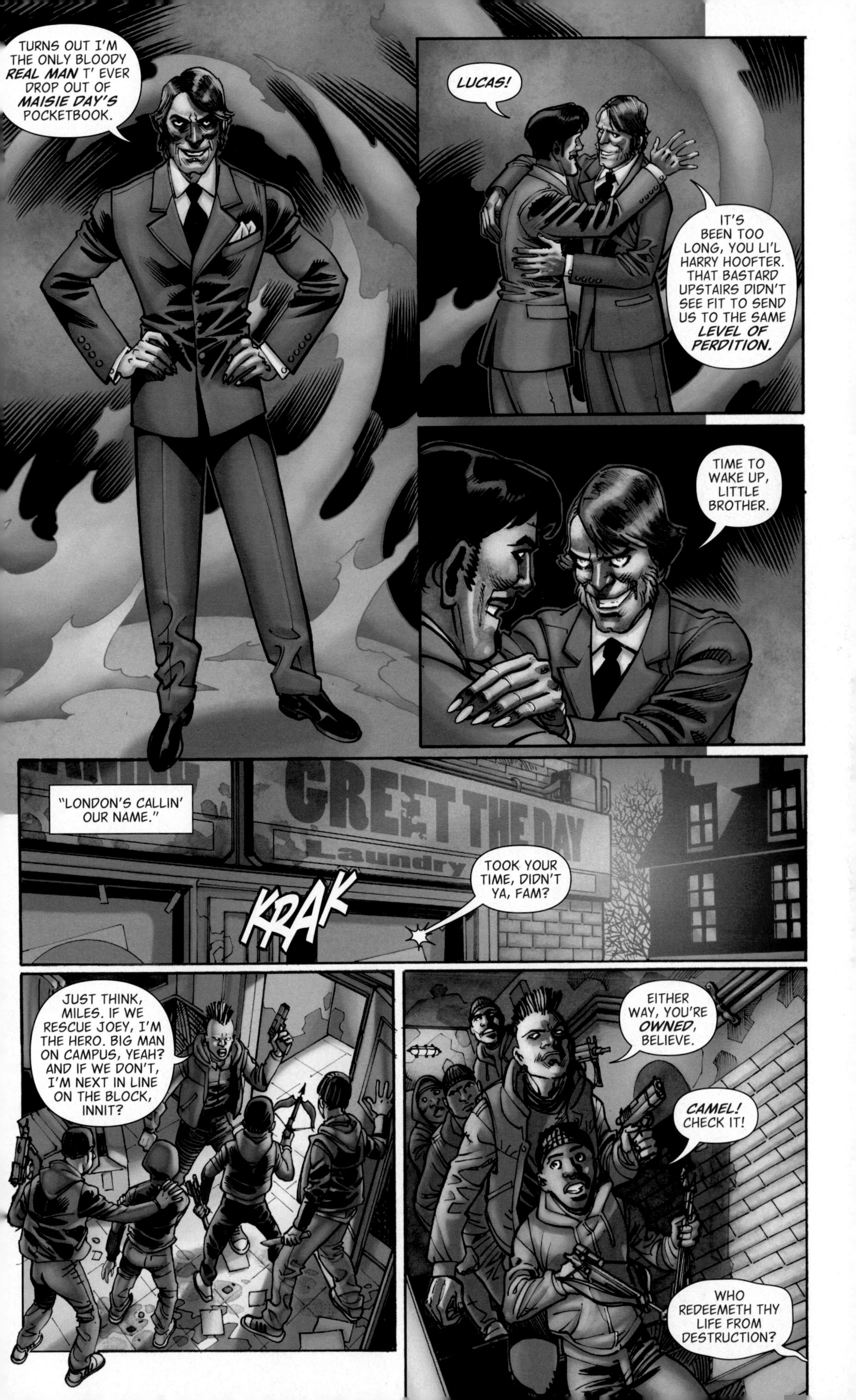
TURNS OUT I'M THE ONLY BLOODY REAL MAN T' EVER DROP OUT OF MAISIE DAY'S POCKETBOOK.
LUCAS!
IT'S BEEN TOO LONG, YOU LI'L HARRY HOOFTER. THAT BASTARD UPSTAIRS DIDN'T SEE FIT TO SEND US TO THE SAME LEVEL OF PERDITION.
TIME TO WAKE UP, LITTLE BROTHER.
"LONDON'S CALLIN' OUR NAME."
GREET THE DAY
Laundry
KRAK
TOOK YOUR TIME, DIDN'T YA, FAM?
JUST THINK, MILES. IF WE RESCUE JOEY, I'M THE HERO. BIG MAN ON CAMPUS, YEAH? AND IF WE DON'T, I'M NEXT IN LINE ON THE BLOCK, INNIT?
EITHER WAY, YOU'RE OWNED, BELIEVE.
CAMEL! CHECK IT!
WHO REDEEMETH THY LIFE FROM DESTRUCTION?

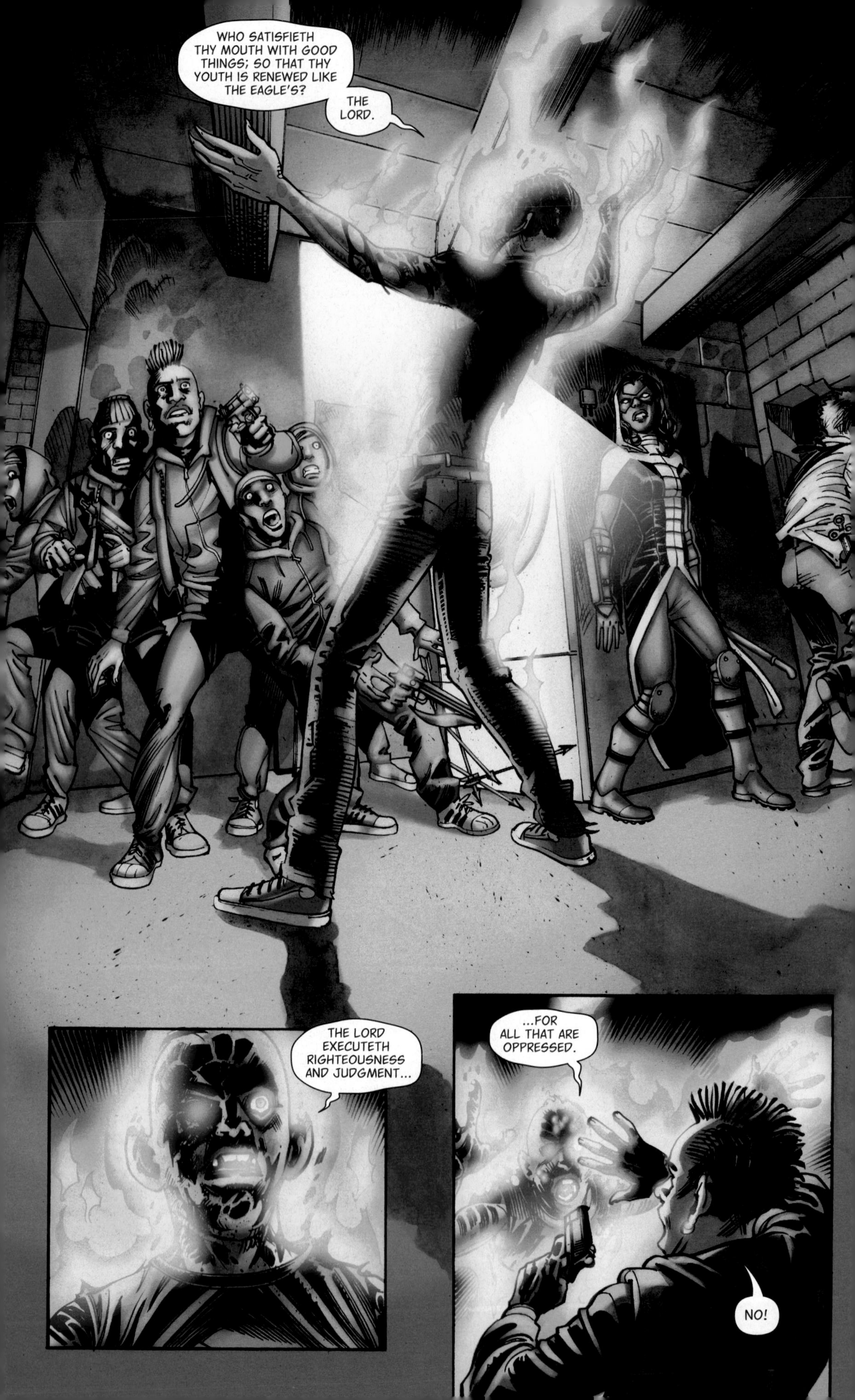
WHO SATISFIETH THY MOUTH WITH GOOD THINGS; SO THAT THY YOUTH IS RENEWED LIKE THE EAGLE'S?
THE LORD.
THE LORD EXECUTETH RIGHTEOUSNESS AND JUDGMENT...
...FOR ALL THAT ARE OPPRESSED.
NO!

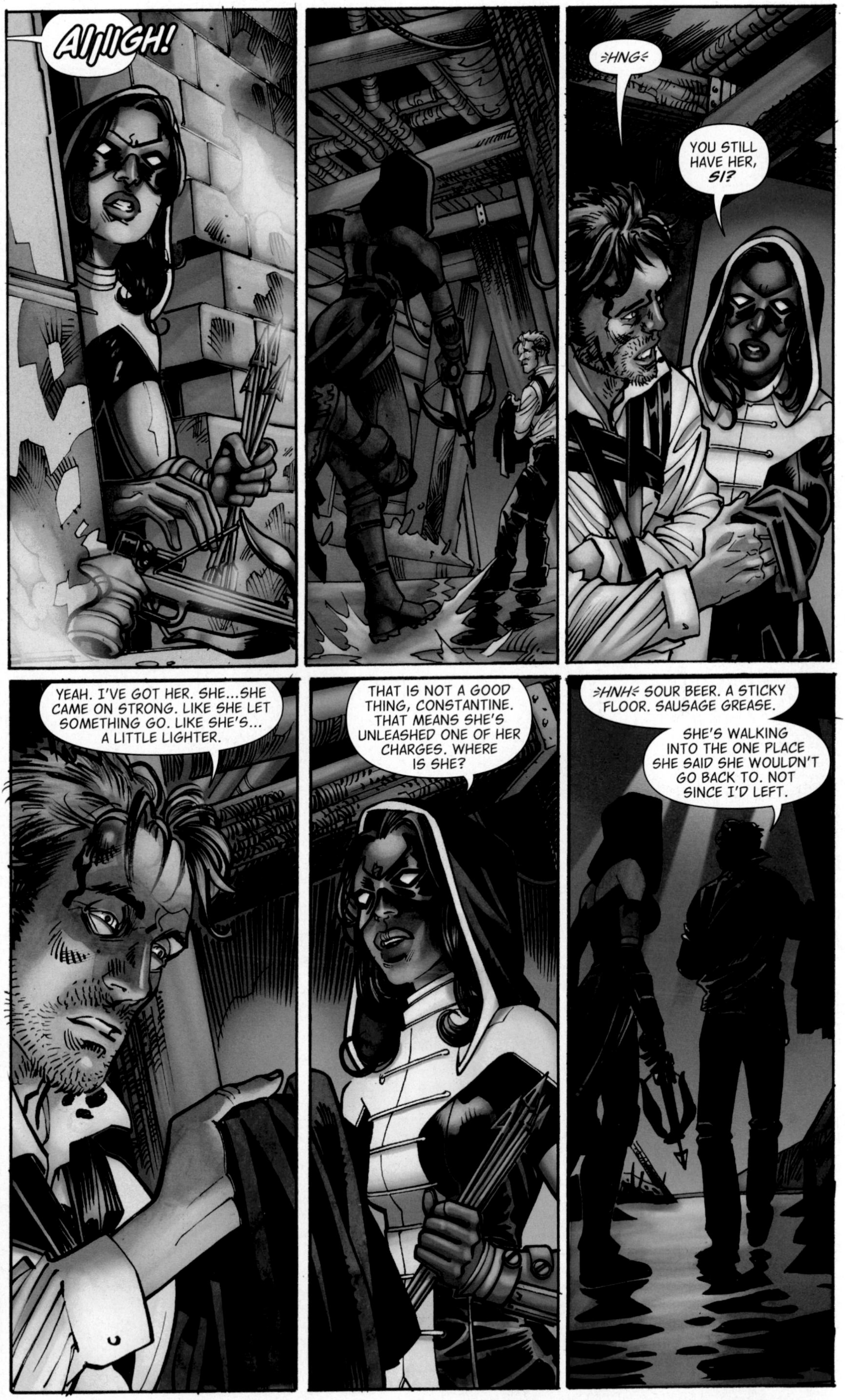
AIIIIGH!
HNG
YOU STILL HAVE HER, SI?
YEAH. I'VE GOT HER. SHE...SHE CAME ON STRONG. LIKE SHE LET SOMETHING GO. LIKE SHE'S... A LITTLE LIGHTER.
THAT IS NOT A GOOD THING, CONSTANTINE. THAT MEANS SHE'S UNLEASHED ONE OF HER CHARGES. WHERE IS SHE?
HNH SOUR BEER. A STICKY FLOOR. SAUSAGE GREASE.
SHE'S WALKING INTO THE ONE PLACE SHE SAID SHE WOULDN'T GO BACK TO. NOT SINCE I'D LEFT.

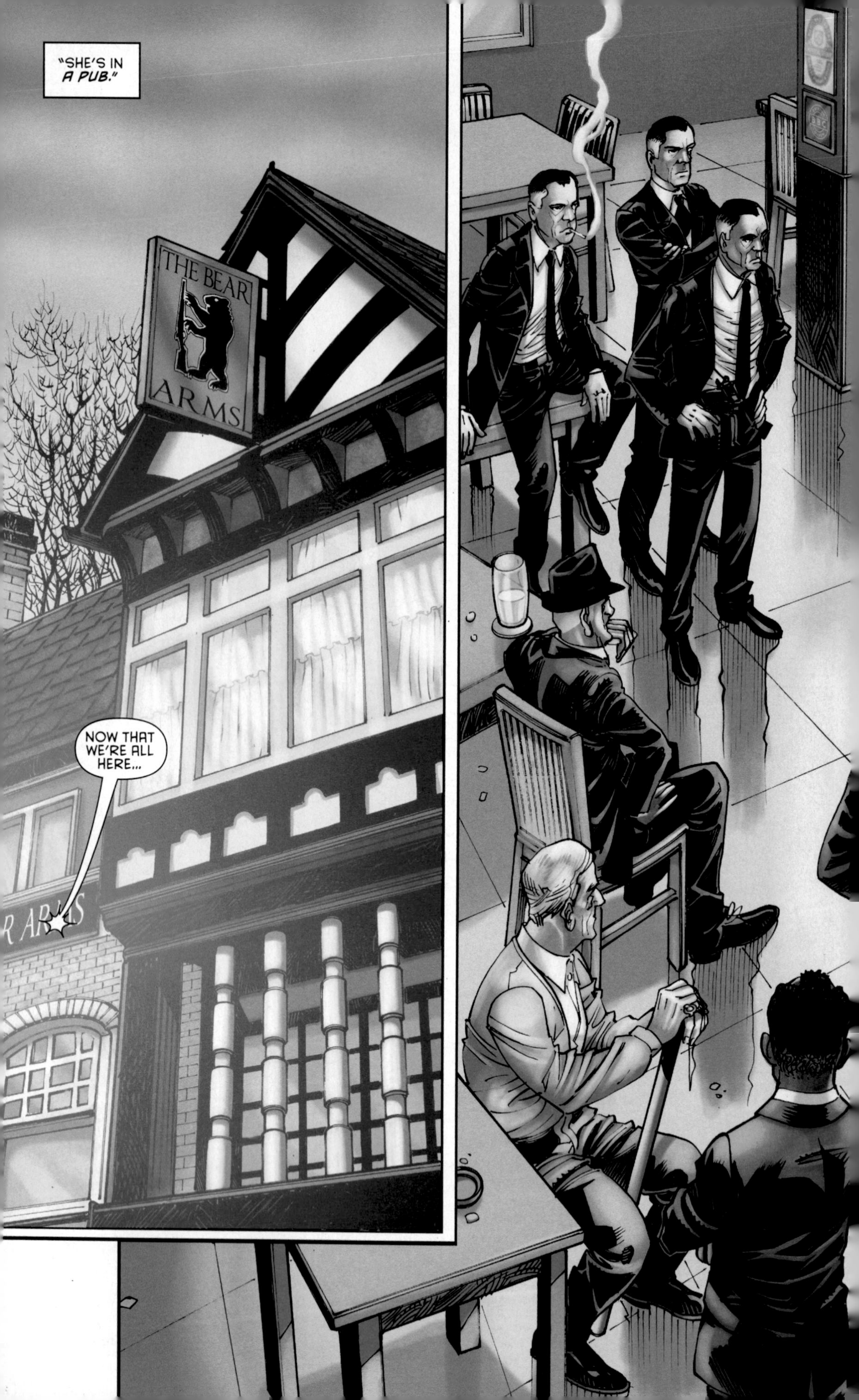
"SHE'S IN A PUB."
THE BEAR ARMS
NOW THAT WE'RE ALL HERE...

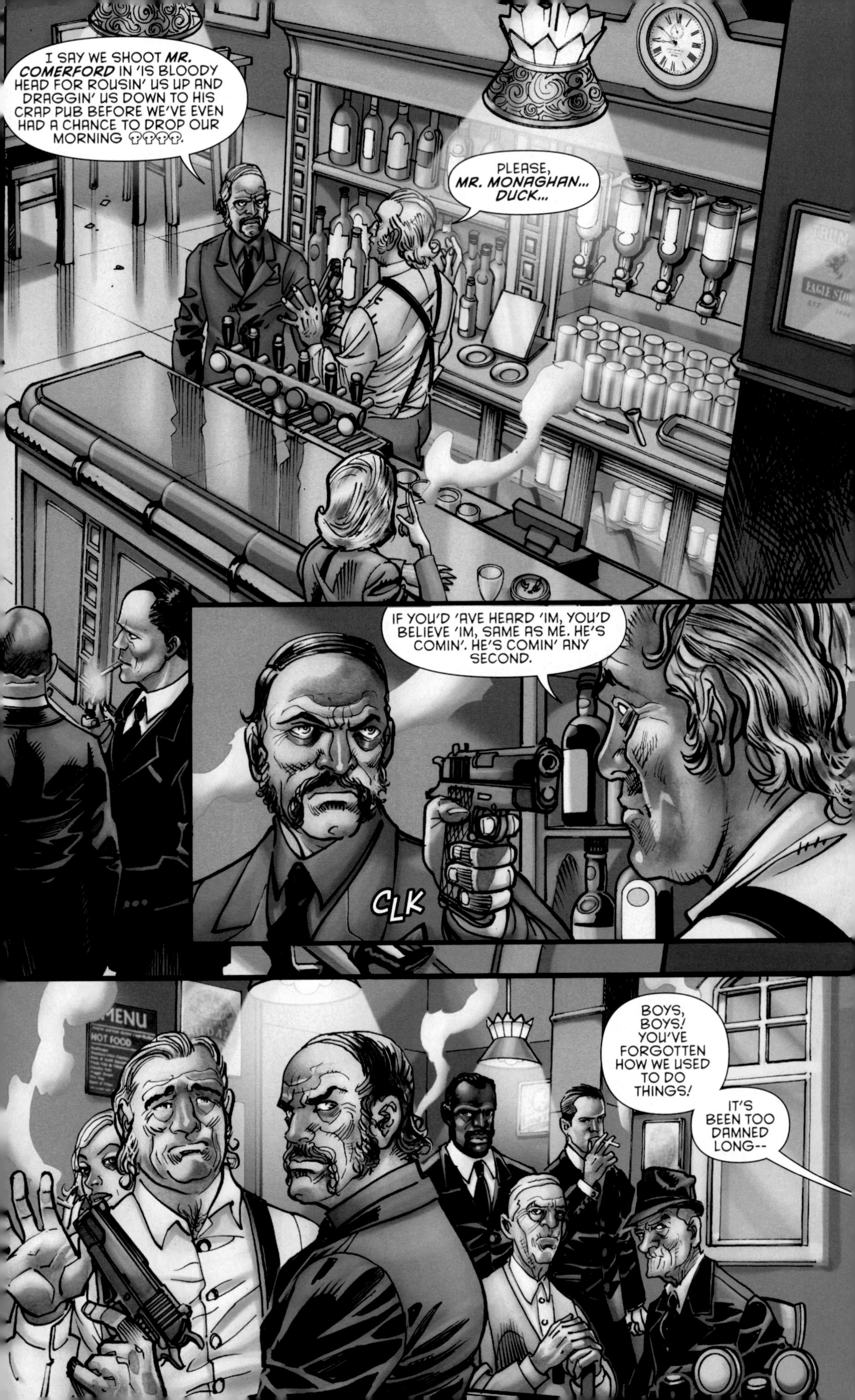
I SAY WE SHOOT MR. COMERFORD IN 'IS BLOODY HEAD FOR ROUSIN' US UP AND DRAGGIN' US DOWN TO HIS CRAP PUB BEFORE WE'VE EVEN HAD A CHANCE TO DROP OUR MORNING ☠☠☠☠.
PLEASE, MR. MONAGHAN... DUCK...
IF YOU'D 'AVE HEARD 'IM, YOU'D BELIEVE 'IM, SAME AS ME. HE'S COMIN'. HE'S COMIN' ANY SECOND.
CLK
BOYS, BOYS! YOU'VE FORGOTTEN HOW WE USED TO DO THINGS!
IT'S BEEN TOO DAMNED LONG--

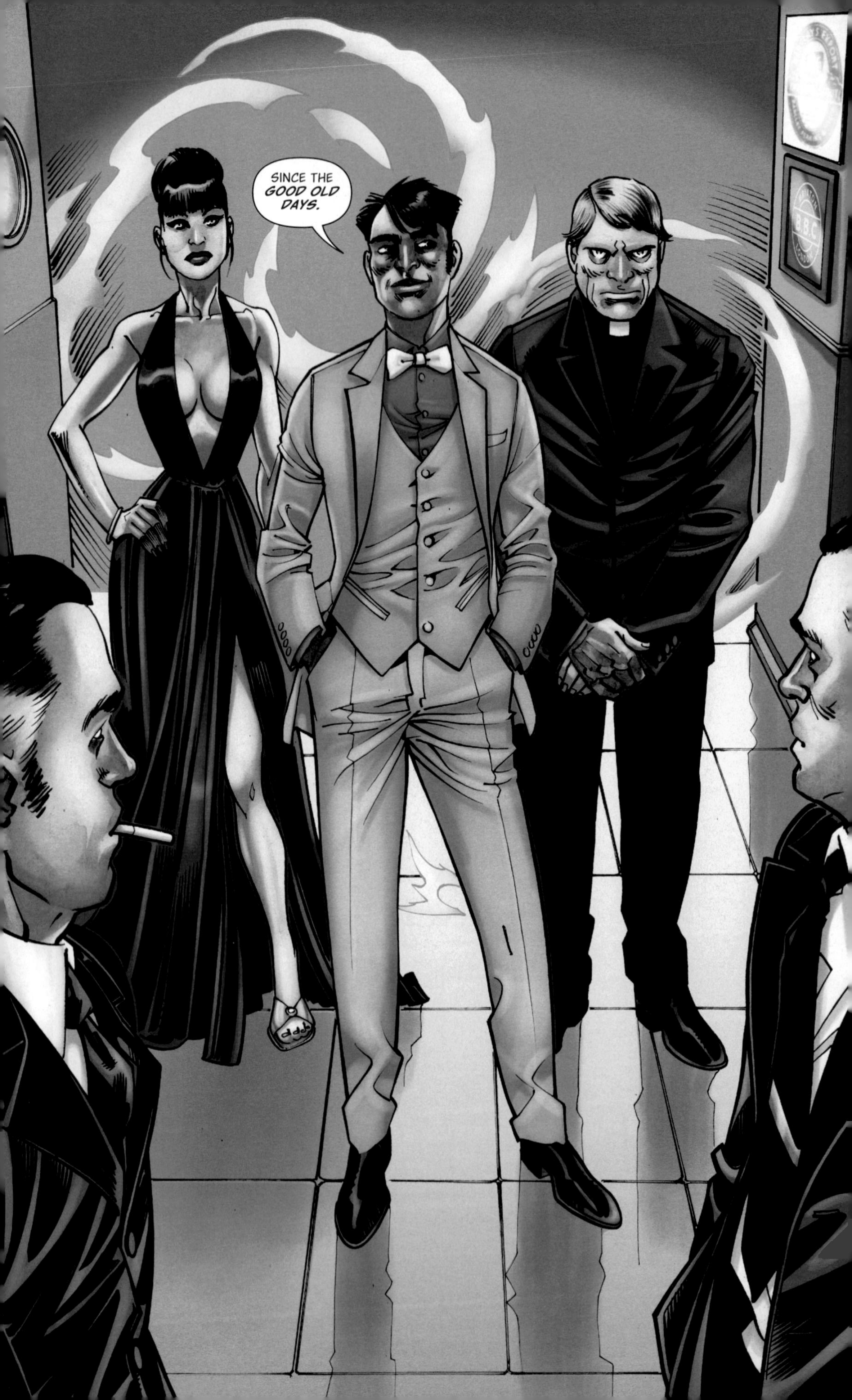
SINCE THE GOOD OLD DAYS.

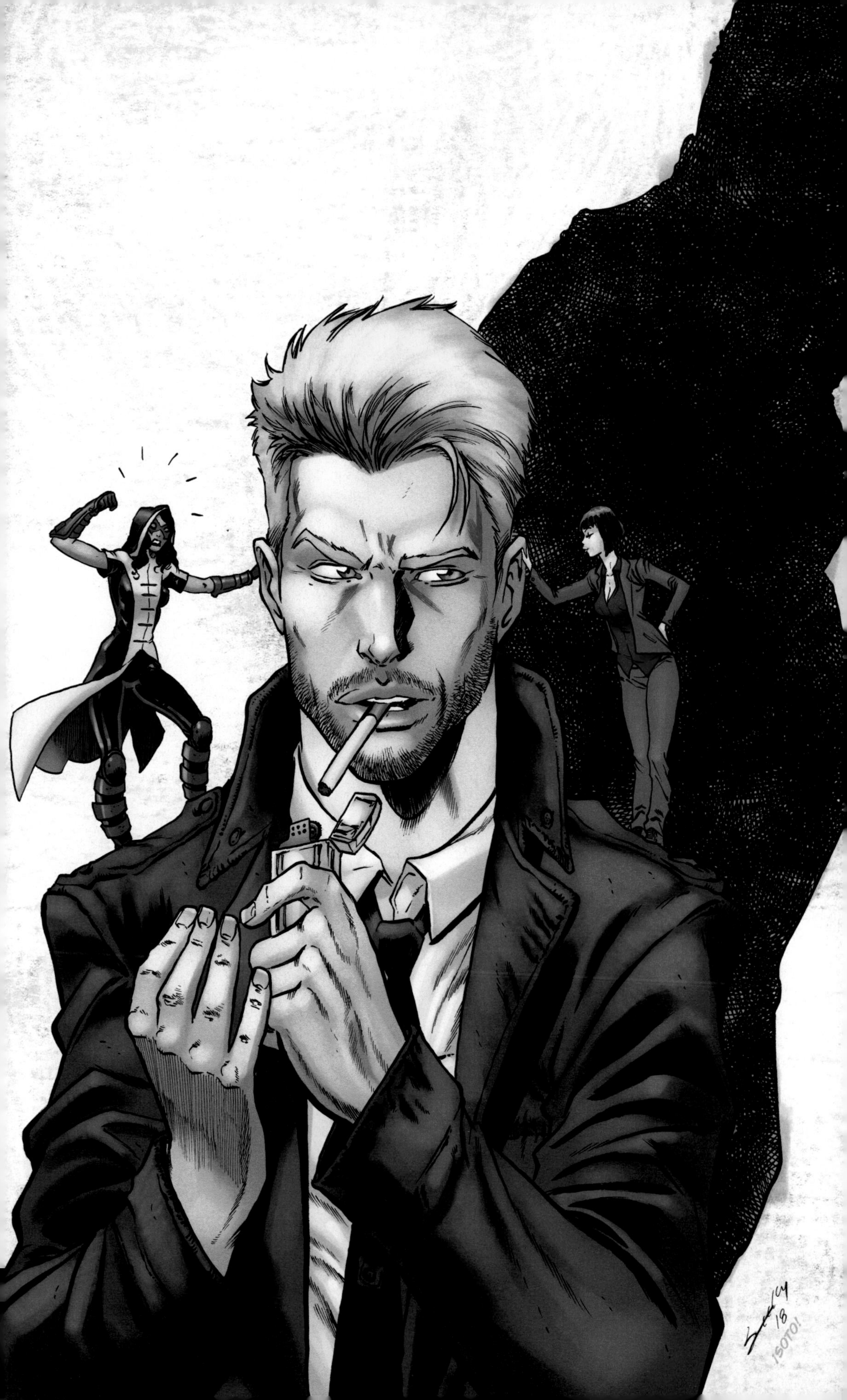
18
iSOTO!

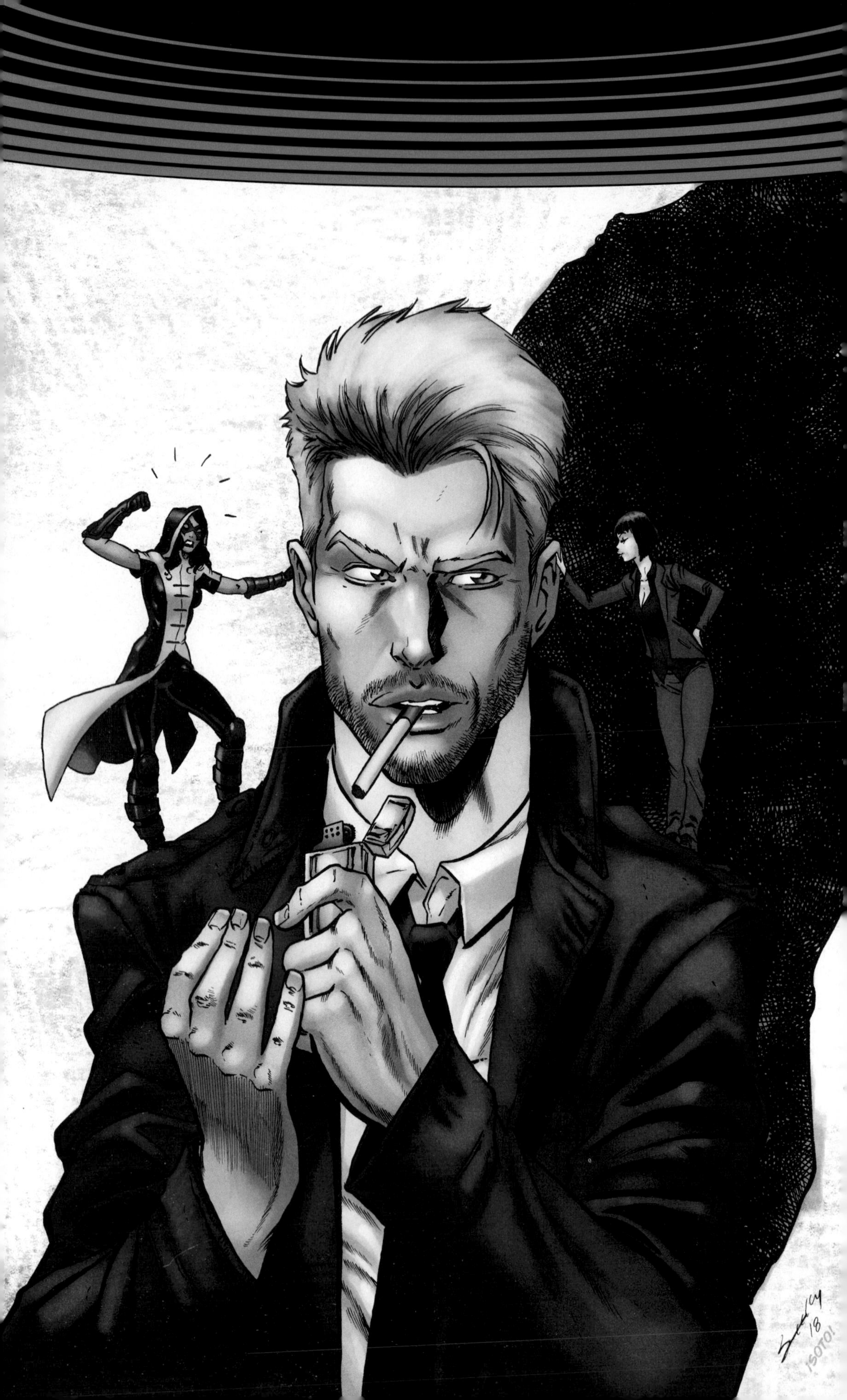
18
¡SOTO!

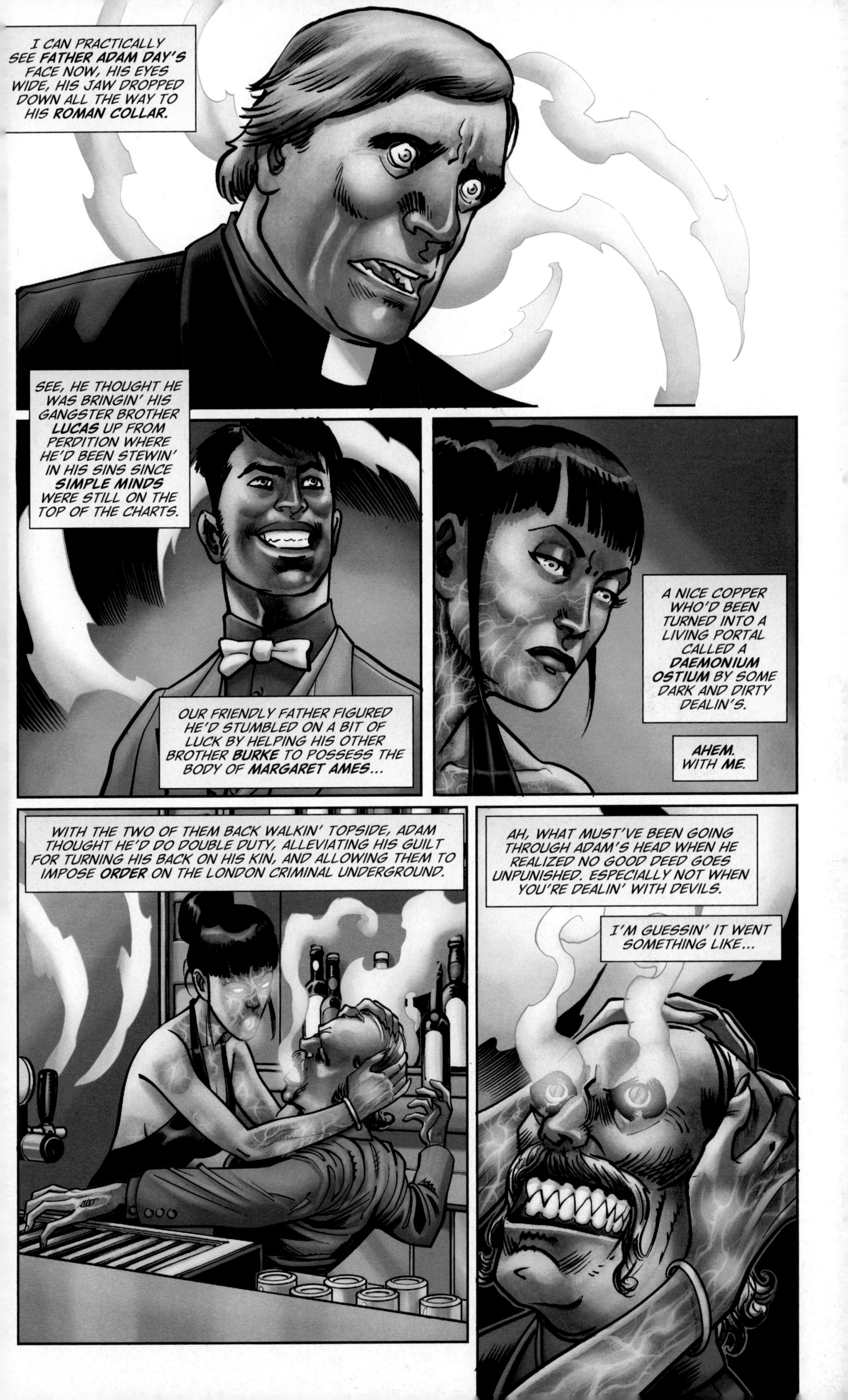
I CAN PRACTICALLY SEE FATHER ADAM DAY'S FACE NOW, HIS EYES WIDE, HIS JAW DROPPED DOWN ALL THE WAY TO HIS ROMAN COLLAR.
SEE, HE THOUGHT HE WAS BRINGIN' HIS GANGSTER BROTHER LUCAS UP FROM PERDITION WHERE HE'D BEEN STEWIN' IN HIS SINS SINCE SIMPLE MINDS WERE STILL ON THE TOP OF THE CHARTS.
OUR FRIENDLY FATHER FIGURED HE'D STUMBLED ON A BIT OF LUCK BY HELPING HIS OTHER BROTHER BURKE TO POSSESS THE BODY OF MARGARET AMES...
A NICE COPPER WHO'D BEEN TURNED INTO A LIVING PORTAL CALLED A DAEMONIUM OSTIUM BY SOME DARK AND DIRTY DEALIN'S.
AHEM. WITH ME.
WITH THE TWO OF THEM BACK WALKIN' TOPSIDE, ADAM THOUGHT HE'D DO DOUBLE DUTY, ALLEVIATING HIS GUILT FOR TURNING HIS BACK ON HIS KIN, AND ALLOWING THEM TO IMPOSE ORDER ON THE LONDON CRIMINAL UNDERGROUND.
AH, WHAT MUST'VE BEEN GOING THROUGH ADAM'S HEAD WHEN HE REALIZED NO GOOD DEED GOES UNPUNISHED. ESPECIALLY NOT WHEN YOU'RE DEALIN' WITH DEVILS.
I'M GUESSIN' IT WENT SOMETHING LIKE...

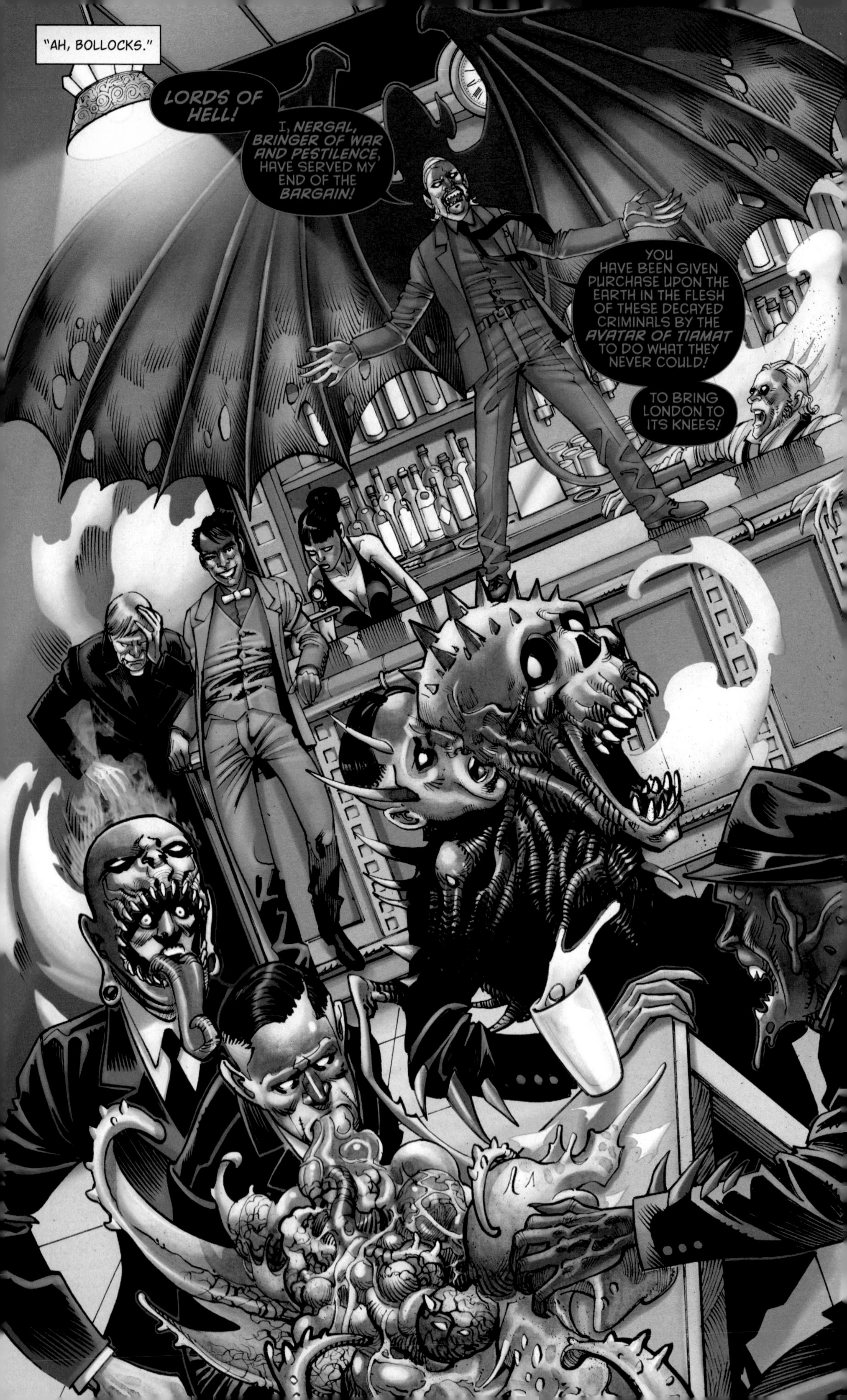
"AH, BOLLOCKS."
LORDS OF HELL!
I, NERGAL, BRINGER OF WAR AND PESTILENCE, HAVE SERVED MY END OF THE BARGAIN!
YOU HAVE BEEN GIVEN PURCHASE UPON THE EARTH IN THE FLESH OF THESE DECAYED CRIMINALS BY THE AVATAR OF TIAMAT TO DO WHAT THEY NEVER COULD!
TO BRING LONDON TO ITS KNEES!

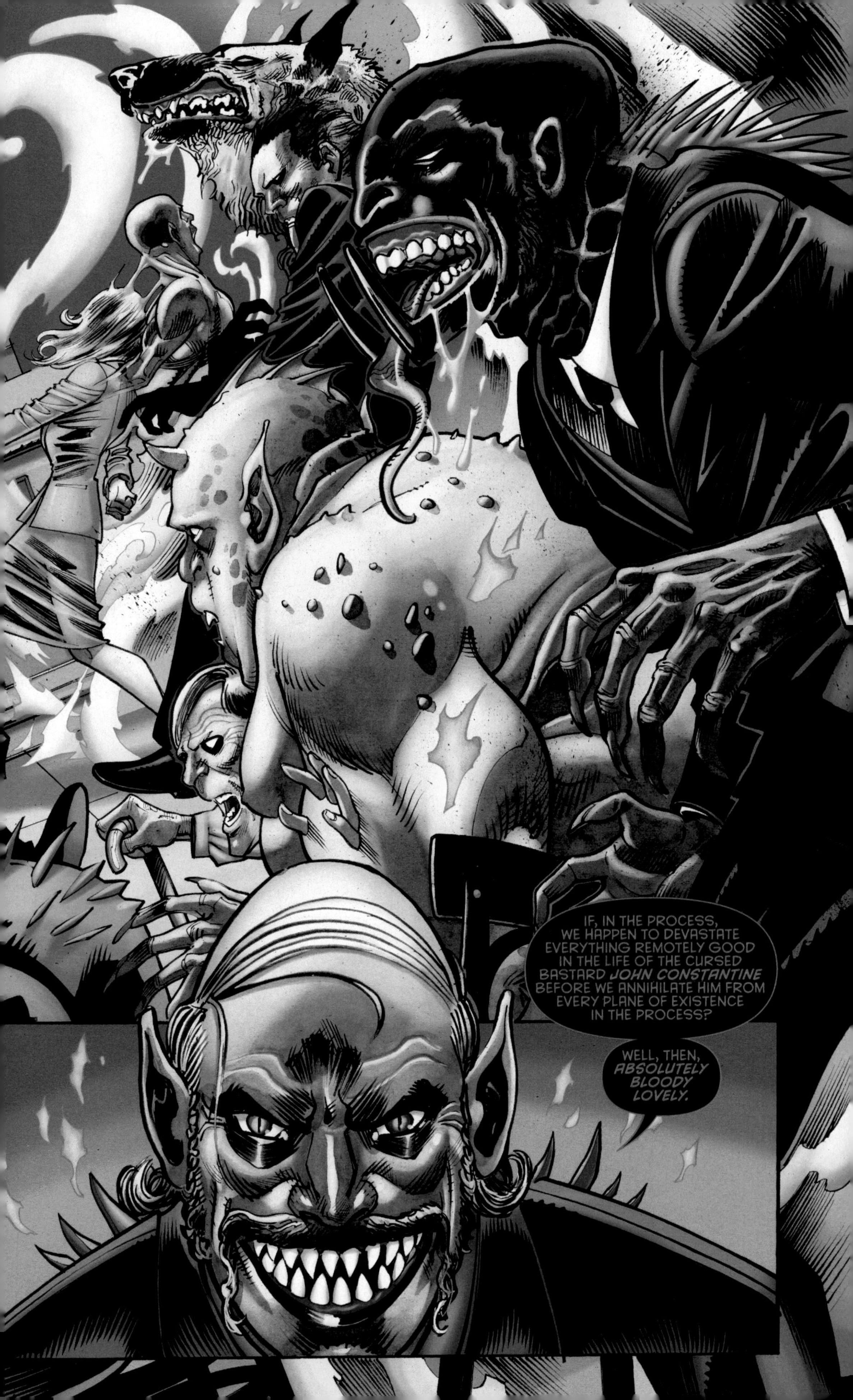
IF, IN THE PROCESS, WE HAPPEN TO DEVASTATE EVERYTHING REMOTELY GOOD IN THE LIFE OF THE CURSED BASTARD *JOHN CONSTANTINE* BEFORE WE ANNIHILATE HIM FROM EVERY PLANE OF EXISTENCE IN THE PROCESS?
WELL, THEN, *ABSOLUTELY BLOODY LOVELY.*

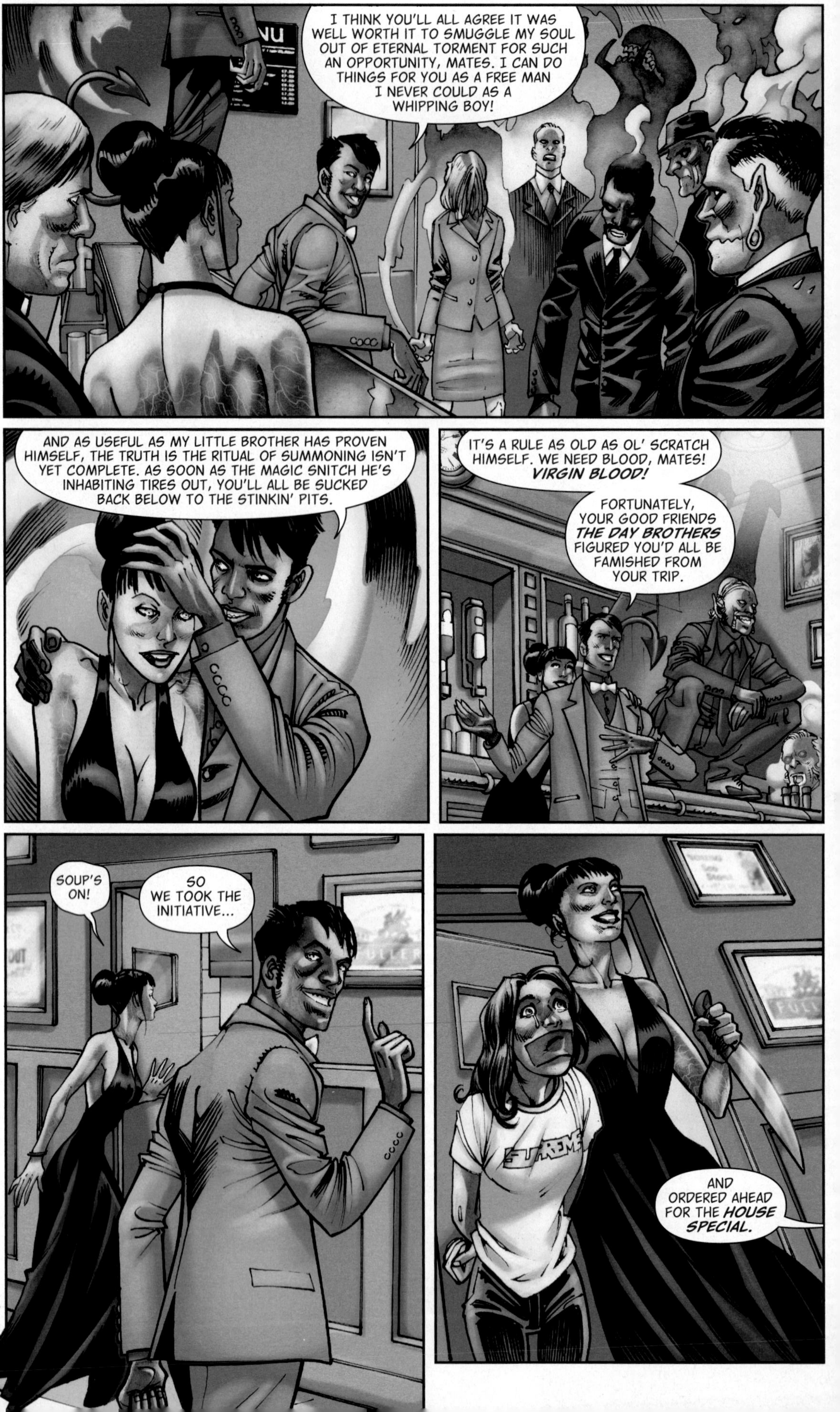

I THINK YOU'LL ALL AGREE IT WAS WELL WORTH IT TO SMUGGLE MY SOUL OUT OF ETERNAL TORMENT FOR SUCH AN OPPORTUNITY, MATES. I CAN DO THINGS FOR YOU AS A FREE MAN I NEVER COULD AS A WHIPPING BOY!
AND AS USEFUL AS MY LITTLE BROTHER HAS PROVEN HIMSELF, THE TRUTH IS THE RITUAL OF SUMMONING ISN'T YET COMPLETE. AS SOON AS THE MAGIC SNITCH HE'S INHABITING TIRES OUT, YOU'LL ALL BE SUCKED BACK BELOW TO THE STINKIN' PITS.
IT'S A RULE AS OLD AS OL' SCRATCH HIMSELF. WE NEED BLOOD, MATES! ***VIRGIN BLOOD!***
FORTUNATELY, YOUR GOOD FRIENDS ***THE DAY BROTHERS*** FIGURED YOU'D ALL BE FAMISHED FROM YOUR TRIP.
SOUP'S ON!
SO WE TOOK THE INITIATIVE...
AND ORDERED AHEAD FOR THE ***HOUSE SPECIAL.***

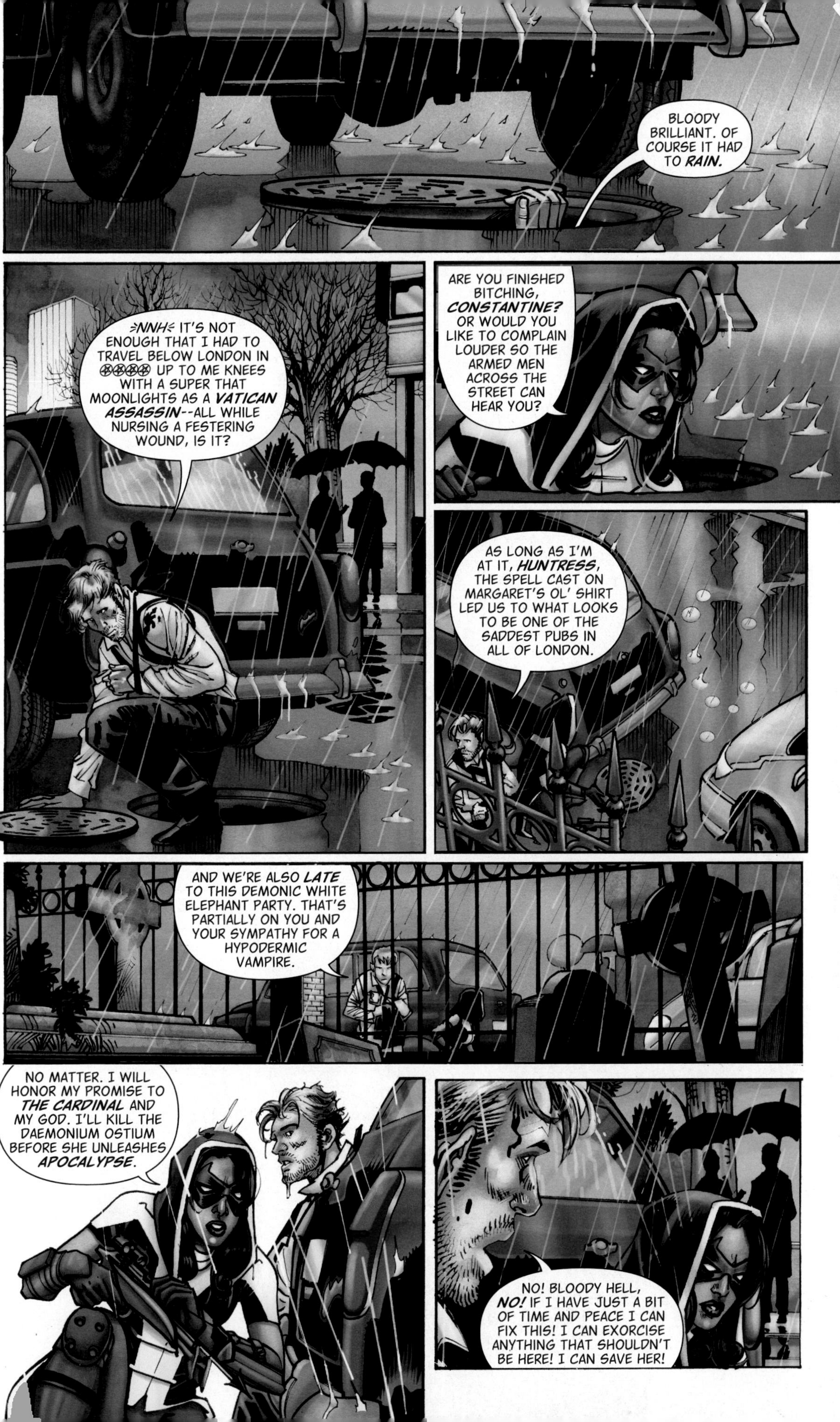
BLOODY BRILLIANT. OF COURSE IT HAD TO RAIN.
>NNH< IT'S NOT ENOUGH THAT I HAD TO TRAVEL BELOW LONDON IN @#$% UP TO ME KNEES WITH A SUPER THAT MOONLIGHTS AS A VATICAN ASSASSIN--ALL WHILE NURSING A FESTERING WOUND, IS IT?
ARE YOU FINISHED BITCHING, CONSTANTINE? OR WOULD YOU LIKE TO COMPLAIN LOUDER SO THE ARMED MEN ACROSS THE STREET CAN HEAR YOU?
AS LONG AS I'M AT IT, HUNTRESS, THE SPELL CAST ON MARGARET'S OL' SHIRT LED US TO WHAT LOOKS TO BE ONE OF THE SADDEST PUBS IN ALL OF LONDON.
AND WE'RE ALSO LATE TO THIS DEMONIC WHITE ELEPHANT PARTY. THAT'S PARTIALLY ON YOU AND YOUR SYMPATHY FOR A HYPODERMIC VAMPIRE.
NO MATTER. I WILL HONOR MY PROMISE TO THE CARDINAL AND MY GOD. I'LL KILL THE DAEMONIUM OSTIUM BEFORE SHE UNLEASHES APOCALYPSE.
NO! BLOODY HELL, NO! IF I HAVE JUST A BIT OF TIME AND PEACE I CAN FIX THIS! I CAN EXORCISE ANYTHING THAT SHOULDN'T BE HERE! I CAN SAVE HER!

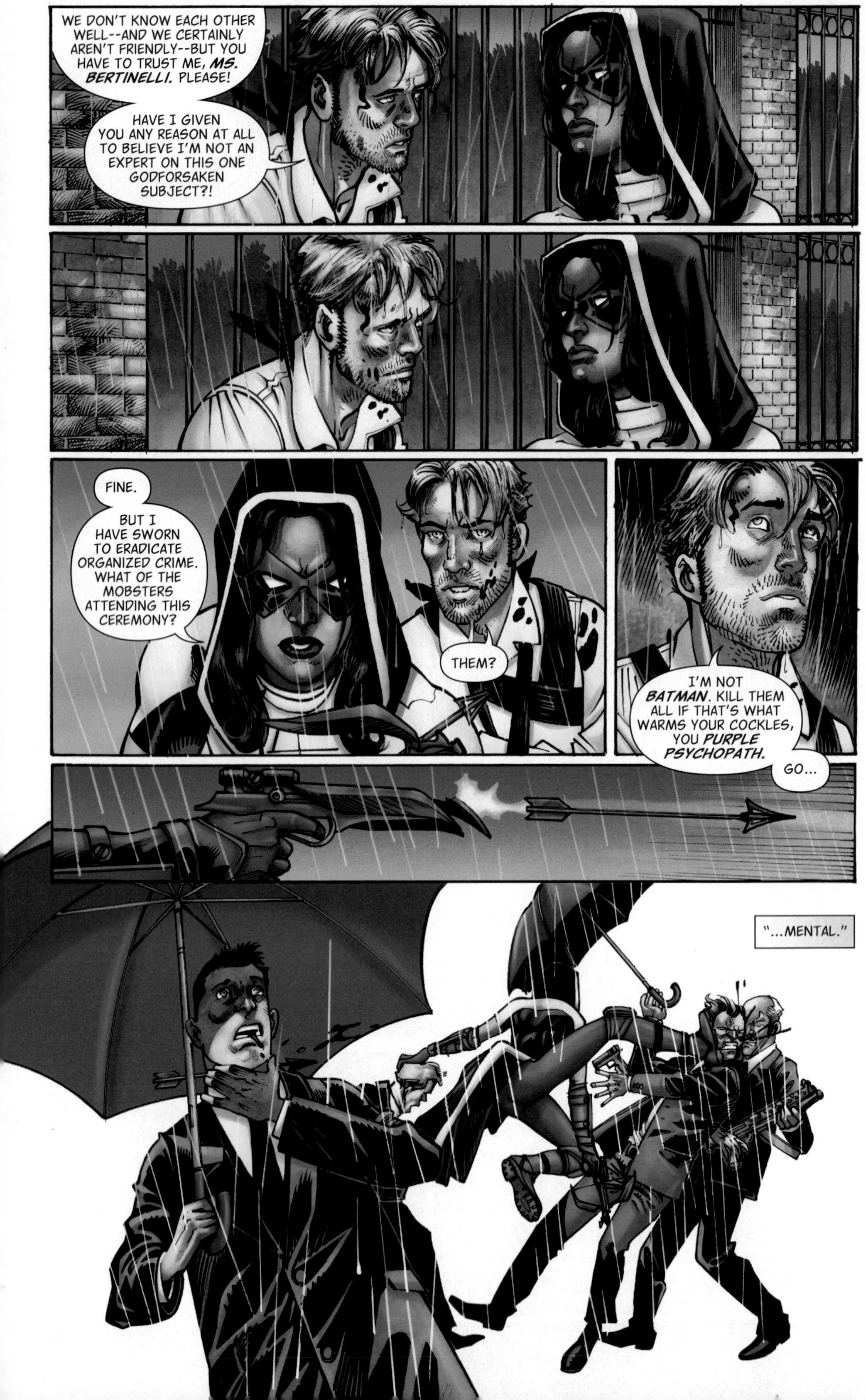
WE DON'T KNOW EACH OTHER WELL--AND WE CERTAINLY AREN'T FRIENDLY--BUT YOU HAVE TO TRUST ME, MS. BERTINELLI. PLEASE!
HAVE I GIVEN YOU ANY REASON AT ALL TO BELIEVE I'M NOT AN EXPERT ON THIS ONE GODFORSAKEN SUBJECT?!
FINE.
BUT I HAVE SWORN TO ERADICATE ORGANIZED CRIME. WHAT OF THE MOBSTERS ATTENDING THIS CEREMONY?
THEM?
I'M NOT BATMAN. KILL THEM ALL IF THAT'S WHAT WARMS YOUR COCKLES, YOU PURPLE PSYCHOPATH.
GO...
"...MENTAL."

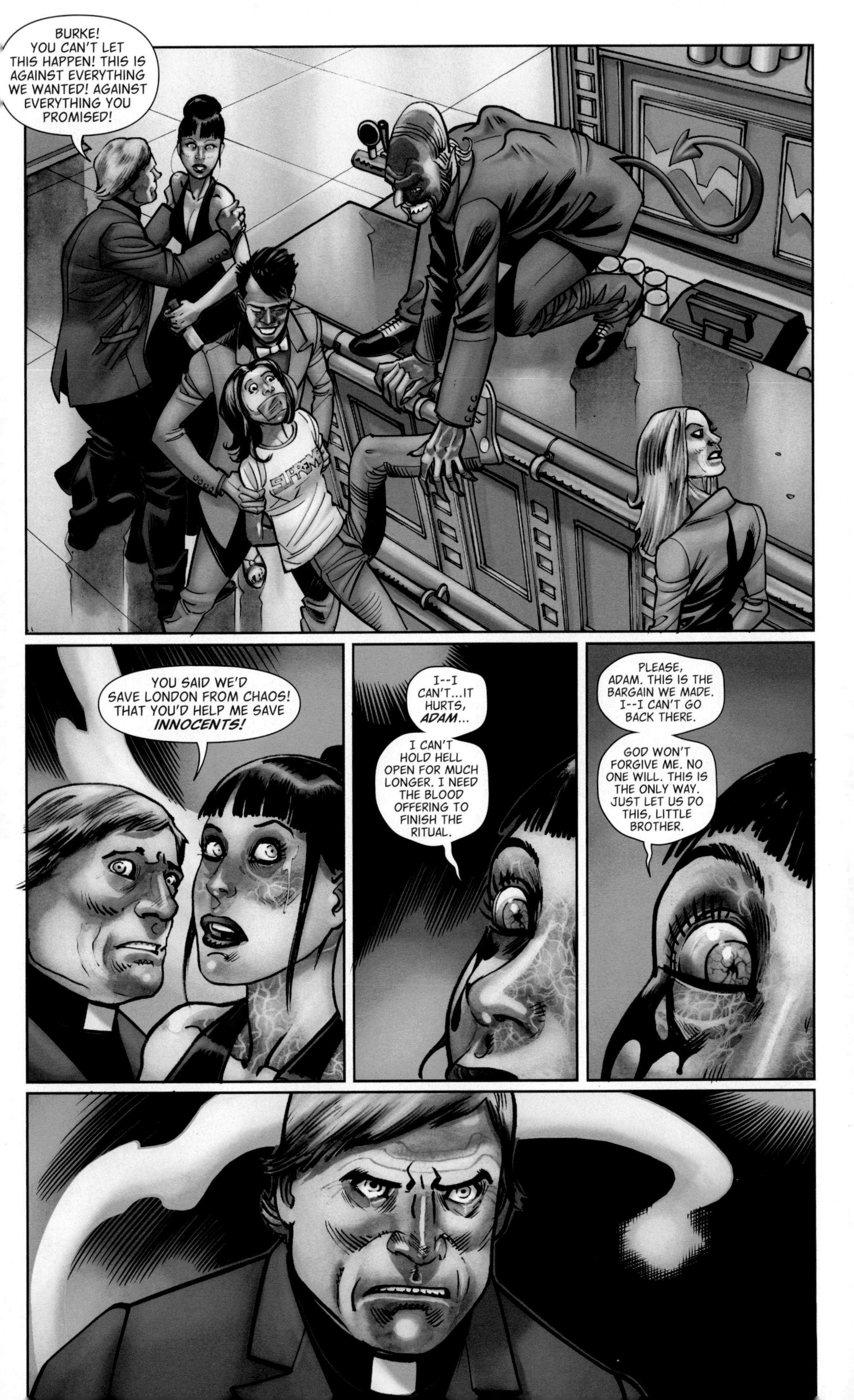
BURKE! YOU CAN'T LET THIS HAPPEN! THIS IS AGAINST EVERYTHING WE WANTED! AGAINST EVERYTHING YOU PROMISED!
YOU SAID WE'D SAVE LONDON FROM CHAOS! THAT YOU'D HELP ME SAVE INNOCENTS!
I--I CAN'T...IT HURTS, ADAM...
I CAN'T HOLD HELL OPEN FOR MUCH LONGER. I NEED THE BLOOD OFFERING TO FINISH THE RITUAL.
PLEASE, ADAM. THIS IS THE BARGAIN WE MADE. I--I CAN'T GO BACK THERE.
GOD WON'T FORGIVE ME. NO ONE WILL. THIS IS THE ONLY WAY. JUST LET US DO THIS, LITTLE BROTHER.

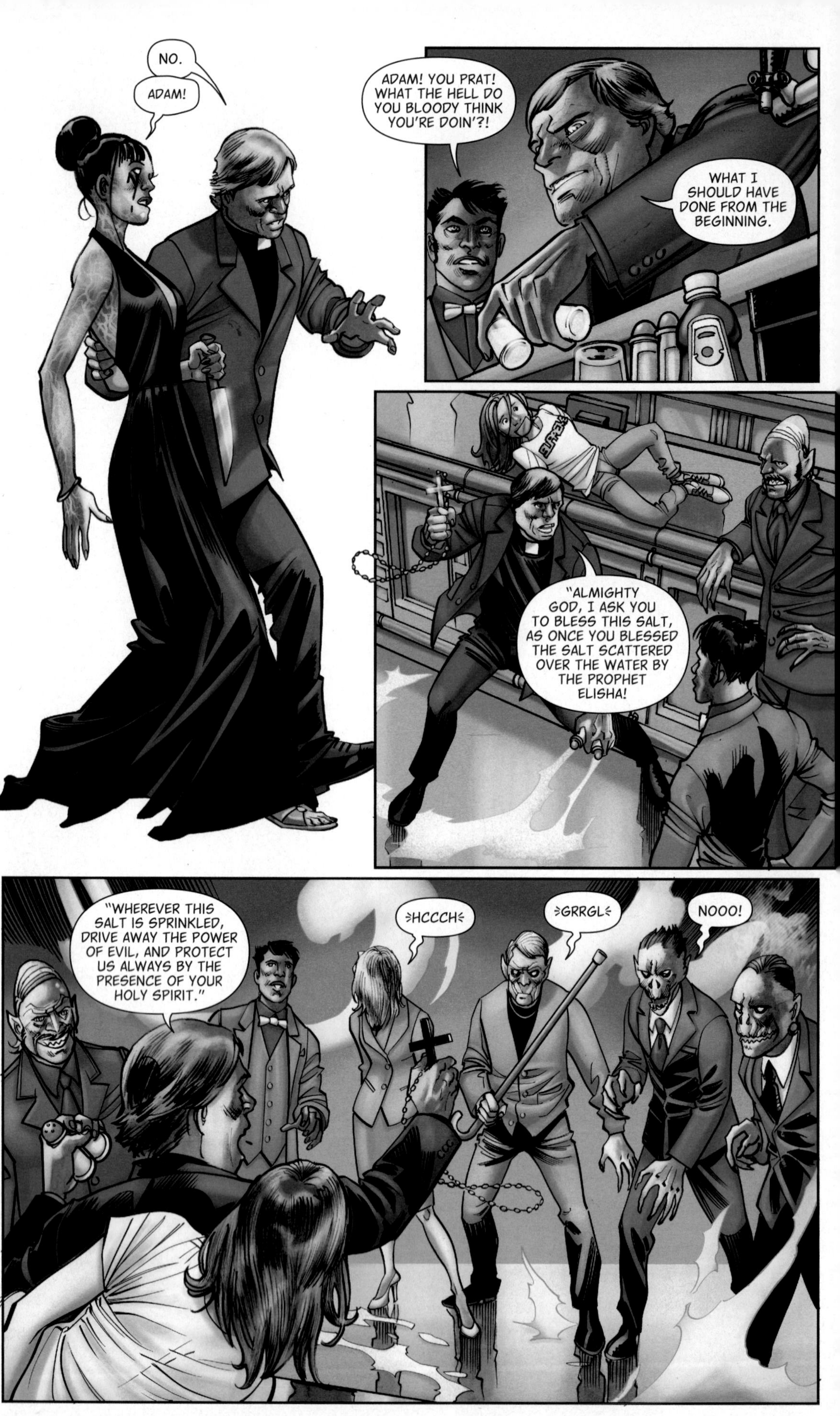
NO.
ADAM!
ADAM! YOU PRAT! WHAT THE HELL DO YOU BLOODY THINK YOU'RE DOIN'?!
WHAT I SHOULD HAVE DONE FROM THE BEGINNING.
"ALMIGHTY GOD, I ASK YOU TO BLESS THIS SALT, AS ONCE YOU BLESSED THE SALT SCATTERED OVER THE WATER BY THE PROPHET ELISHA!
"WHEREVER THIS SALT IS SPRINKLED, DRIVE AWAY THE POWER OF EVIL, AND PROTECT US ALWAYS BY THE PRESENCE OF YOUR HOLY SPIRIT."
HCCCH
GRRGL
NOOO!

ADAM! CHRIST ON A BIKE! A LINE OF SALT?! WE DON'T HAVE TIME FOR ONE OF YOUR FANCY SHOWS! WHAT DO YOU THINK YOU'RE DOING, MAN?!

I'M DOING WHAT'S RIGHT. NOTHING OF SATAN'S REALM CAN ENTER HERE, INCLUDING YOU. I'LL PROTECT THIS CHILD OF GOD AS LONG AS *MY FAITH* WILL ALLOW.

YOUR FAITH.

AND HOW *GREAT* CAN THAT FAITH BE, FATHER?

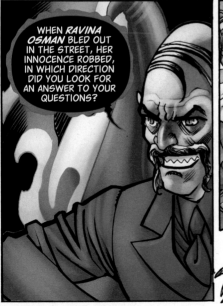

WHEN *RAVINA OSMAN* BLED OUT IN THE STREET, HER INNOCENCE ROBBED, IN WHICH DIRECTION DID YOU LOOK FOR AN ANSWER TO YOUR QUESTIONS?

LET ME GIVE YOU A CLUE, FATHER DAY.

IT WAS NOT *UP.*

≥TT≤

SHUNK

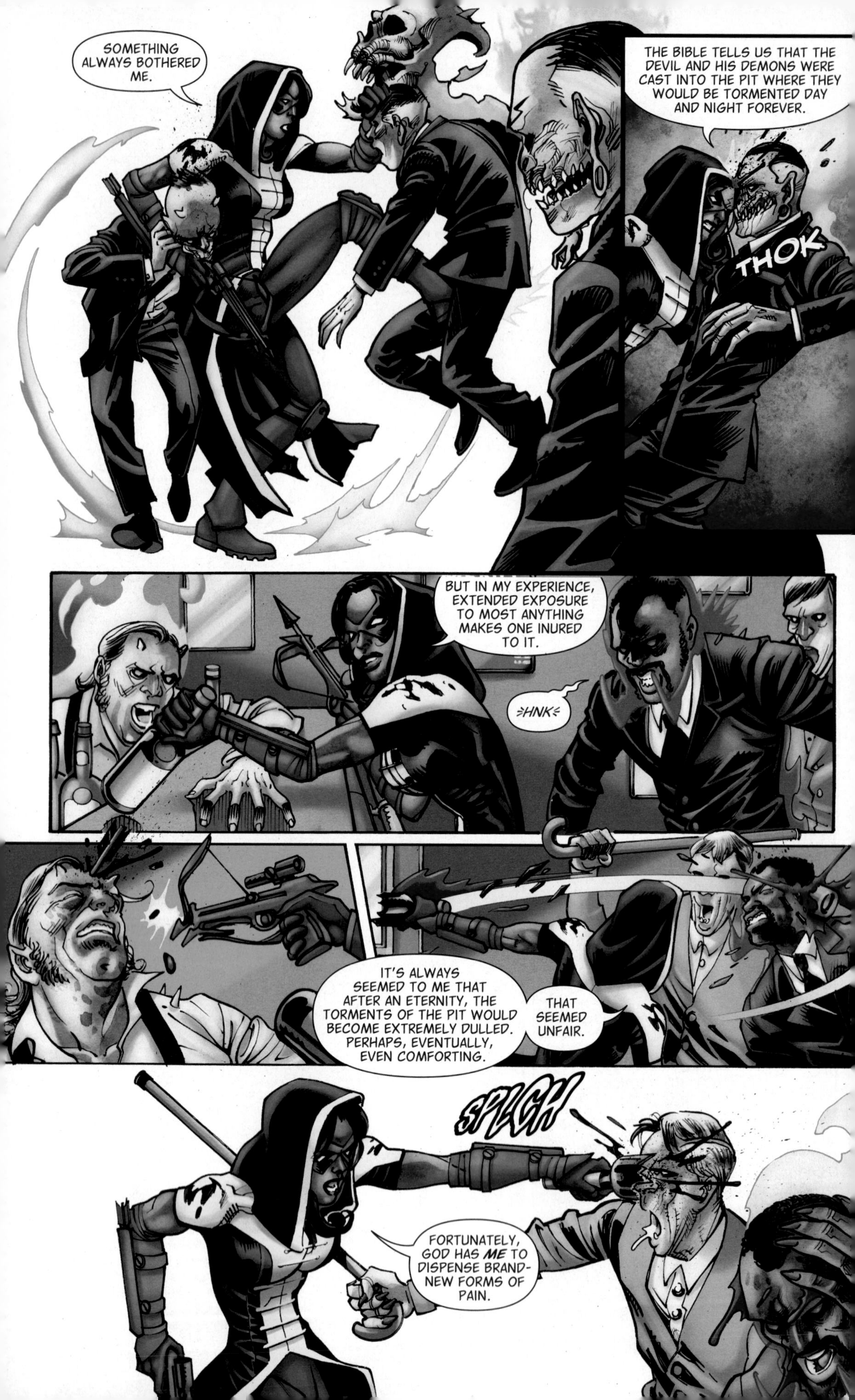
SOMETHING ALWAYS BOTHERED ME.
THE BIBLE TELLS US THAT THE DEVIL AND HIS DEMONS WERE CAST INTO THE PIT WHERE THEY WOULD BE TORMENTED DAY AND NIGHT FOREVER.
THOK
BUT IN MY EXPERIENCE, EXTENDED EXPOSURE TO MOST ANYTHING MAKES ONE INURED TO IT.
HNK
IT'S ALWAYS SEEMED TO ME THAT AFTER AN ETERNITY, THE TORMENTS OF THE PIT WOULD BECOME EXTREMELY DULLED. PERHAPS, EVENTUALLY, EVEN COMFORTING.
THAT SEEMED UNFAIR.
SPLCH
FORTUNATELY, GOD HAS *ME* TO DISPENSE BRAND-NEW FORMS OF PAIN.

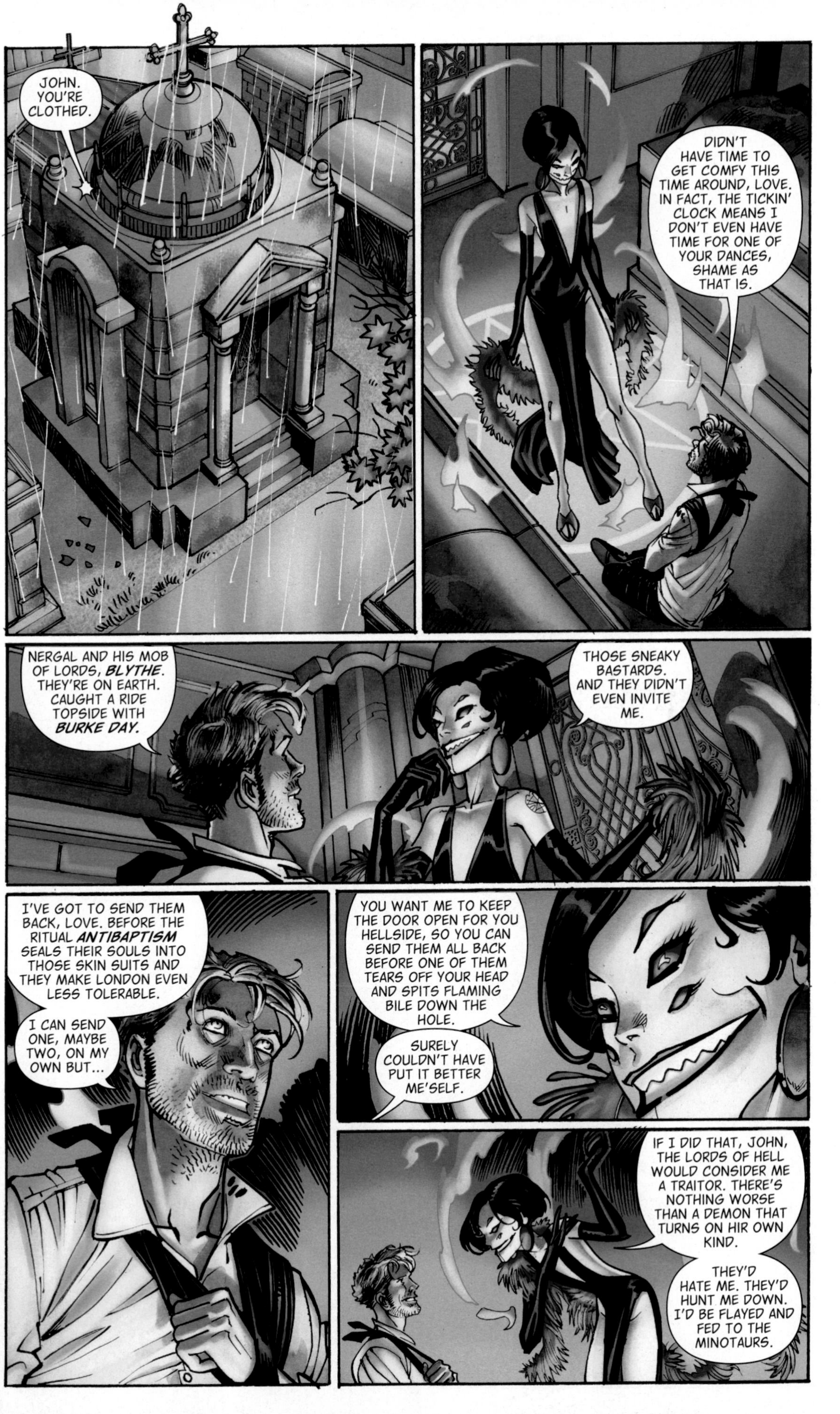

JOHN. YOU'RE CLOTHED.
DIDN'T HAVE TIME TO GET COMFY THIS TIME AROUND, LOVE. IN FACT, THE TICKIN' CLOCK MEANS I DON'T EVEN HAVE TIME FOR ONE OF YOUR DANCES, SHAME AS THAT IS.
NERGAL AND HIS MOB OF LORDS, BLYTHE. THEY'RE ON EARTH. CAUGHT A RIDE TOPSIDE WITH BURKE DAY.
THOSE SNEAKY BASTARDS. AND THEY DIDN'T EVEN INVITE ME.
I'VE GOT TO SEND THEM BACK, LOVE. BEFORE THE RITUAL ANTIBAPTISM SEALS THEIR SOULS INTO THOSE SKIN SUITS AND THEY MAKE LONDON EVEN LESS TOLERABLE.
I CAN SEND ONE, MAYBE TWO, ON MY OWN BUT...
YOU WANT ME TO KEEP THE DOOR OPEN FOR YOU HELLSIDE, SO YOU CAN SEND THEM ALL BACK BEFORE ONE OF THEM TEARS OFF YOUR HEAD AND SPITS FLAMING BILE DOWN THE HOLE.
SURELY COULDN'T HAVE PUT IT BETTER ME'SELF.
IF I DID THAT, JOHN, THE LORDS OF HELL WOULD CONSIDER ME A TRAITOR. THERE'S NOTHING WORSE THAN A DEMON THAT TURNS ON HIR OWN KIND.
THEY'D HATE ME. THEY'D HUNT ME DOWN. I'D BE FLAYED AND FED TO THE MINOTAURS.

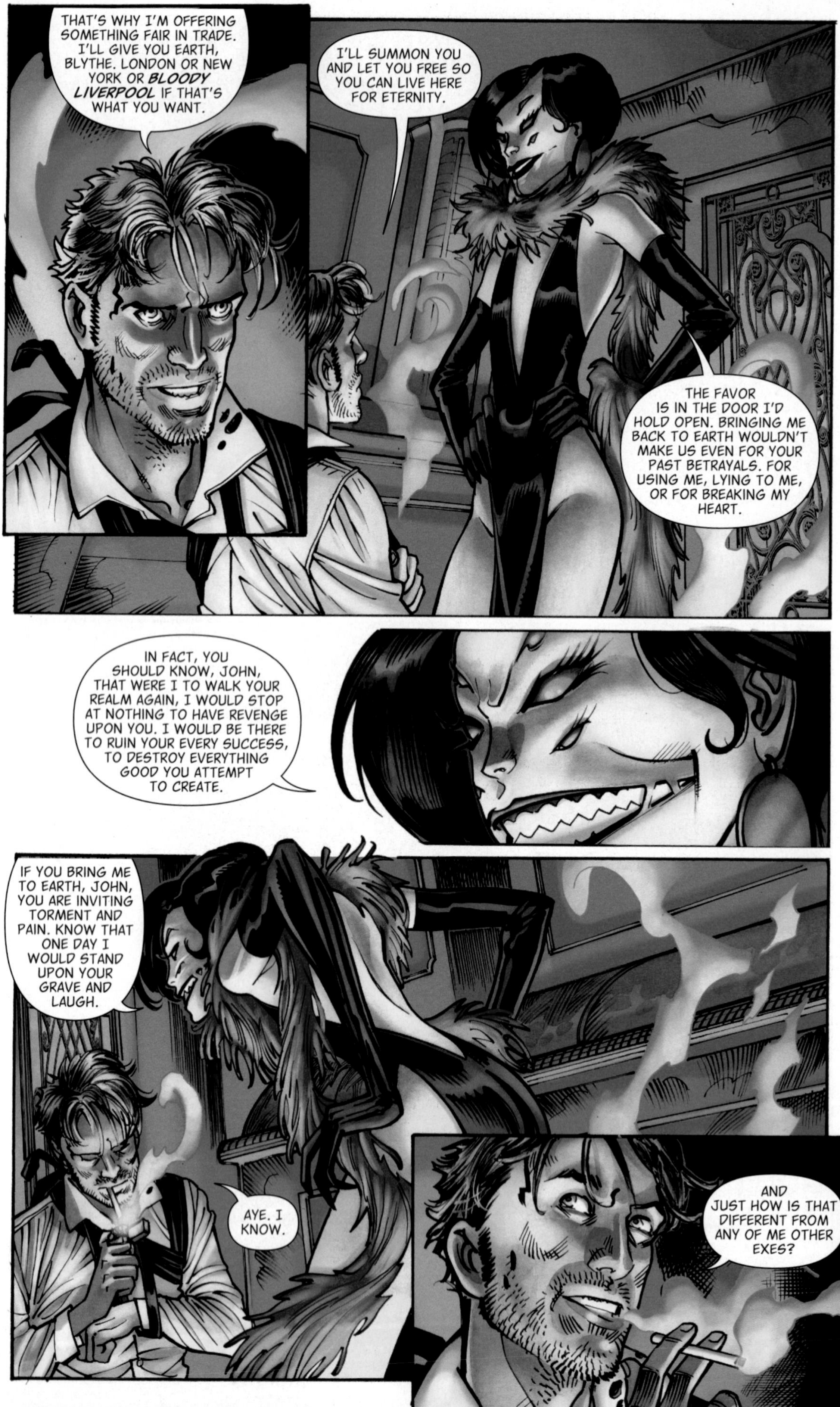
THAT'S WHY I'M OFFERING SOMETHING FAIR IN TRADE. I'LL GIVE YOU EARTH, BLYTHE. LONDON OR NEW YORK OR BLOODY LIVERPOOL IF THAT'S WHAT YOU WANT.
I'LL SUMMON YOU AND LET YOU FREE SO YOU CAN LIVE HERE FOR ETERNITY.
THE FAVOR IS IN THE DOOR I'D HOLD OPEN. BRINGING ME BACK TO EARTH WOULDN'T MAKE US EVEN FOR YOUR PAST BETRAYALS. FOR USING ME, LYING TO ME, OR FOR BREAKING MY HEART.
IN FACT, YOU SHOULD KNOW, JOHN, THAT WERE I TO WALK YOUR REALM AGAIN, I WOULD STOP AT NOTHING TO HAVE REVENGE UPON YOU. I WOULD BE THERE TO RUIN YOUR EVERY SUCCESS, TO DESTROY EVERYTHING GOOD YOU ATTEMPT TO CREATE.
IF YOU BRING ME TO EARTH, JOHN, YOU ARE INVITING TORMENT AND PAIN. KNOW THAT ONE DAY I WOULD STAND UPON YOUR GRAVE AND LAUGH.
AYE. I KNOW.
AND JUST HOW IS THAT DIFFERENT FROM ANY OF ME OTHER EXES?

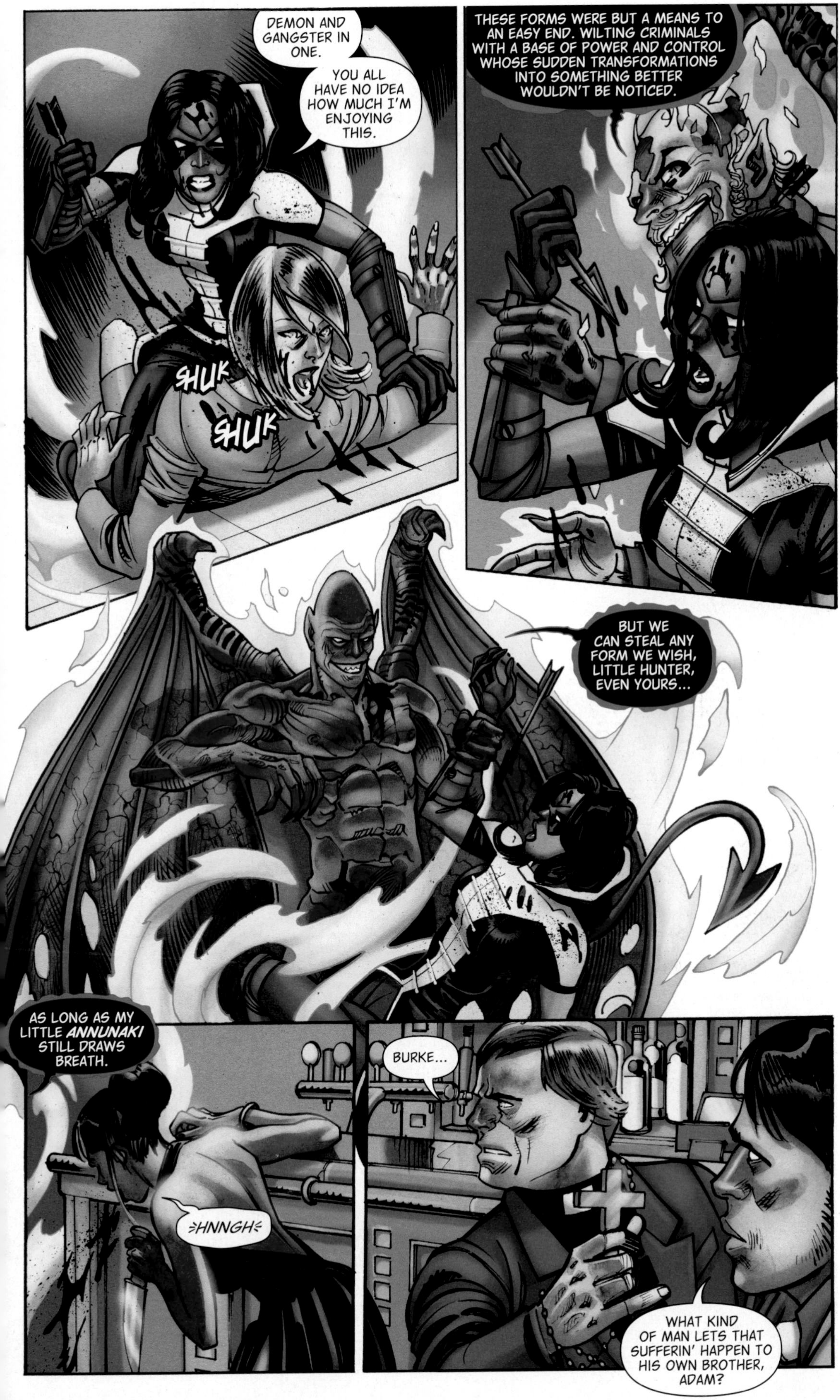
DEMON AND GANGSTER IN ONE.
YOU ALL HAVE NO IDEA HOW MUCH I'M ENJOYING THIS.
SHUK
SHUK
THESE FORMS WERE BUT A MEANS TO AN EASY END. WILTING CRIMINALS WITH A BASE OF POWER AND CONTROL WHOSE SUDDEN TRANSFORMATIONS INTO SOMETHING BETTER WOULDN'T BE NOTICED.
BUT WE CAN STEAL ANY FORM WE WISH, LITTLE HUNTER, EVEN YOURS...
AS LONG AS MY LITTLE *ANNUNAKI* STILL DRAWS BREATH.
HNNGH
BURKE...
WHAT KIND OF MAN LETS THAT SUFFERIN' HAPPEN TO HIS OWN BROTHER, ADAM?

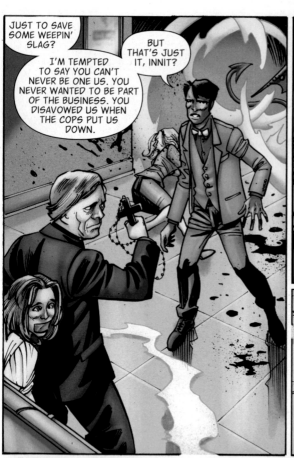

JUST TO SAVE SOME WEEPIN' SLAG?

BUT THAT'S JUST IT, INNIT?

I'M TEMPTED TO SAY YOU CAN'T NEVER BE ONE US. YOU NEVER WANTED TO BE PART OF THE BUSINESS. YOU DISAVOWED US WHEN THE COPS PUT US DOWN.

YOU PLEDGED YOURSELF TO GOD BECAUSE YOU WANTED HIM TO SAVE YOU FROM WHAT YOU KNOW RESIDES INSIDE YOU, ADAM.

A MURDERER. A RAPIST. A GANGSTER.

A BLOODY *DAY* BROTHER!

WHEN YOU GET TO THE PITS, SAY "CHEERS" TO ALL OF MY OLD COWORKERS WOULD YOU?

LUCAS! NO!

TELL 'EM I'M NEVER COMIN' BACK! HAHAHA!

≥NGH-- NUH≤

HA--

SPLUK

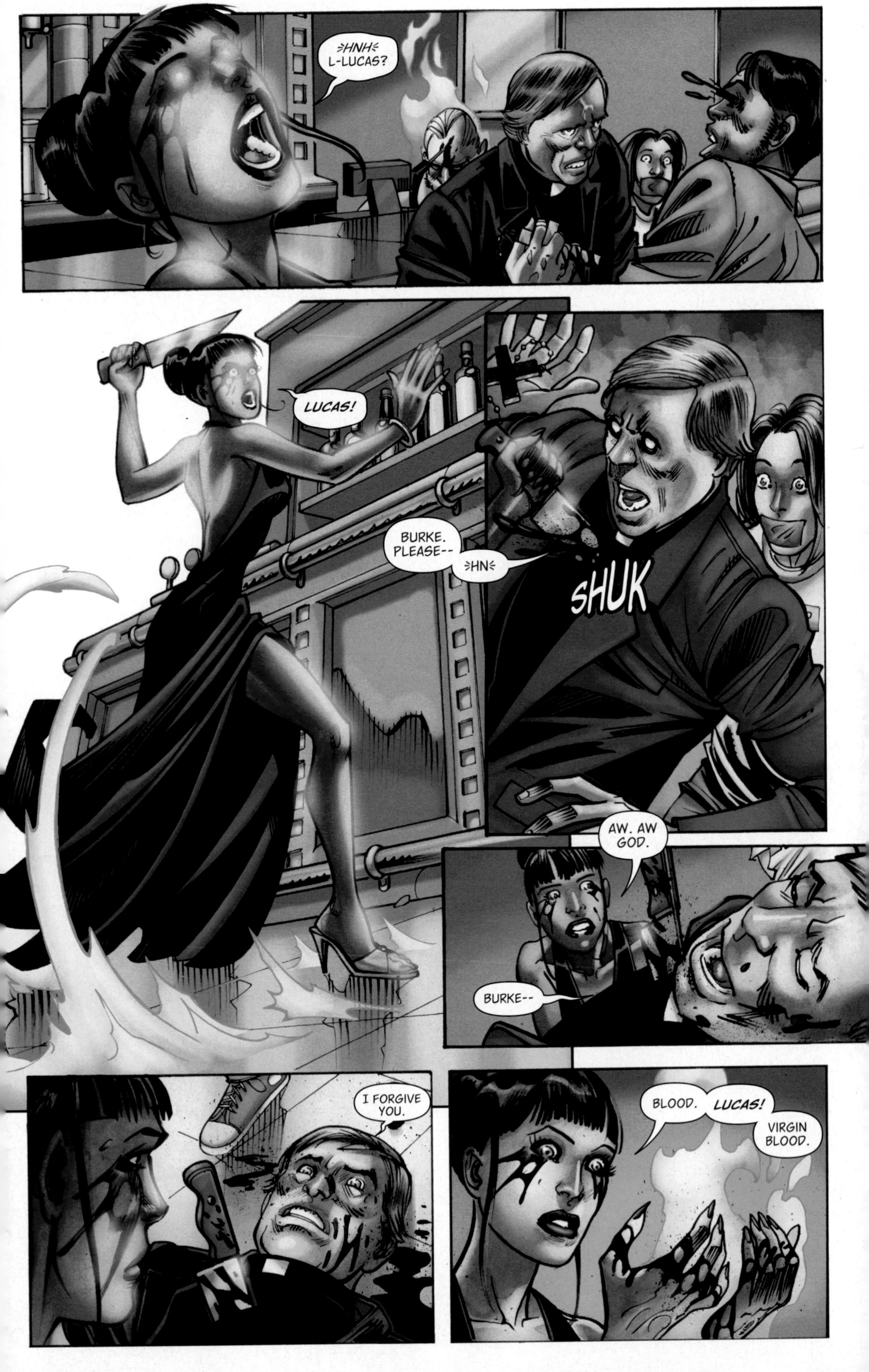
HNH L-LUCAS?
LUCAS!
BURKE. PLEASE--
HN
SHUK
AW. AW GOD.
BURKE--
I FORGIVE YOU.
BLOOD. LUCAS!
VIRGIN BLOOD.

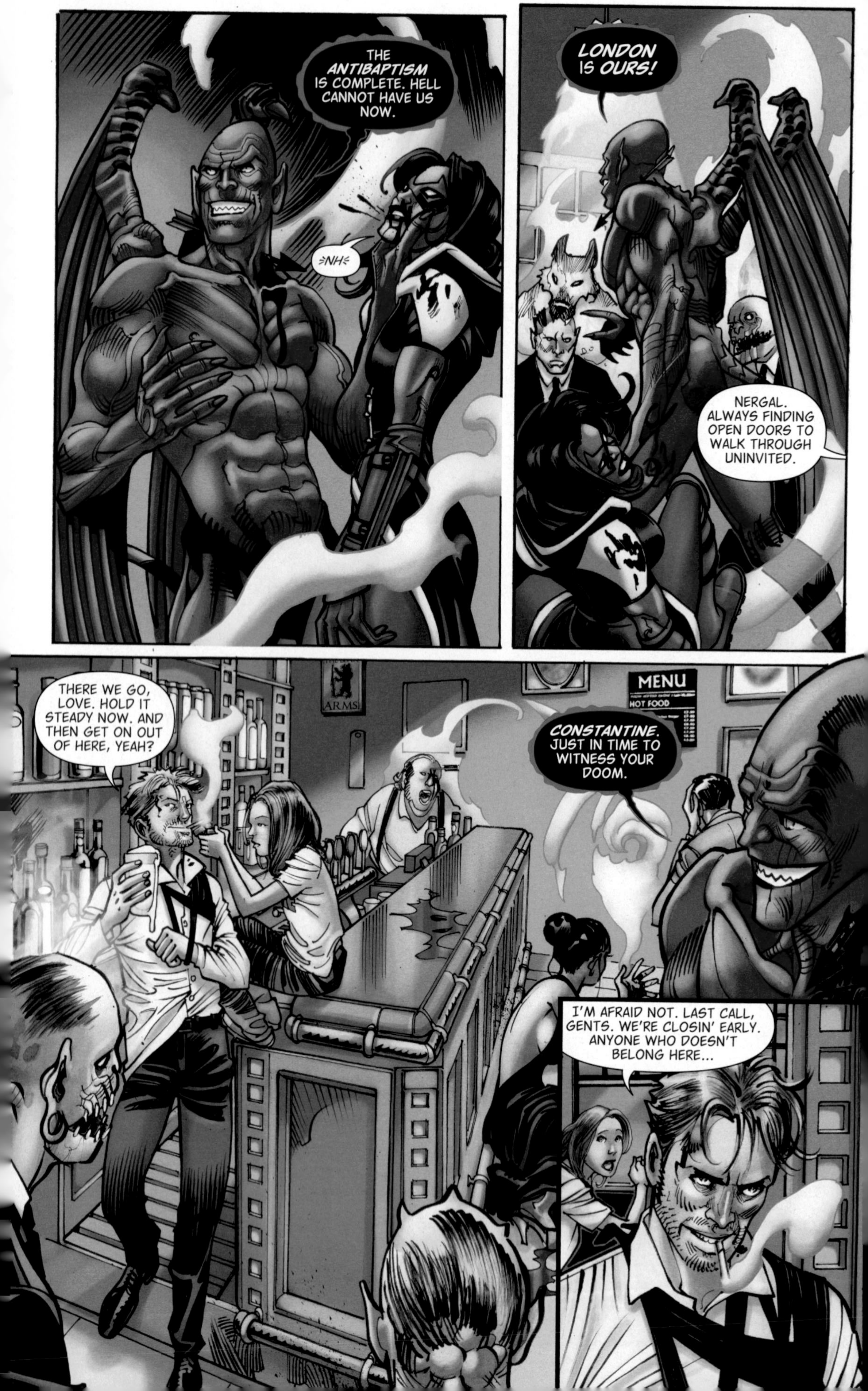
THE *ANTIBAPTISM* IS COMPLETE. HELL CANNOT HAVE US NOW.
NH
LONDON IS *OURS!*
NERGAL. ALWAYS FINDING OPEN DOORS TO WALK THROUGH UNINVITED.
ARMS
MENU
HOT FOOD
THERE WE GO, LOVE. HOLD IT STEADY NOW. AND THEN GET ON OUT OF HERE, YEAH?
CONSTANTINE. JUST IN TIME TO WITNESS YOUR DOOM.
I'M AFRAID NOT. LAST CALL, GENTS. WE'RE CLOSIN' EARLY. ANYONE WHO DOESN'T BELONG HERE...

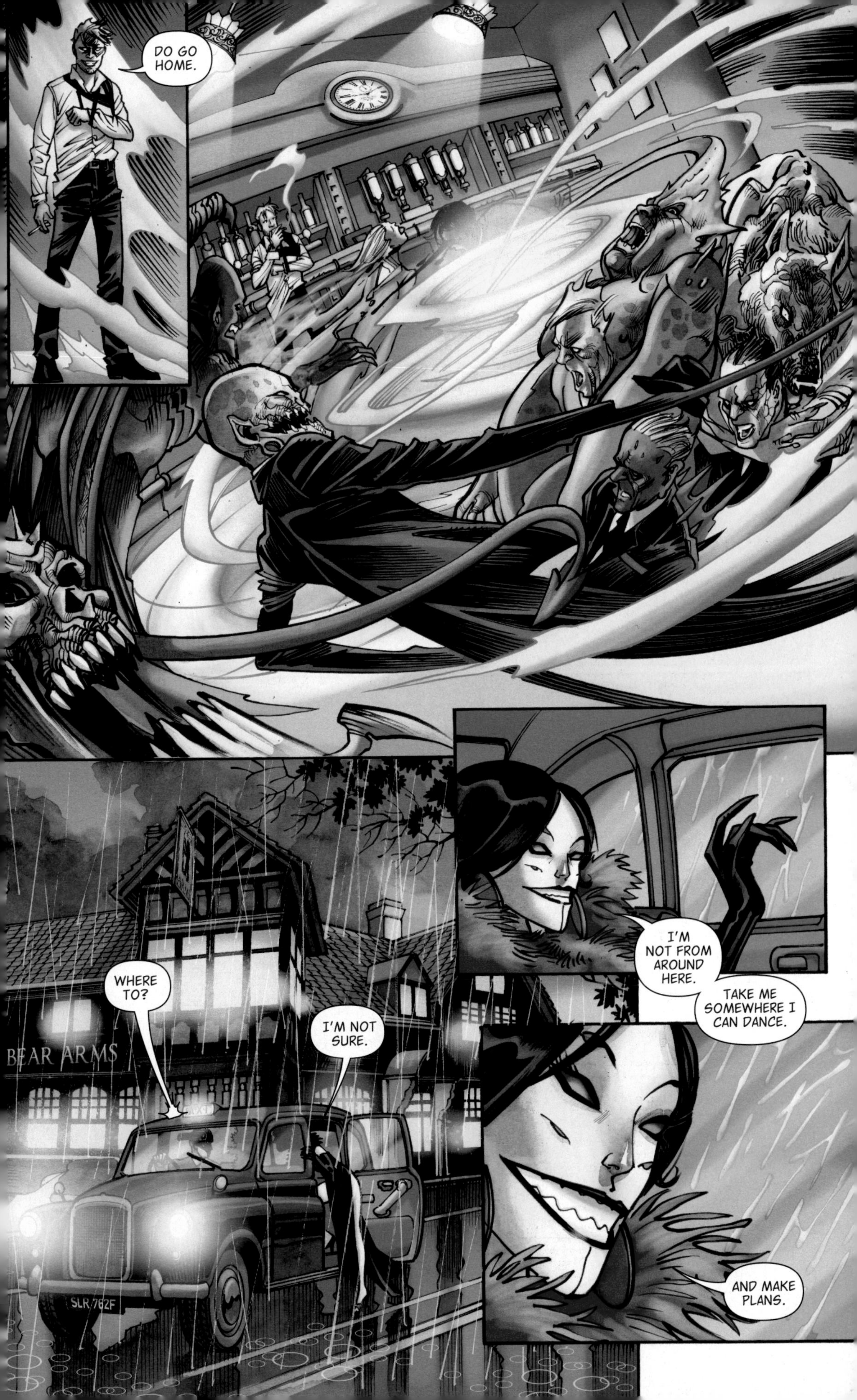
DO GO HOME.
WHERE TO?
I'M NOT SURE.
BEAR ARMS
SLR 762F
I'M NOT FROM AROUND HERE.
TAKE ME SOMEWHERE I CAN DANCE.
AND MAKE PLANS.

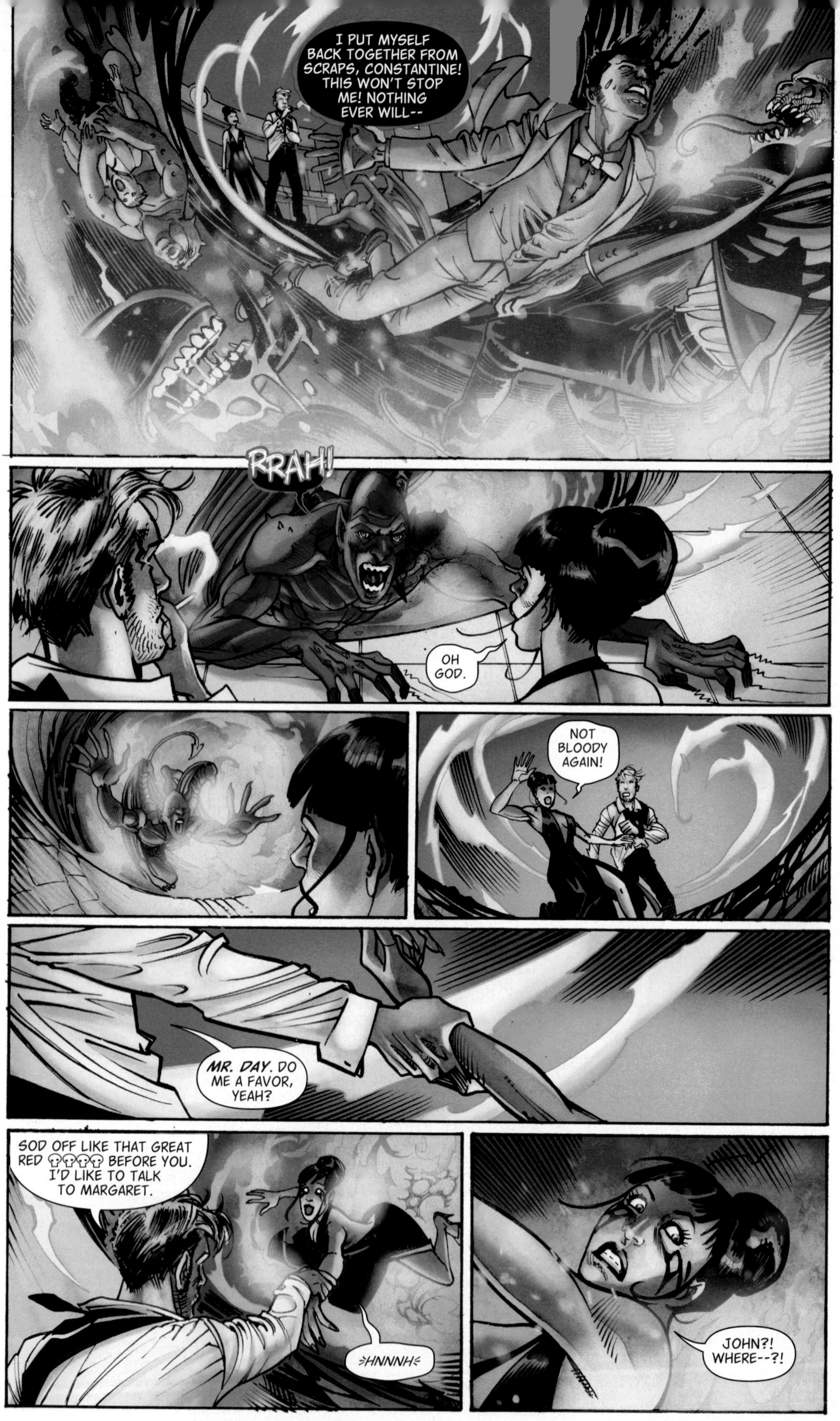
I PUT MYSELF BACK TOGETHER FROM SCRAPS, CONSTANTINE! THIS WON'T STOP ME! NOTHING EVER WILL--
RRAH!
OH GOD.
NOT BLOODY AGAIN!
MR. DAY. DO ME A FAVOR, YEAH?
SOD OFF LIKE THAT GREAT RED 💀💀💀💀 BEFORE YOU. I'D LIKE TO TALK TO MARGARET.
HNNNH
JOHN?! WHERE--?!

YOU'VE GOT A SPECIAL POWER, LOVE. YOU'RE A VESSEL, LIKE AN URN THAT CAN COLLECT RAIN, AND THEN POUR IT BACK OUT.

YOU'VE GOT JUST A BIT LEFT IN YOU. I JUST NEED YOU TO EJECT THIS ONE LAST PASSENGER. ONE BIG PUSH OUGHT TO DO IT.

JUST TRUST ME, LOVE.

≥NNH≤

NO.

YOU KNOW SHE BLAMES YOU FOR ALL THIS. SHE DOESN'T TRUST YOU, JOHN-BOY. NOT ENOUGH TO GIVE HERSELF UP TO YOU.

AND NOT ENOUGH TO GET RID OF ME WITHOUT A FIGHT.

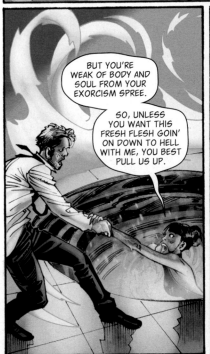

BUT YOU'RE WEAK OF BODY AND SOUL FROM YOUR EXORCISM SPREE.

SO, UNLESS YOU WANT THIS FRESH FLESH GOIN' ON DOWN TO HELL WITH ME, YOU BEST PULL US UP.

DAMN!

THAT'S RIGHT, YOU SCOUSER SCUM. SHE CAN'T KICK ME, AND I SURE AS BLOODY HELL AIN'T GIVIN' HER UP.

≥HN-GH≤

SEE, YOU'RE RIGHT ABOUT ONE THING, JOHNNY. SHE IS SPECIAL.

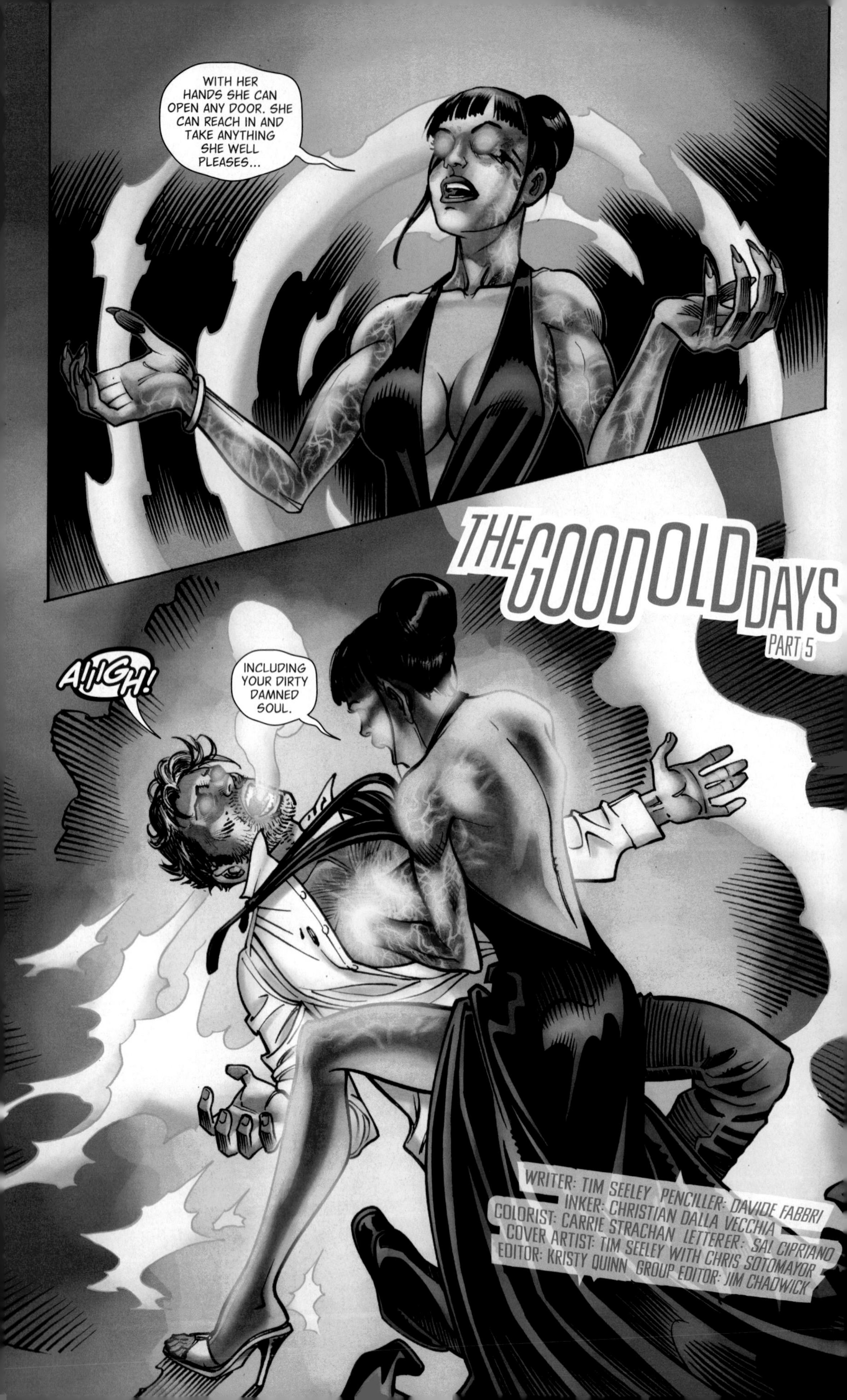

WITH HER HANDS SHE CAN OPEN ANY DOOR. SHE CAN REACH IN AND TAKE ANYTHING SHE WELL PLEASES...
THE GOOD OLD DAYS
PART 5
AIIIGH!
INCLUDING YOUR DIRTY DAMNED SOUL.
WRITER: TIM SEELEY PENCILLER: DAVIDE FABBRI
INKER: CHRISTIAN DALLA VECCHIA
COLORIST: CARRIE STRACHAN LETTERER: SAL CIPRIANO
COVER ARTIST: TIM SEELEY WITH CHRIS SOTOMAYOR
EDITOR: KRISTY QUINN GROUP EDITOR: JIM CHADWICK

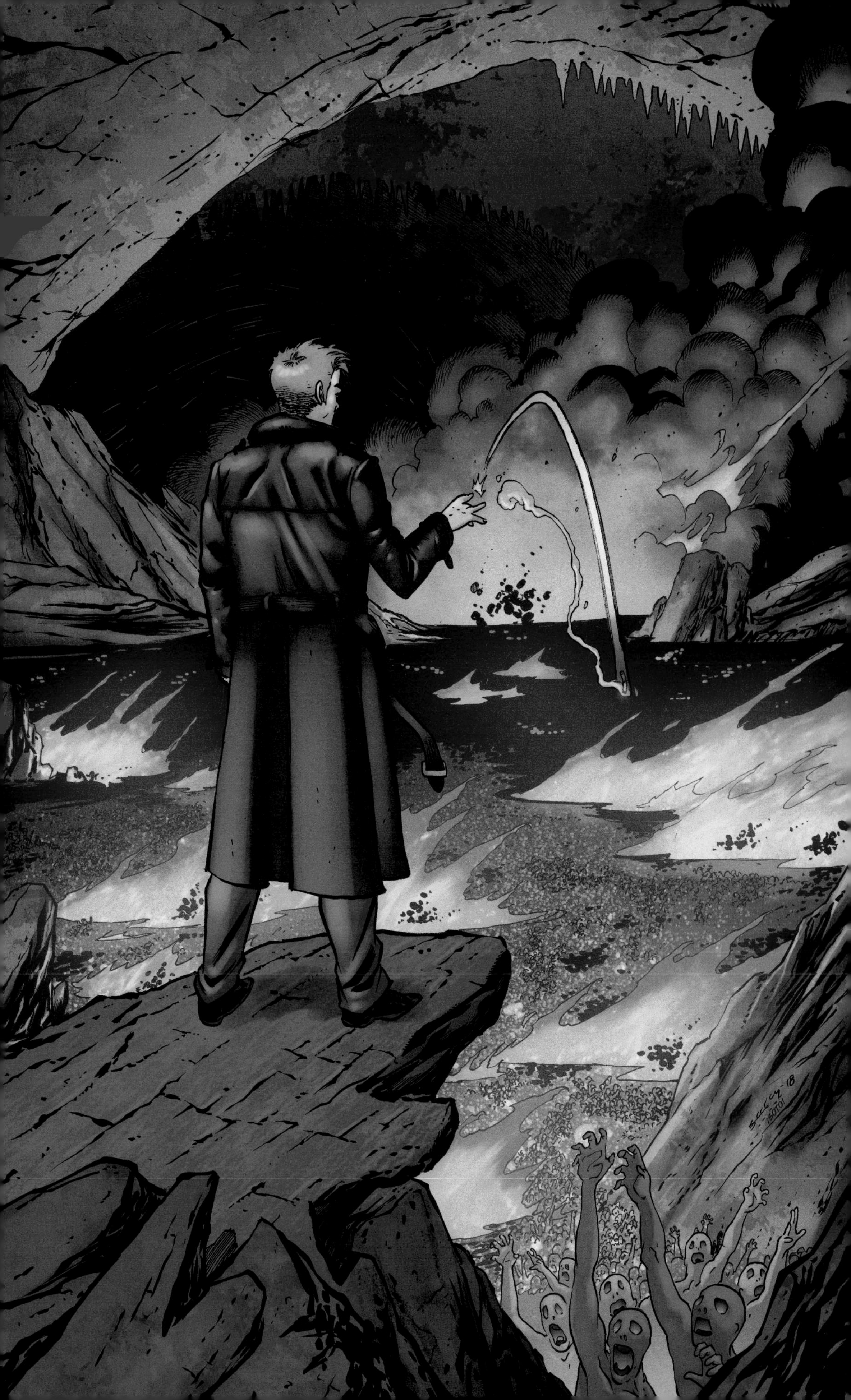

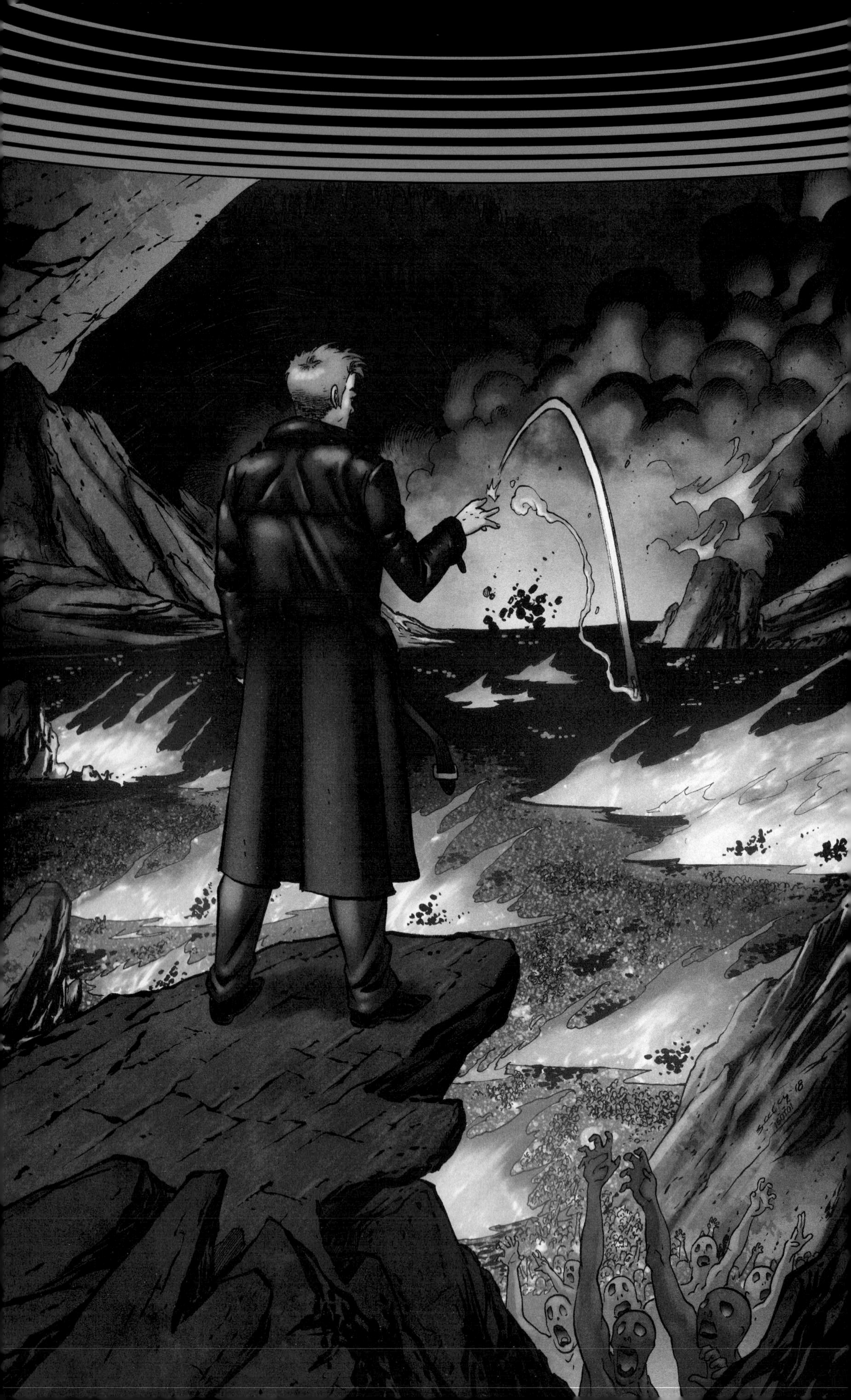

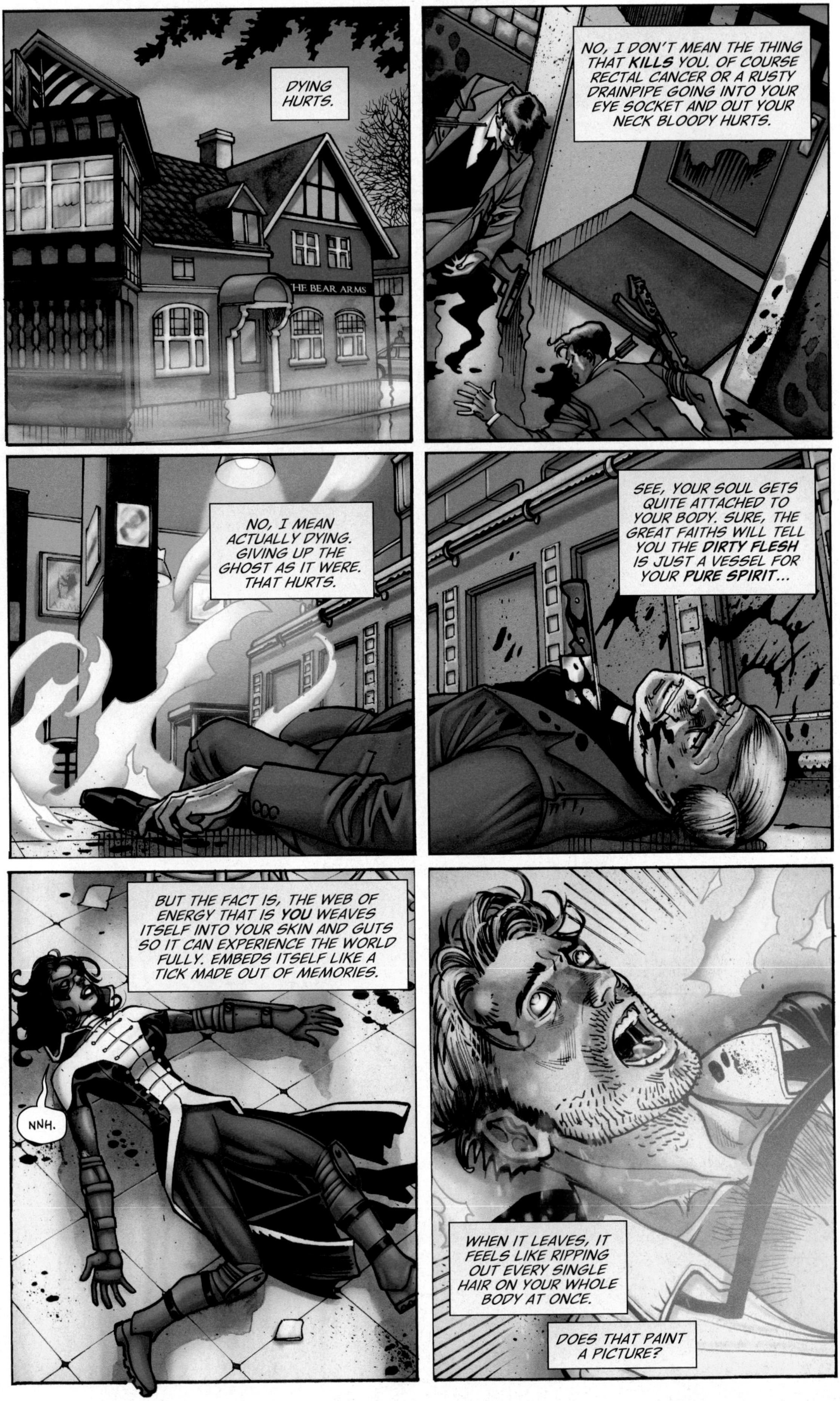

DYING HURTS.
THE BEAR ARMS
NO, I DON'T MEAN THE THING THAT KILLS YOU. OF COURSE RECTAL CANCER OR A RUSTY DRAINPIPE GOING INTO YOUR EYE SOCKET AND OUT YOUR NECK BLOODY HURTS.
NO, I MEAN ACTUALLY DYING. GIVING UP THE GHOST AS IT WERE. THAT HURTS.
SEE, YOUR SOUL GETS QUITE ATTACHED TO YOUR BODY. SURE, THE GREAT FAITHS WILL TELL YOU THE DIRTY FLESH IS JUST A VESSEL FOR YOUR PURE SPIRIT...
BUT THE FACT IS, THE WEB OF ENERGY THAT IS YOU WEAVES ITSELF INTO YOUR SKIN AND GUTS SO IT CAN EXPERIENCE THE WORLD FULLY. EMBEDS ITSELF LIKE A TICK MADE OUT OF MEMORIES.
NNH.
WHEN IT LEAVES, IT FEELS LIKE RIPPING OUT EVERY SINGLE HAIR ON YOUR WHOLE BODY AT ONCE.
DOES THAT PAINT A PICTURE?

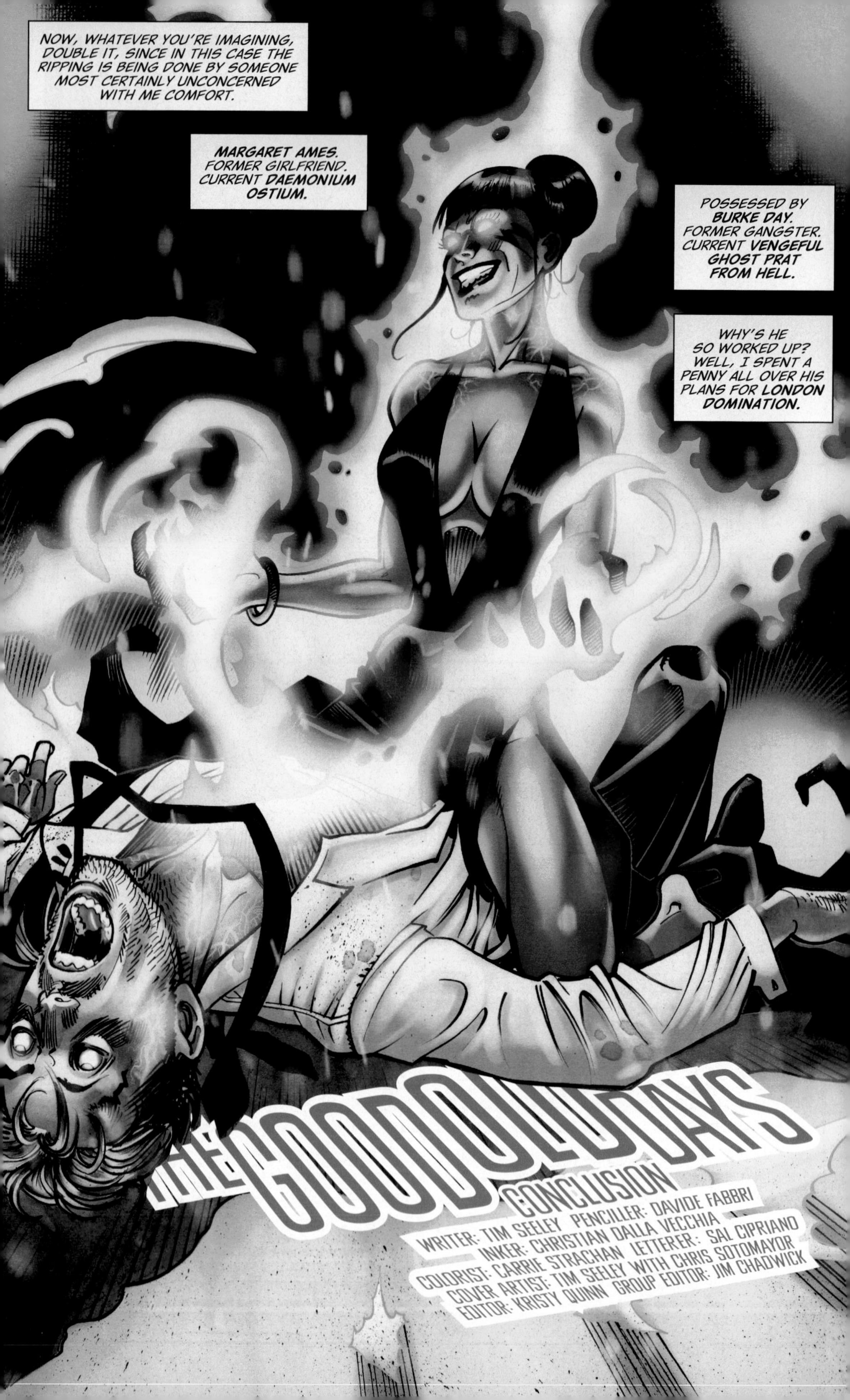
NOW, WHATEVER YOU'RE IMAGINING, DOUBLE IT, SINCE IN THIS CASE THE RIPPING IS BEING DONE BY SOMEONE MOST CERTAINLY UNCONCERNED WITH ME COMFORT.
MARGARET AMES. FORMER GIRLFRIEND. CURRENT DAEMONIUM OSTIUM.
POSSESSED BY BURKE DAY. FORMER GANGSTER. CURRENT VENGEFUL GHOST PRAT FROM HELL.
WHY'S HE SO WORKED UP? WELL, I SPENT A PENNY ALL OVER HIS PLANS FOR LONDON DOMINATION.
THE GOOD OLD DAYS
CONCLUSION
WRITER: TIM SEELEY PENCILLER: DAVIDE FABBRI
INKER: CHRISTIAN DALLA VECCHIA
COLORIST: CARRIE STRACHAN LETTERER: SAL CIPRIANO
COVER ARTIST: TIM SEELEY WITH CHRIS SOTOMAYOR
EDITOR: KRISTY QUINN GROUP EDITOR: JIM CHADWICK

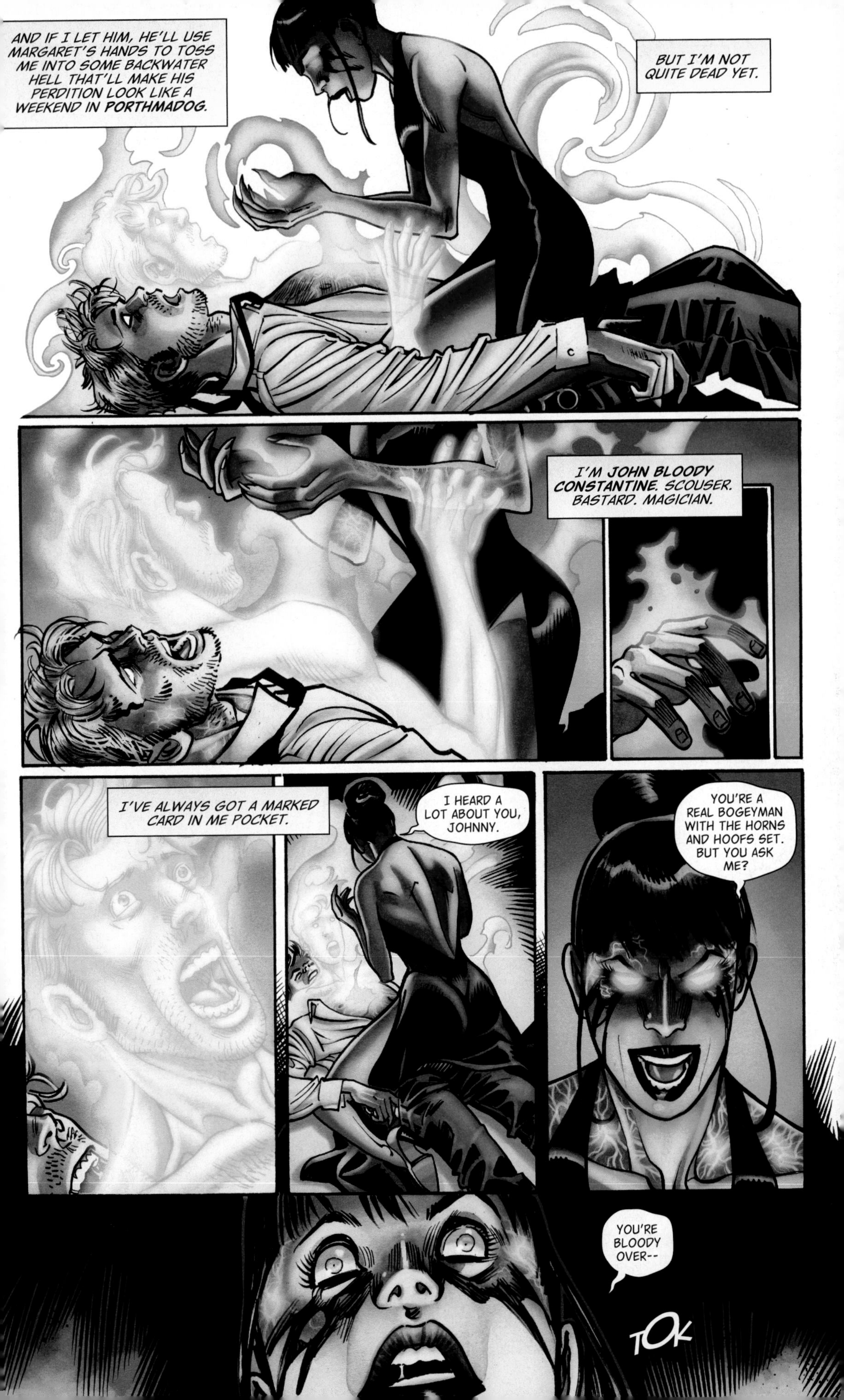
AND IF I LET HIM, HE'LL USE MARGARET'S HANDS TO TOSS ME INTO SOME BACKWATER HELL THAT'LL MAKE HIS PERDITION LOOK LIKE A WEEKEND IN PORTHMADOG.
BUT I'M NOT QUITE DEAD YET.
I'M JOHN BLOODY CONSTANTINE. SCOUSER. BASTARD. MAGICIAN.
I'VE ALWAYS GOT A MARKED CARD IN ME POCKET.
I HEARD A LOT ABOUT YOU, JOHNNY.
YOU'RE A REAL BOGEYMAN WITH THE HORNS AND HOOFS SET. BUT YOU ASK ME?
YOU'RE BLOODY OVER--
TOK

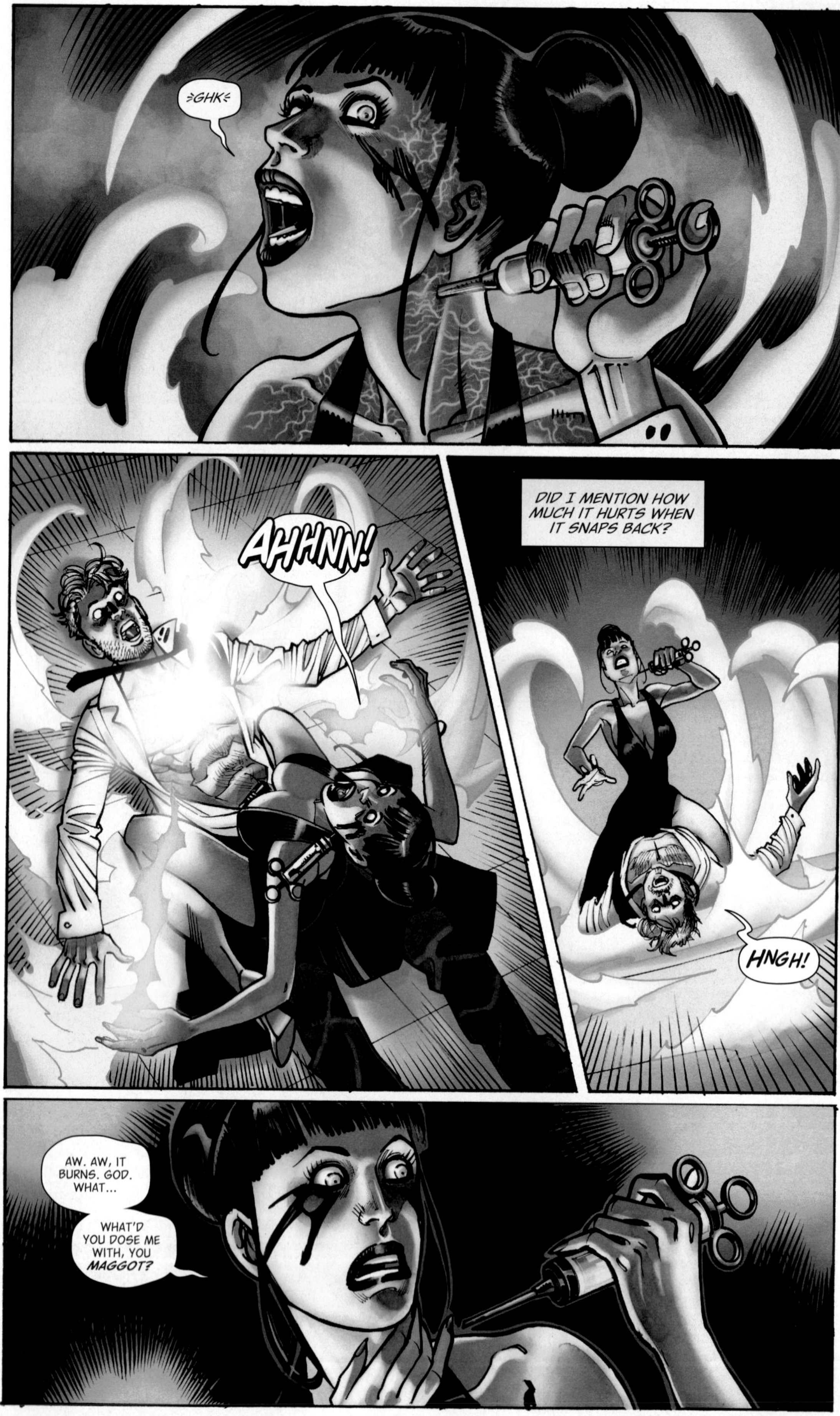

GHK
AHHNN!
DID I MENTION HOW MUCH IT HURTS WHEN IT SNAPS BACK?
HNGH!
AW. AW, IT BURNS. GOD. WHAT...
WHAT'D YOU DOSE ME WITH, YOU MAGGOT?

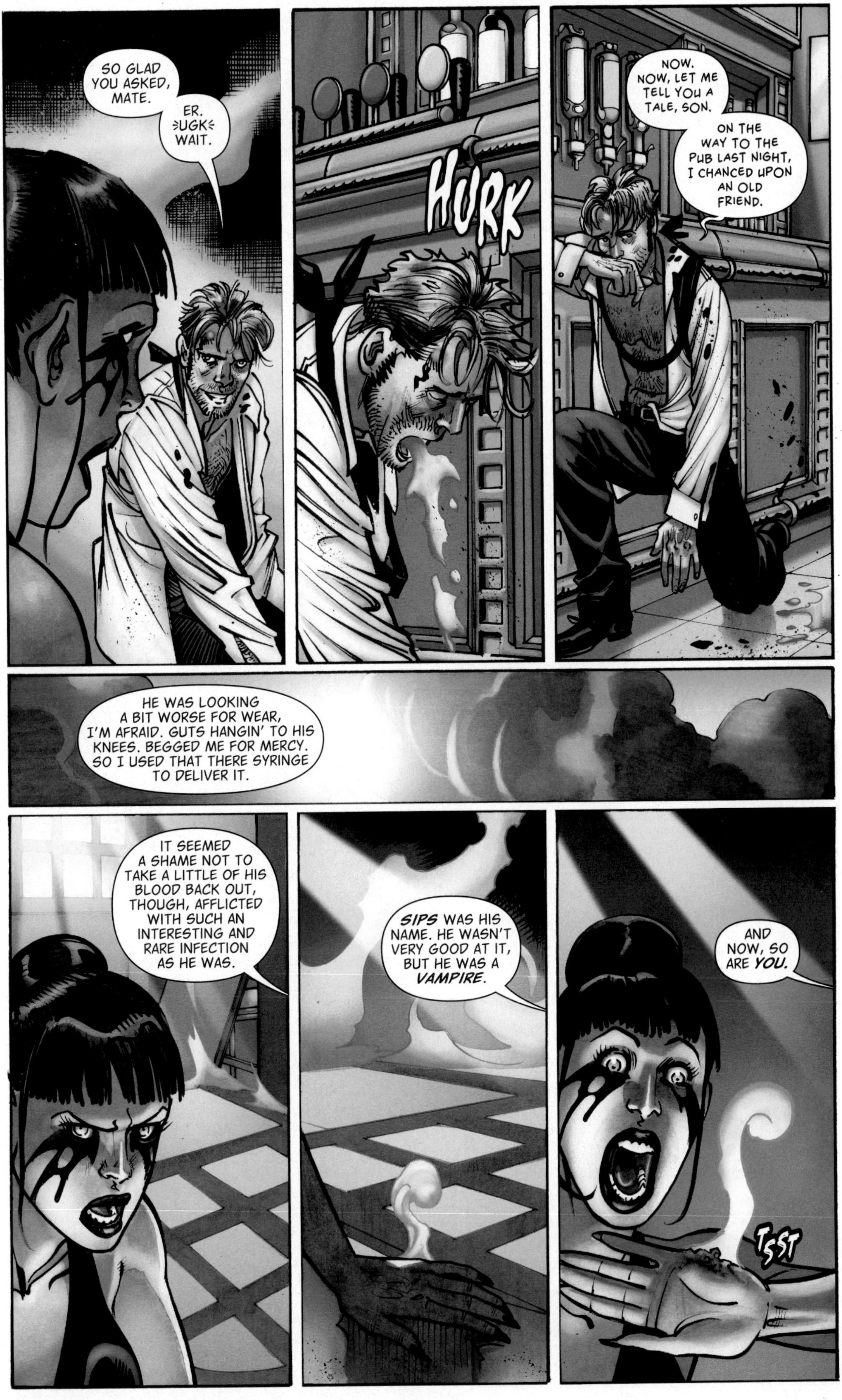
SO GLAD YOU ASKED, MATE.
ER. UGK WAIT.
HURK
NOW. NOW, LET ME TELL YOU A TALE, SON.
ON THE WAY TO THE PUB LAST NIGHT, I CHANCED UPON AN OLD FRIEND.
HE WAS LOOKING A BIT WORSE FOR WEAR, I'M AFRAID. GUTS HANGIN' TO HIS KNEES. BEGGED ME FOR MERCY. SO I USED THAT THERE SYRINGE TO DELIVER IT.
IT SEEMED A SHAME NOT TO TAKE A LITTLE OF HIS BLOOD BACK OUT, THOUGH, AFFLICTED WITH SUCH AN INTERESTING AND RARE INFECTION AS HE WAS.
SIPS WAS HIS NAME. HE WASN'T VERY GOOD AT IT, BUT HE WAS A *VAMPIRE*.
AND NOW, SO ARE *YOU*.
TSST

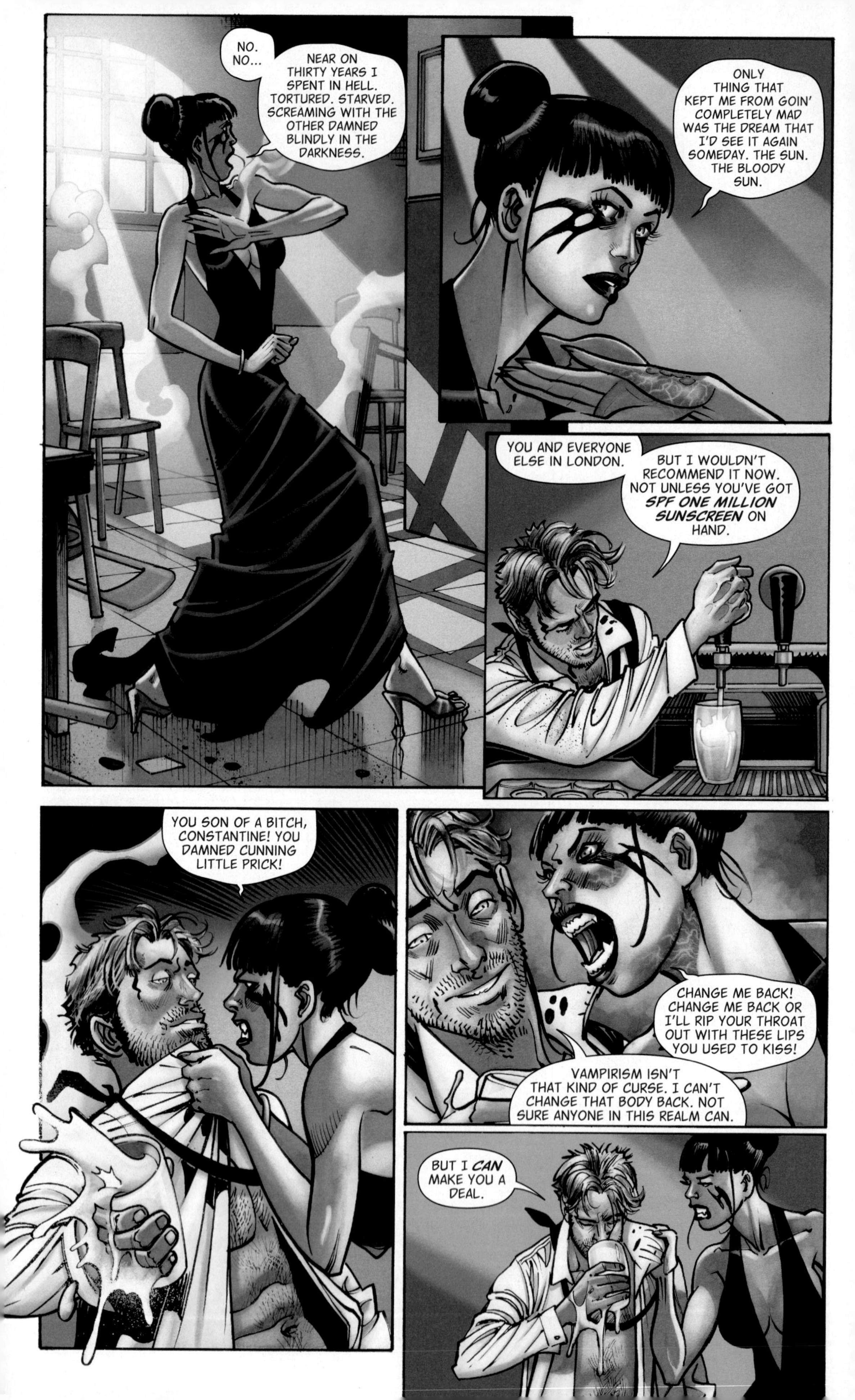
NO. NO...
NEAR ON THIRTY YEARS I SPENT IN HELL. TORTURED. STARVED. SCREAMING WITH THE OTHER DAMNED BLINDLY IN THE DARKNESS.
ONLY THING THAT KEPT ME FROM GOIN' COMPLETELY MAD WAS THE DREAM THAT I'D SEE IT AGAIN SOMEDAY. THE SUN. THE BLOODY SUN.
YOU AND EVERYONE ELSE IN LONDON.
BUT I WOULDN'T RECOMMEND IT NOW. NOT UNLESS YOU'VE GOT ***SPF ONE MILLION SUNSCREEN*** ON HAND.
YOU SON OF A BITCH, CONSTANTINE! YOU DAMNED CUNNING LITTLE PRICK!
CHANGE ME BACK! CHANGE ME BACK OR I'LL RIP YOUR THROAT OUT WITH THESE LIPS YOU USED TO KISS!
VAMPIRISM ISN'T THAT KIND OF CURSE. I CAN'T CHANGE THAT BODY BACK. NOT SURE ANYONE IN THIS REALM CAN.
BUT I ***CAN*** MAKE YOU A DEAL.

I'LL ADMIT IT. I FEEL A BIT RESPONSIBLE FOR WHAT HAPPENED TO MARGARET, HER BEING SO SUSCEPTIBLE TO YOUR PISSANT GANGSTER'S SOUL AS SHE WAS.

SHE WAS NEVER ANYTHING BUT GOOD TO ME. BELIEVED I MIGHT BE A BETTER MAN. LEFT ME WITH NOTHING BUT GOOD MEMORIES, AND A SHIRT THAT STILL SMELLS LIKE HER SKIN.

SO, YOU GIVE ME MY MARGARET BACK, *BURKE*. SHE'LL BE A LITTLE WORSE FOR WEAR, SURE, BUT STILL ME PLUCKY IRISH COPPER.

IT'S NOT LIKE SHE'S MUCH USE TO YOU ANYMORE ANYWAY

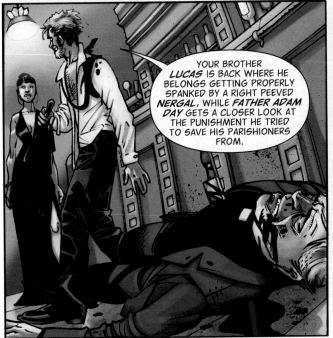

YOUR BROTHER *LUCAS* IS BACK WHERE HE BELONGS GETTING PROPERLY SPANKED BY A RIGHT PEEVED *NERGAL*, WHILE *FATHER ADAM DAY* GETS A CLOSER LOOK AT THE PUNISHMENT HE TRIED TO SAVE HIS PARISHIONERS FROM.

IN RETURN, I'LL GIVE YOU WHAT YOU REALLY WANT--A HEALTHY, PERFECT, BEAUTIFUL BODY.

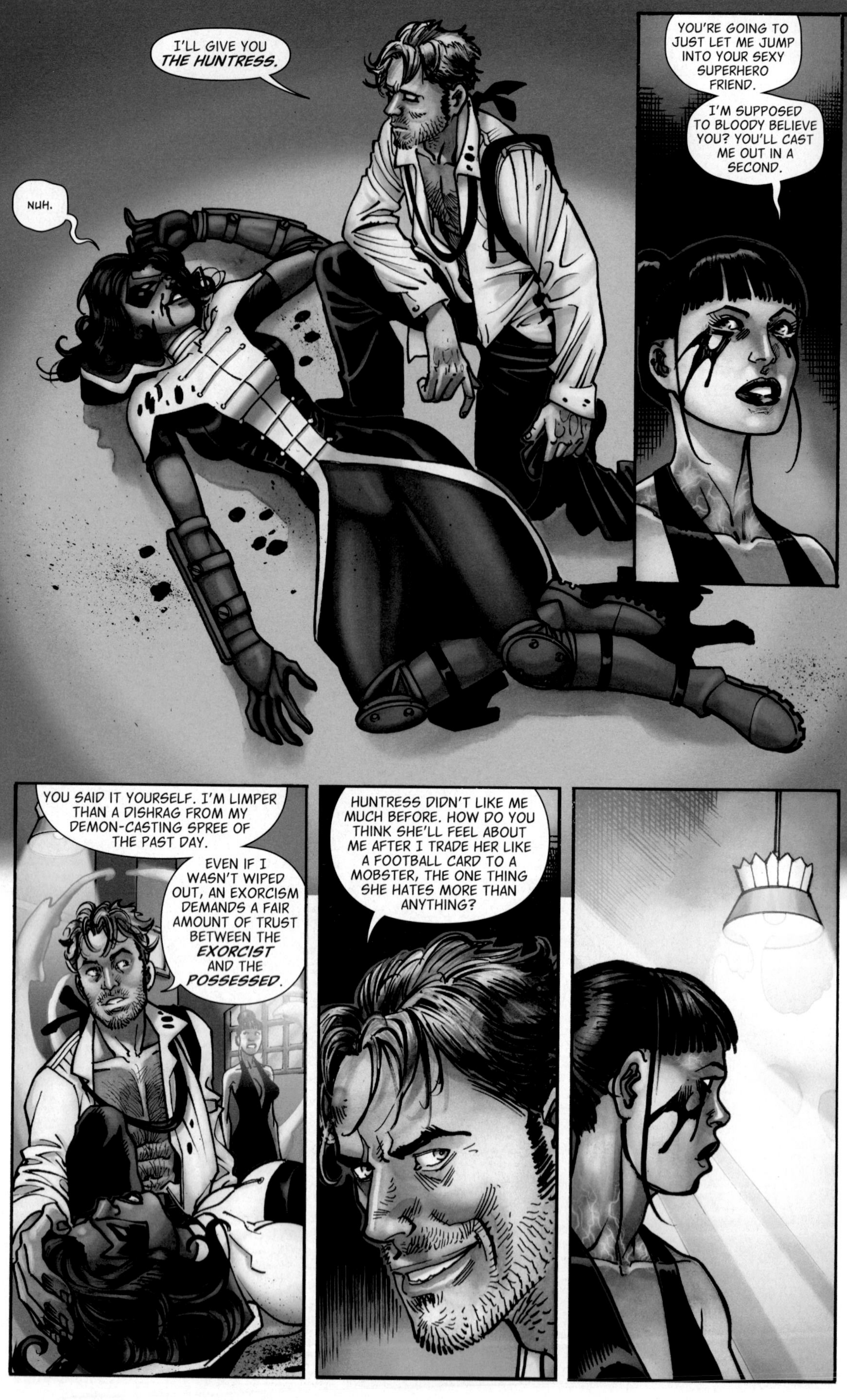
I'LL GIVE YOU THE HUNTRESS.
NUH.
YOU'RE GOING TO JUST LET ME JUMP INTO YOUR SEXY SUPERHERO FRIEND.
I'M SUPPOSED TO BLOODY BELIEVE YOU? YOU'LL CAST ME OUT IN A SECOND.
YOU SAID IT YOURSELF. I'M LIMPER THAN A DISHRAG FROM MY DEMON-CASTING SPREE OF THE PAST DAY.
EVEN IF I WASN'T WIPED OUT, AN EXORCISM DEMANDS A FAIR AMOUNT OF TRUST BETWEEN THE EXORCIST AND THE POSSESSED.
HUNTRESS DIDN'T LIKE ME MUCH BEFORE. HOW DO YOU THINK SHE'LL FEEL ABOUT ME AFTER I TRADE HER LIKE A FOOTBALL CARD TO A MOBSTER, THE ONE THING SHE HATES MORE THAN ANYTHING?

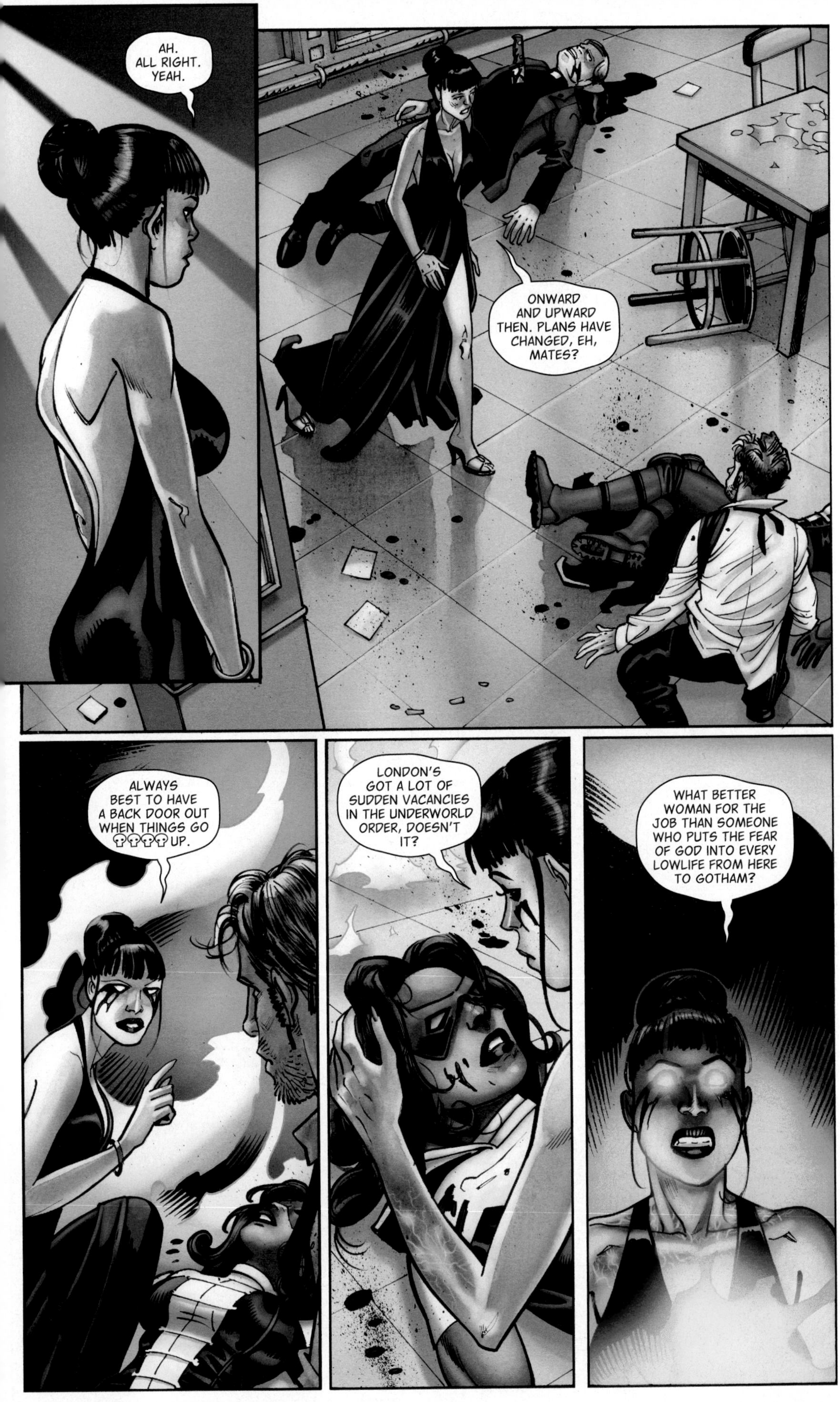
AH. ALL RIGHT. YEAH.
ONWARD AND UPWARD THEN. PLANS HAVE CHANGED, EH, MATES?
ALWAYS BEST TO HAVE A BACK DOOR OUT WHEN THINGS GO UP.
LONDON'S GOT A LOT OF SUDDEN VACANCIES IN THE UNDERWORLD ORDER, DOESN'T IT?
WHAT BETTER WOMAN FOR THE JOB THAN SOMEONE WHO PUTS THE FEAR OF GOD INTO EVERY LOWLIFE FROM HERE TO GOTHAM?

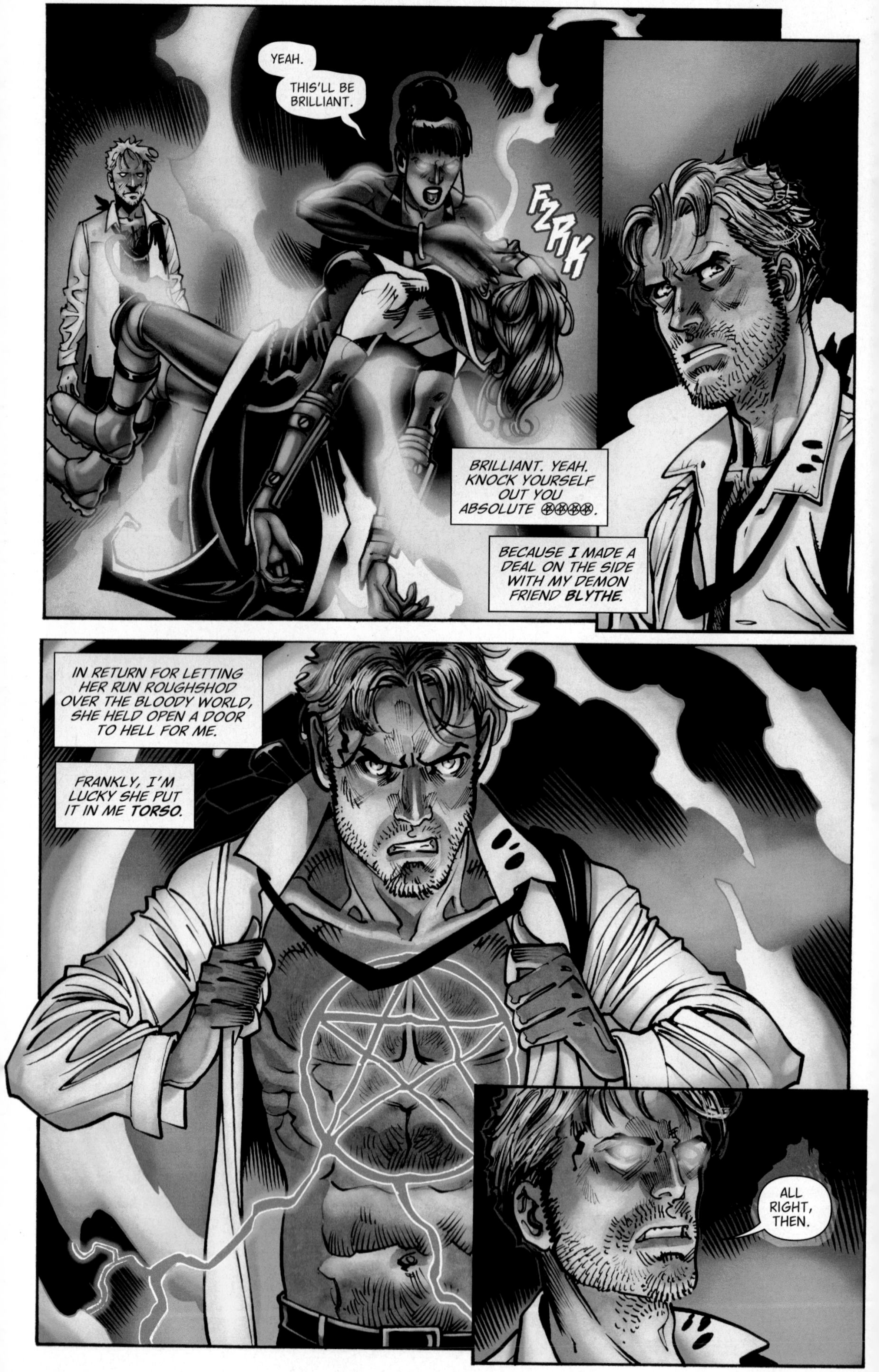
YEAH.
THIS'LL BE BRILLIANT.
FZRK
BRILLIANT. YEAH. KNOCK YOURSELF OUT YOU ABSOLUTE ✪✪✪✪.
BECAUSE I MADE A DEAL ON THE SIDE WITH MY DEMON FRIEND BLYTHE.
IN RETURN FOR LETTING HER RUN ROUGHSHOD OVER THE BLOODY WORLD, SHE HELD OPEN A DOOR TO HELL FOR ME.
FRANKLY, I'M LUCKY SHE PUT IT IN ME TORSO.
ALL RIGHT, THEN.

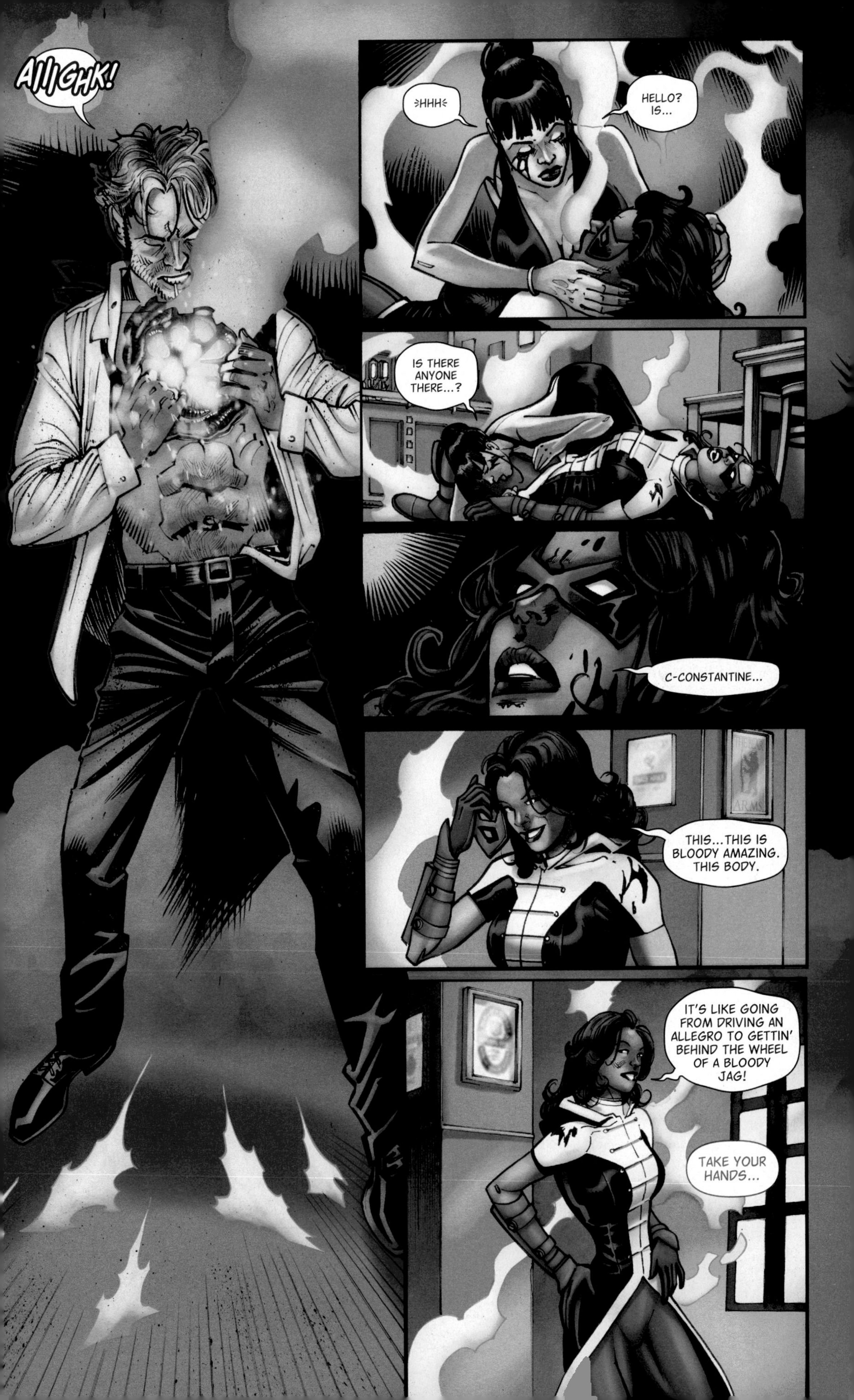
AIIIGHK!
HELLO? IS...
≥HHH≤
IS THERE ANYONE THERE...?
C-CONSTANTINE...
THIS...THIS IS BLOODY AMAZING. THIS BODY.
IT'S LIKE GOING FROM DRIVING AN ALLEGRO TO GETTIN' BEHIND THE WHEEL OF A BLOODY JAG!
TAKE YOUR HANDS...

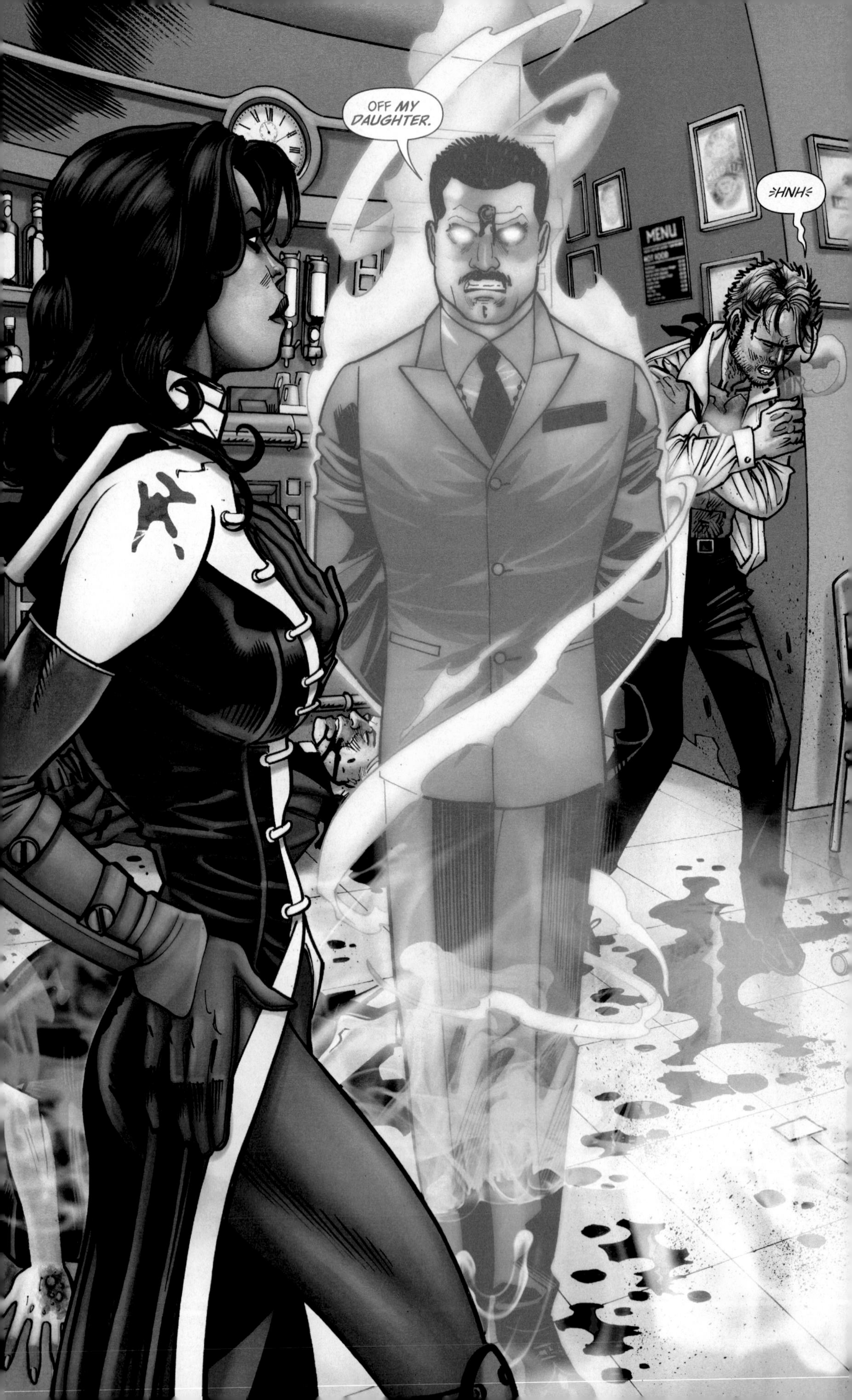
OFF MY DAUGHTER.
HNH
MENU

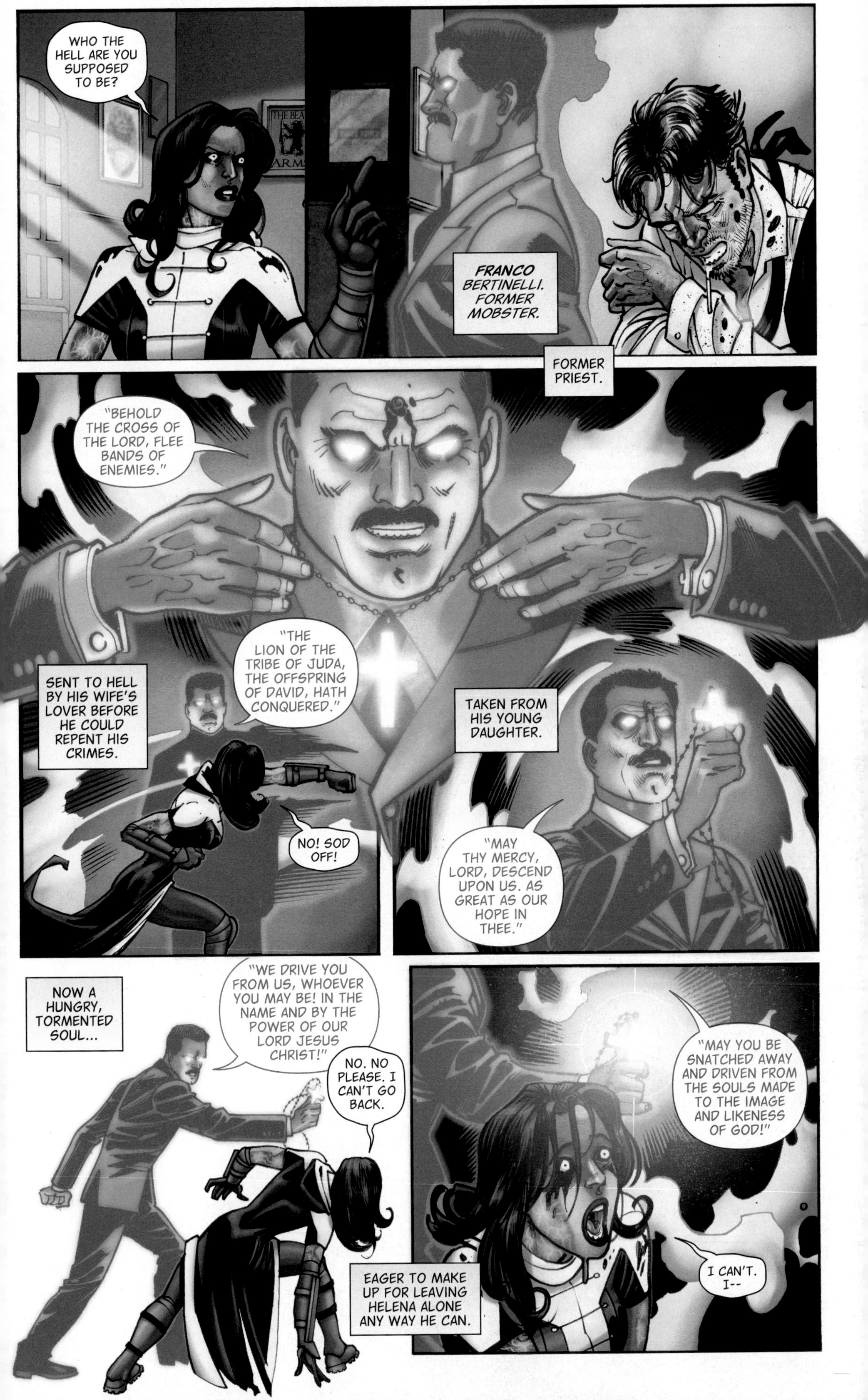

WHO THE HELL ARE YOU SUPPOSED TO BE?
THE BEA ARMS
FRANCO BERTINELLI. FORMER MOBSTER.
FORMER PRIEST.
"BEHOLD THE CROSS OF THE LORD, FLEE BANDS OF ENEMIES."
"THE LION OF THE TRIBE OF JUDA, THE OFFSPRING OF DAVID, HATH CONQUERED."
SENT TO HELL BY HIS WIFE'S LOVER BEFORE HE COULD REPENT HIS CRIMES.
NO! SOD OFF!
TAKEN FROM HIS YOUNG DAUGHTER.
"MAY THY MERCY, LORD, DESCEND UPON US. AS GREAT AS OUR HOPE IN THEE."
NOW A HUNGRY, TORMENTED SOUL...
"WE DRIVE YOU FROM US, WHOEVER YOU MAY BE! IN THE NAME AND BY THE POWER OF OUR LORD JESUS CHRIST!"
NO. NO PLEASE. I CAN'T GO BACK.
EAGER TO MAKE UP FOR LEAVING HELENA ALONE ANY WAY HE CAN.
"MAY YOU BE SNATCHED AWAY AND DRIVEN FROM THE SOULS MADE TO THE IMAGE AND LIKENESS OF GOD!"
I CAN'T. I--

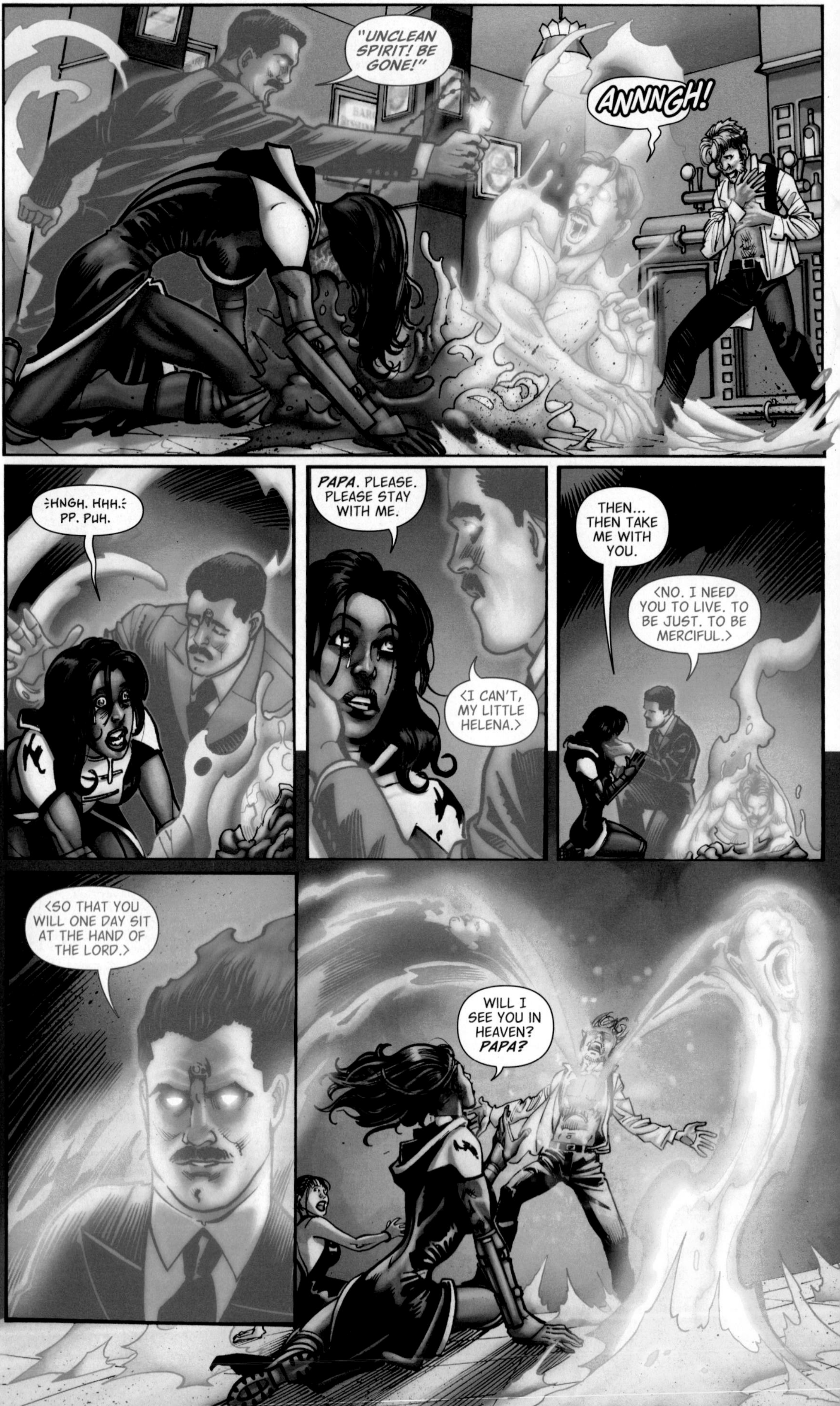
"UNCLEAN SPIRIT! BE GONE!"
ANNNGH!
HNGH. HHH. PP. PUH.
PAPA. PLEASE. PLEASE STAY WITH ME.
<I CAN'T, MY LITTLE HELENA.>
THEN... THEN TAKE ME WITH YOU.
<NO. I NEED YOU TO LIVE. TO BE JUST. TO BE MERCIFUL.>
<SO THAT YOU WILL ONE DAY SIT AT THE HAND OF THE LORD.>
WILL I SEE YOU IN HEAVEN? PAPA?

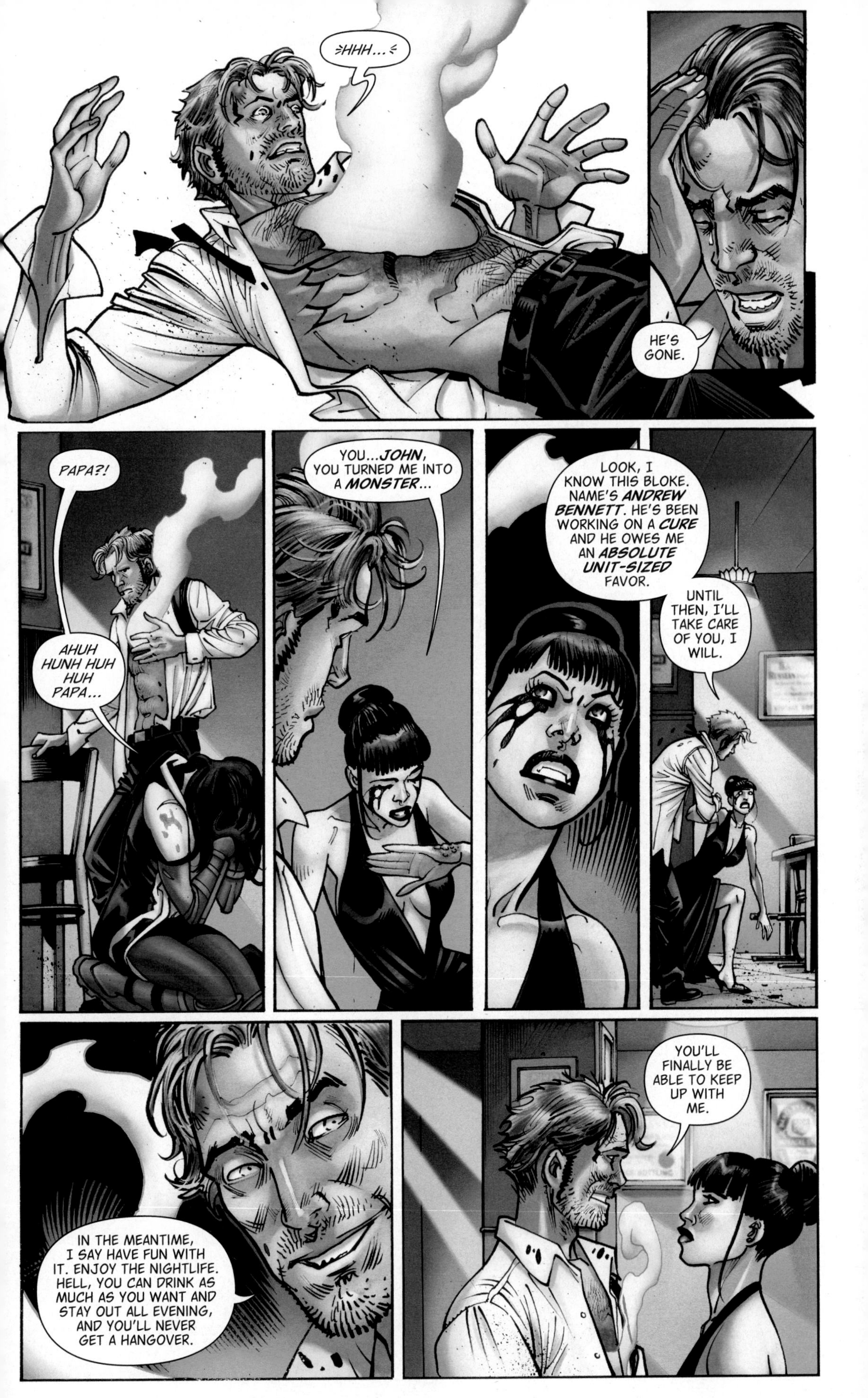

HHH...
HE'S GONE.
PAPA?!
AHUH HUNH HUH HUH PAPA...
YOU...*JOHN*, YOU TURNED ME INTO A *MONSTER*...
LOOK, I KNOW THIS BLOKE. NAME'S *ANDREW BENNETT*. HE'S BEEN WORKING ON A *CURE* AND HE OWES ME AN *ABSOLUTE UNIT-SIZED* FAVOR.
UNTIL THEN, I'LL TAKE CARE OF YOU, I WILL.
IN THE MEANTIME, I SAY HAVE FUN WITH IT. ENJOY THE NIGHTLIFE. HELL, YOU CAN DRINK AS MUCH AS YOU WANT AND STAY OUT ALL EVENING, AND YOU'LL NEVER GET A HANGOVER.
YOU'LL FINALLY BE ABLE TO KEEP UP WITH ME.

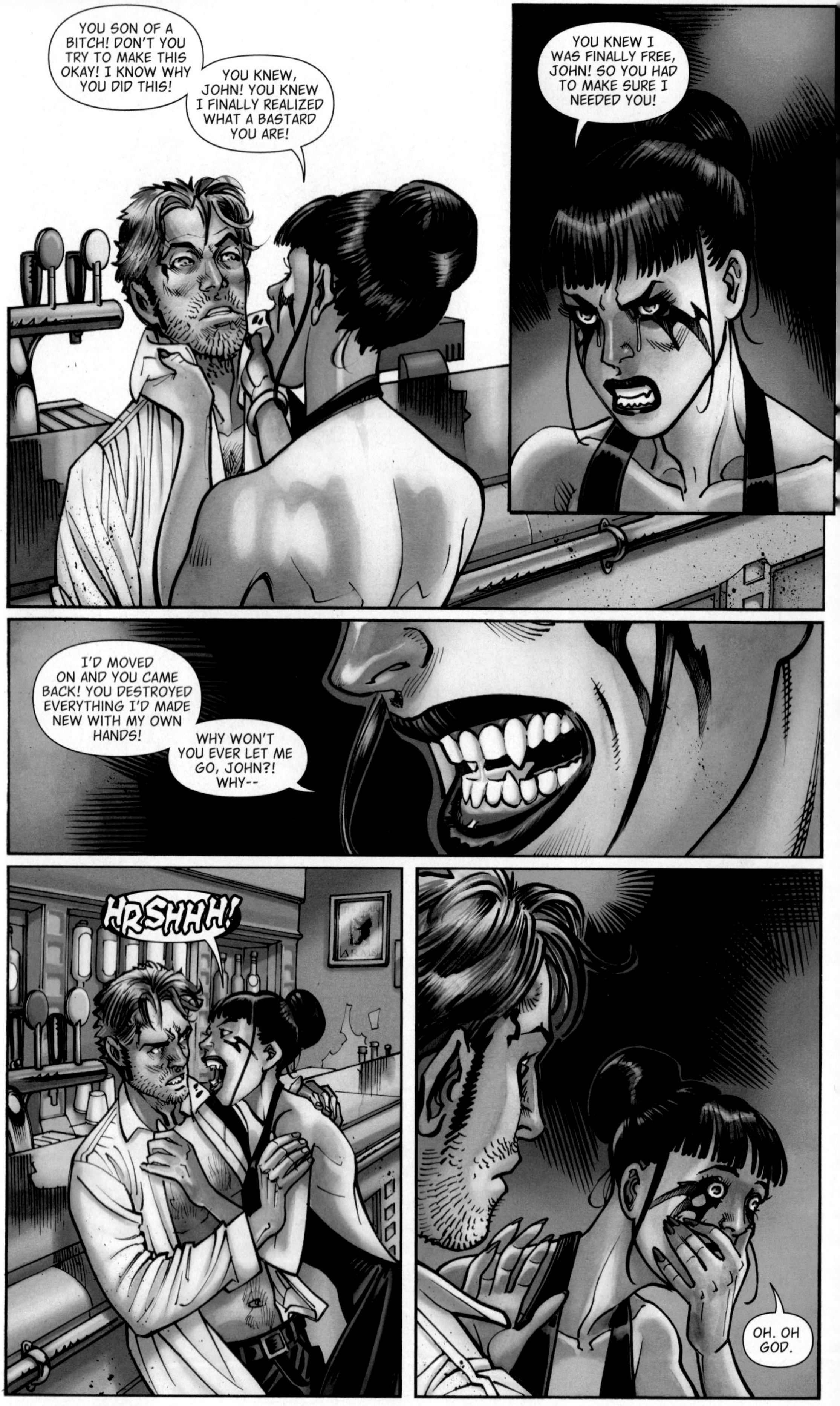
YOU SON OF A BITCH! DON'T YOU TRY TO MAKE THIS OKAY! I KNOW WHY YOU DID THIS!
YOU KNEW, JOHN! YOU KNEW I FINALLY REALIZED WHAT A BASTARD YOU ARE!
YOU KNEW I WAS FINALLY FREE, JOHN! SO YOU HAD TO MAKE SURE I NEEDED YOU!
I'D MOVED ON AND YOU CAME BACK! YOU DESTROYED EVERYTHING I'D MADE NEW WITH MY OWN HANDS!
WHY WON'T YOU EVER LET ME GO, JOHN?! WHY--
HRSHHH!
OH. OH GOD.

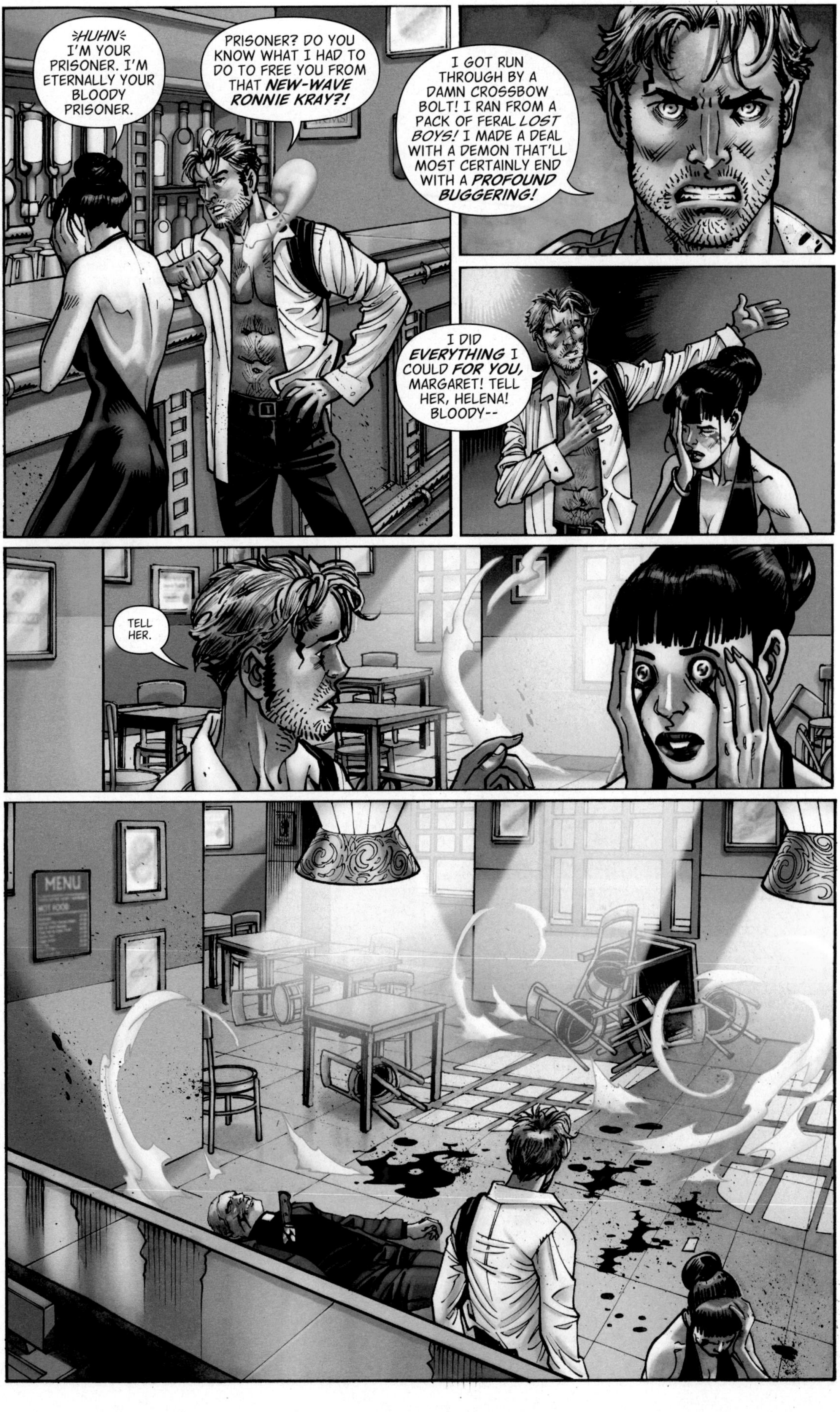

HUHN
I'M YOUR PRISONER. I'M ETERNALLY YOUR BLOODY PRISONER.
PRISONER? DO YOU KNOW WHAT I HAD TO DO TO FREE YOU FROM THAT NEW-WAVE RONNIE KRAY?!
I GOT RUN THROUGH BY A DAMN CROSSBOW BOLT! I RAN FROM A PACK OF FERAL LOST BOYS! I MADE A DEAL WITH A DEMON THAT'LL MOST CERTAINLY END WITH A PROFOUND BUGGERING!
I DID EVERYTHING I COULD FOR YOU, MARGARET! TELL HER, HELENA! BLOODY--
TELL HER.
MENU

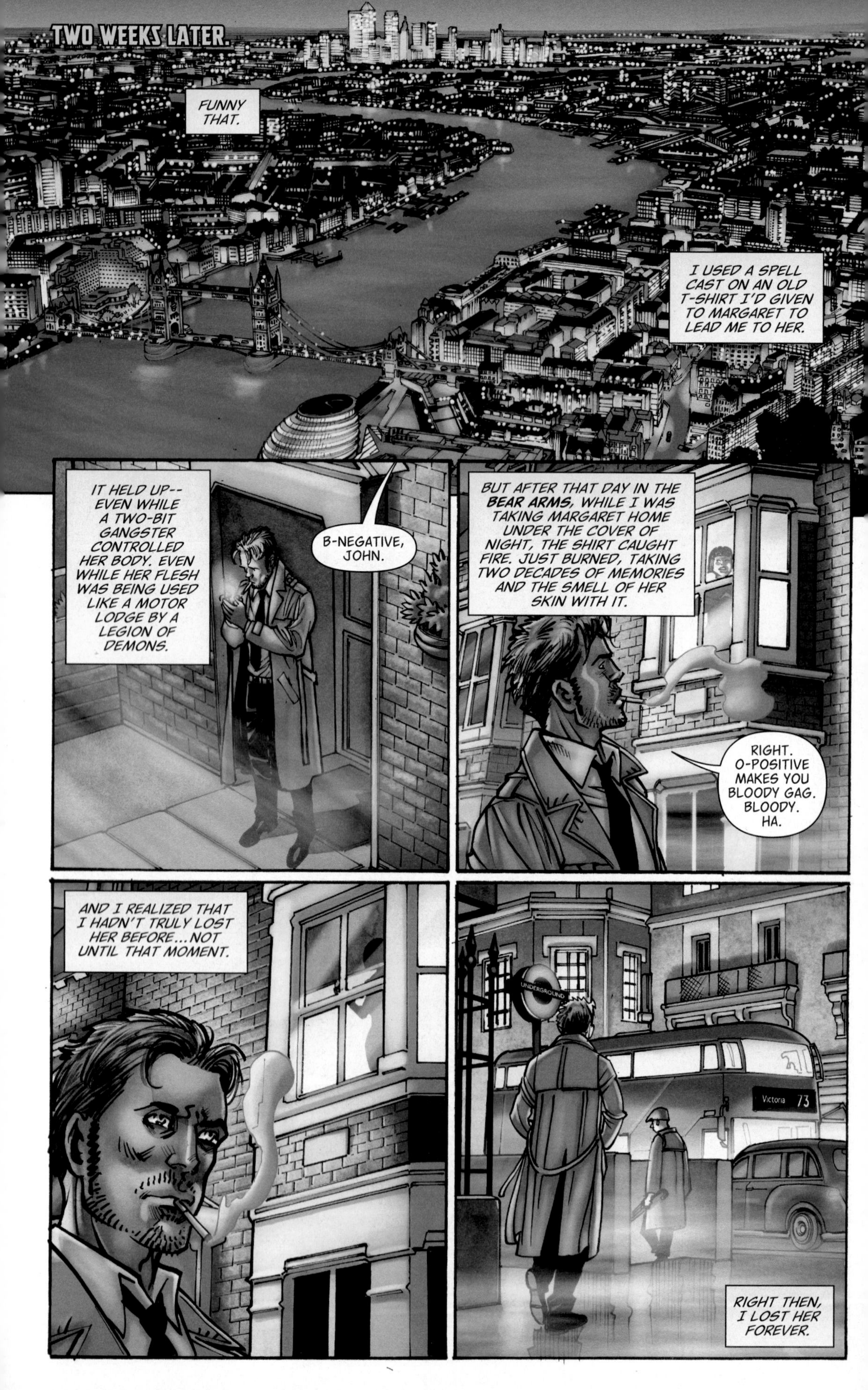
TWO WEEKS LATER.
FUNNY THAT.
I USED A SPELL CAST ON AN OLD T-SHIRT I'D GIVEN TO MARGARET TO LEAD ME TO HER.
IT HELD UP-- EVEN WHILE A TWO-BIT GANGSTER CONTROLLED HER BODY. EVEN WHILE HER FLESH WAS BEING USED LIKE A MOTOR LODGE BY A LEGION OF DEMONS.
B-NEGATIVE, JOHN.
BUT AFTER THAT DAY IN THE BEAR ARMS, WHILE I WAS TAKING MARGARET HOME UNDER THE COVER OF NIGHT, THE SHIRT CAUGHT FIRE. JUST BURNED, TAKING TWO DECADES OF MEMORIES AND THE SMELL OF HER SKIN WITH IT.
RIGHT. O-POSITIVE MAKES YOU BLOODY GAG. BLOODY. HA.
AND I REALIZED THAT I HADN'T TRULY LOST HER BEFORE... NOT UNTIL THAT MOMENT.
UNDERGROUND
Victoria 73
RIGHT THEN, I LOST HER FOREVER.

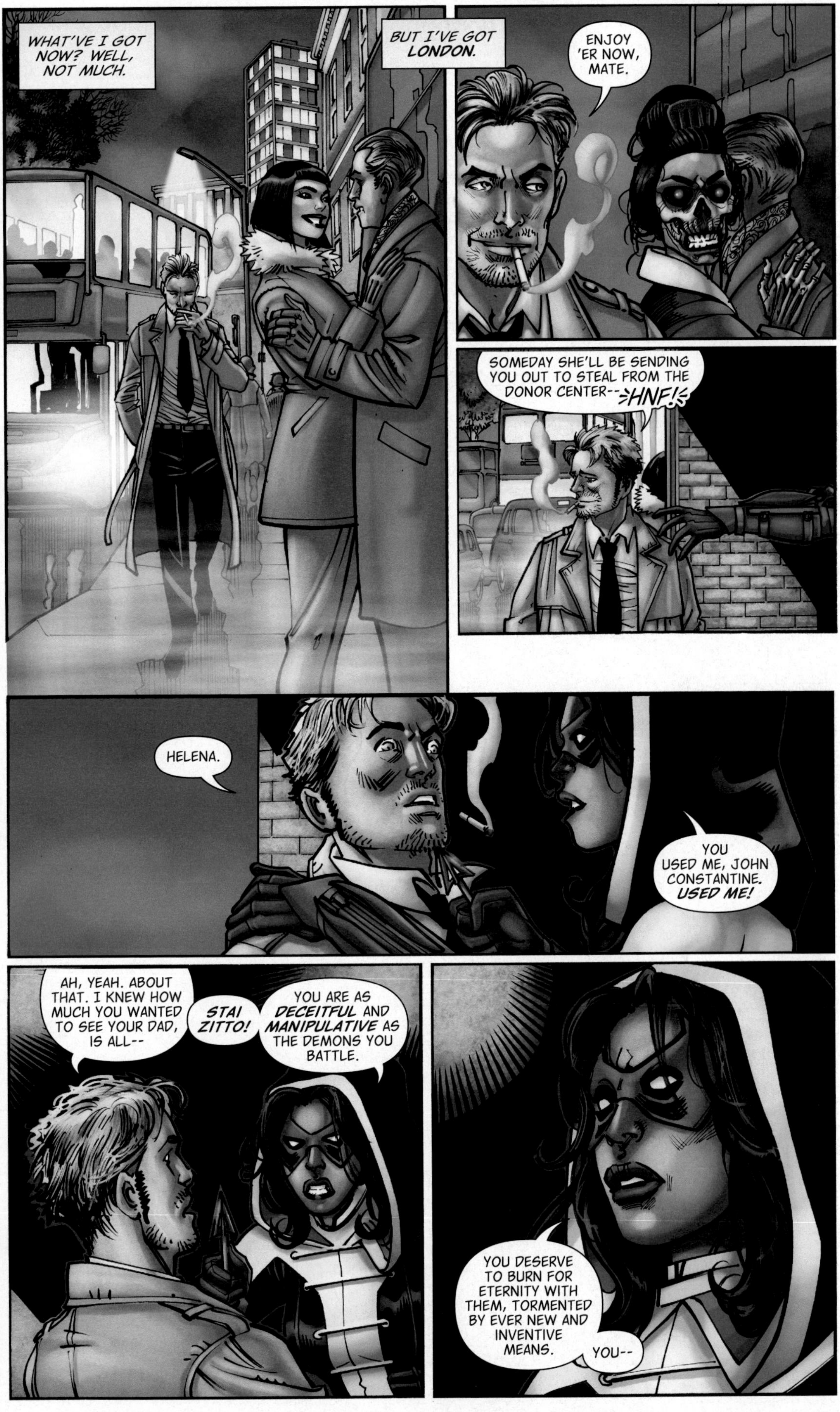
WHAT'VE I GOT NOW? WELL, NOT MUCH.
BUT I'VE GOT LONDON.
ENJOY 'ER NOW, MATE.
SOMEDAY SHE'LL BE SENDING YOU OUT TO STEAL FROM THE DONOR CENTER-- HNF!
HELENA.
YOU USED ME, JOHN CONSTANTINE. USED ME!
AH, YEAH. ABOUT THAT. I KNEW HOW MUCH YOU WANTED TO SEE YOUR DAD, IS ALL--
STAI ZITTO!
YOU ARE AS DECEITFUL AND MANIPULATIVE AS THE DEMONS YOU BATTLE.
YOU DESERVE TO BURN FOR ETERNITY WITH THEM, TORMENTED BY EVER NEW AND INVENTIVE MEANS.
YOU--

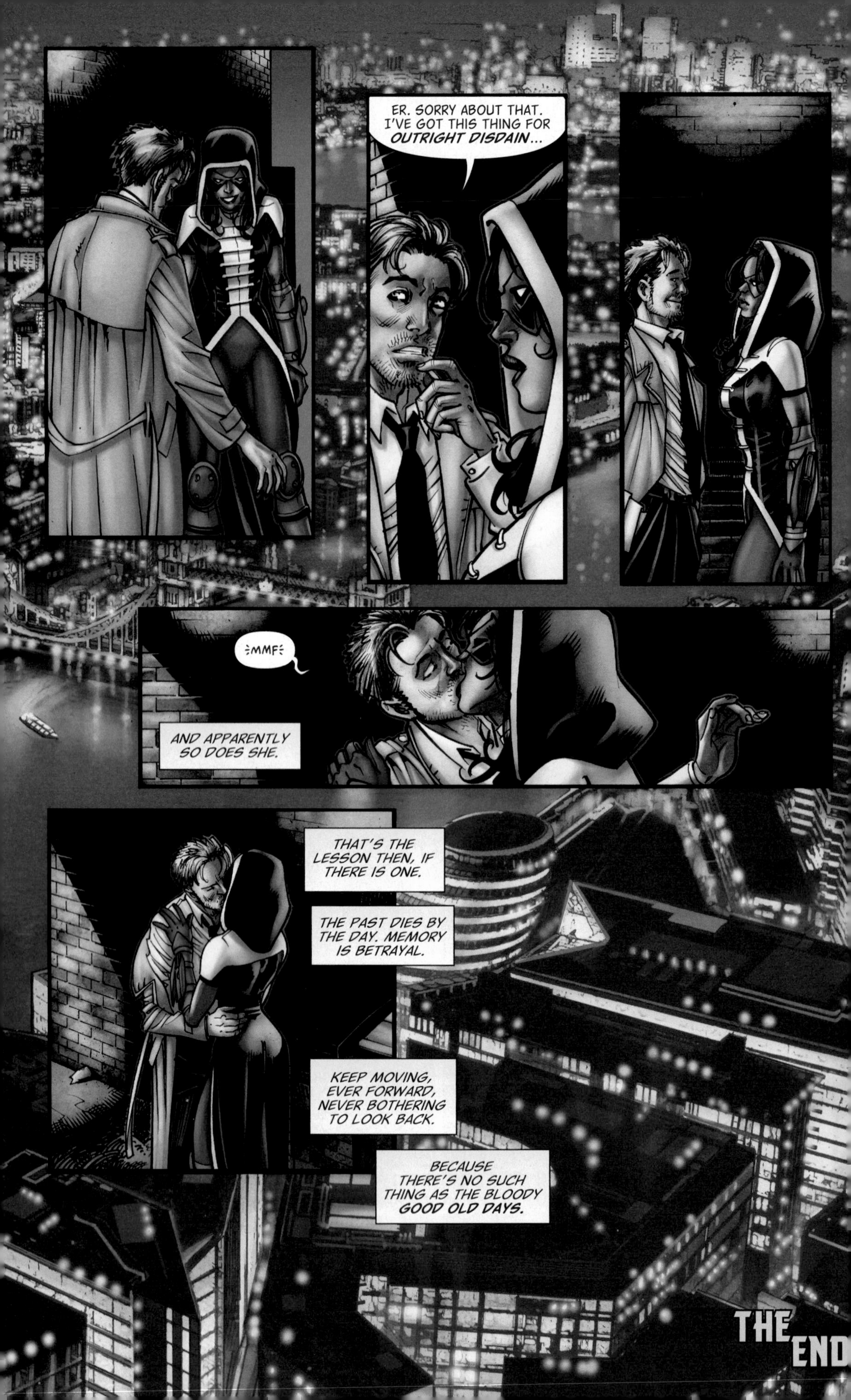
ER. SORRY ABOUT THAT. I'VE GOT THIS THING FOR OUTRIGHT DISDAIN...
MMF
AND APPARENTLY SO DOES SHE.
THAT'S THE LESSON THEN, IF THERE IS ONE.
THE PAST DIES BY THE DAY. MEMORY IS BETRAYAL.
KEEP MOVING, EVER FORWARD, NEVER BOTHERING TO LOOK BACK.
BECAUSE THERE'S NO SUCH THING AS THE BLOODY GOOD OLD DAYS.
THE END

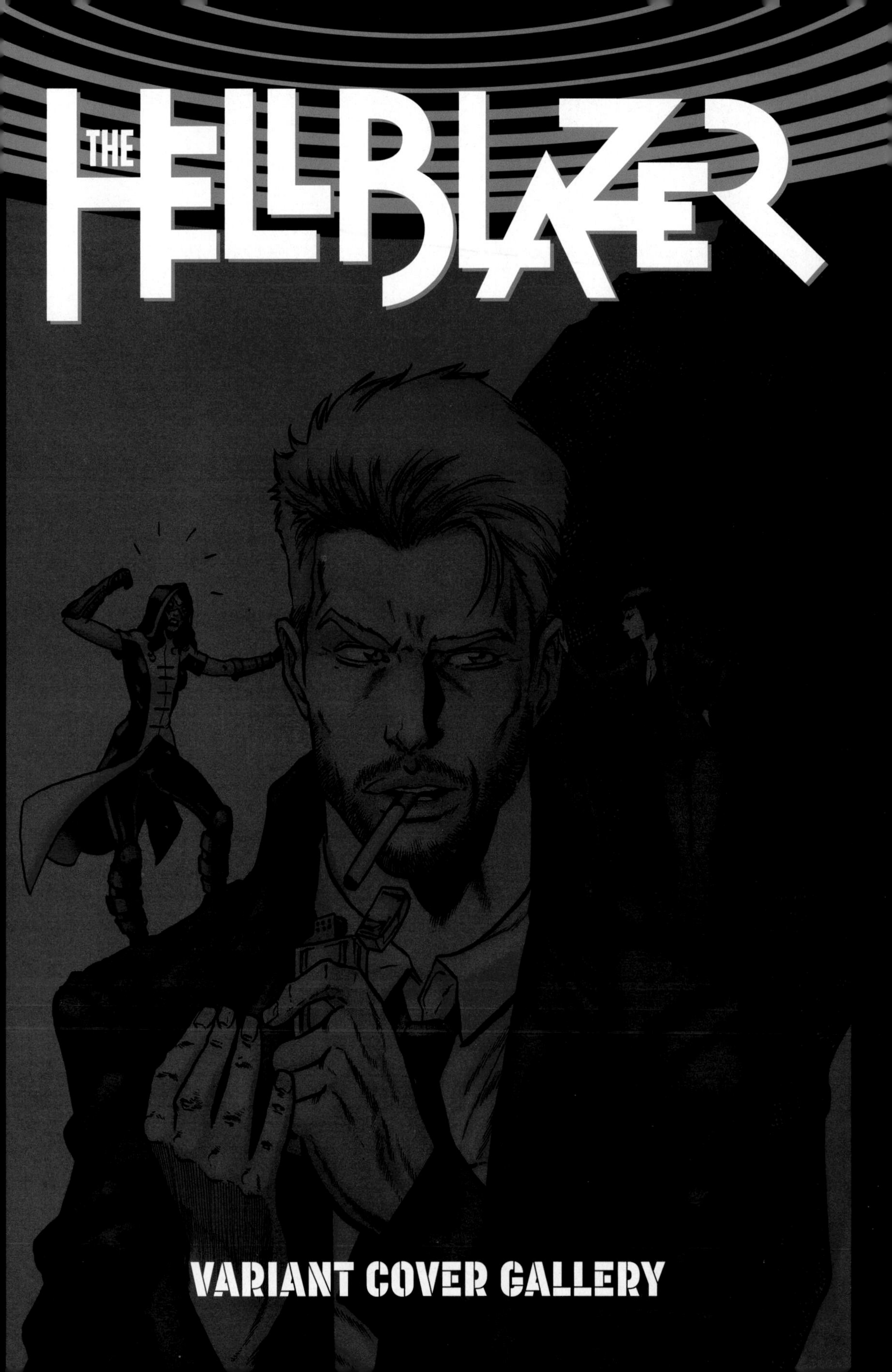
THE HELLBLAZER

VARIANT COVER GALLERY

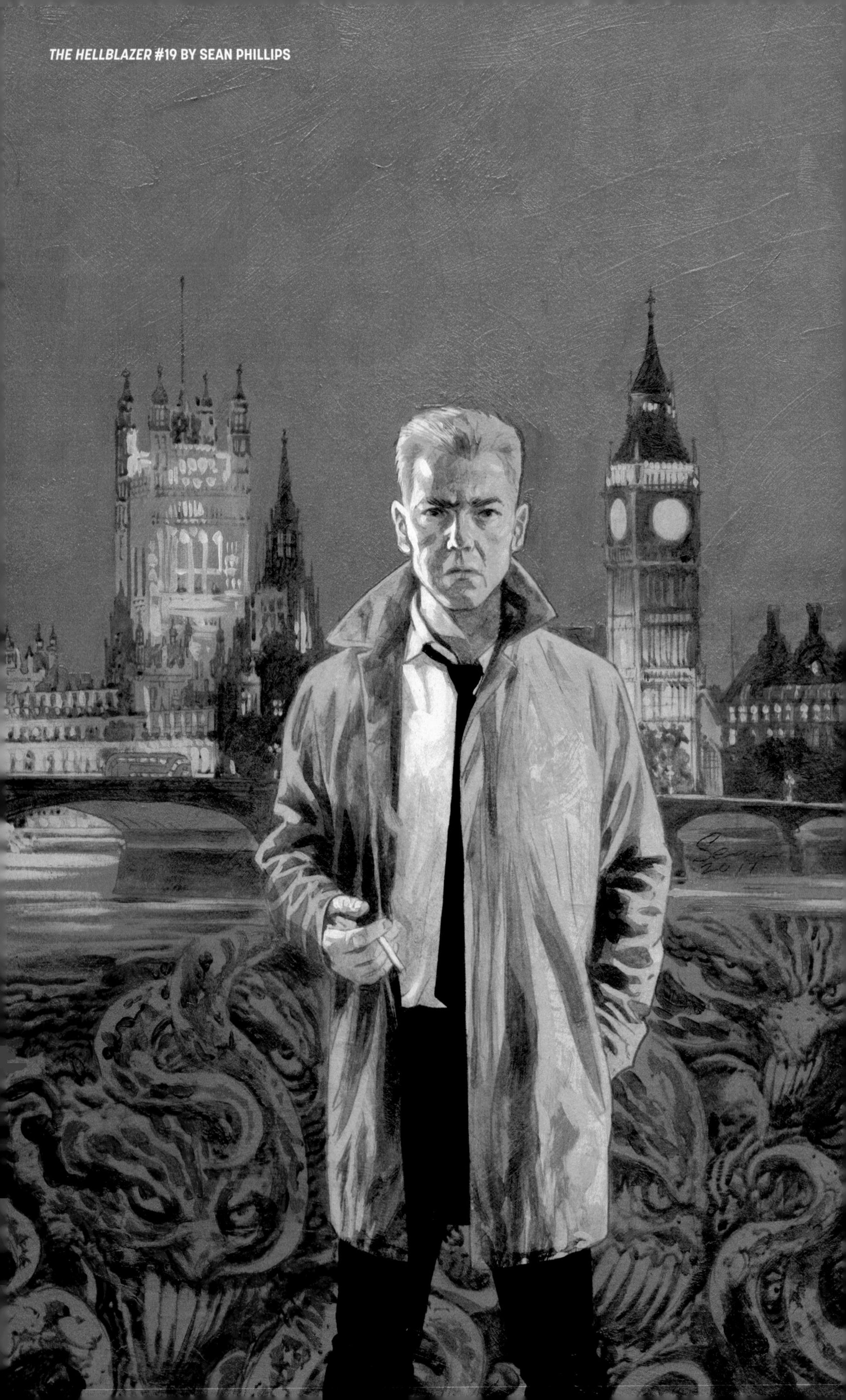

THE HELLBLAZER #19 BY SEAN PHILLIPS

THE HELLBLAZER #20 BY SEAN PHILLIPS

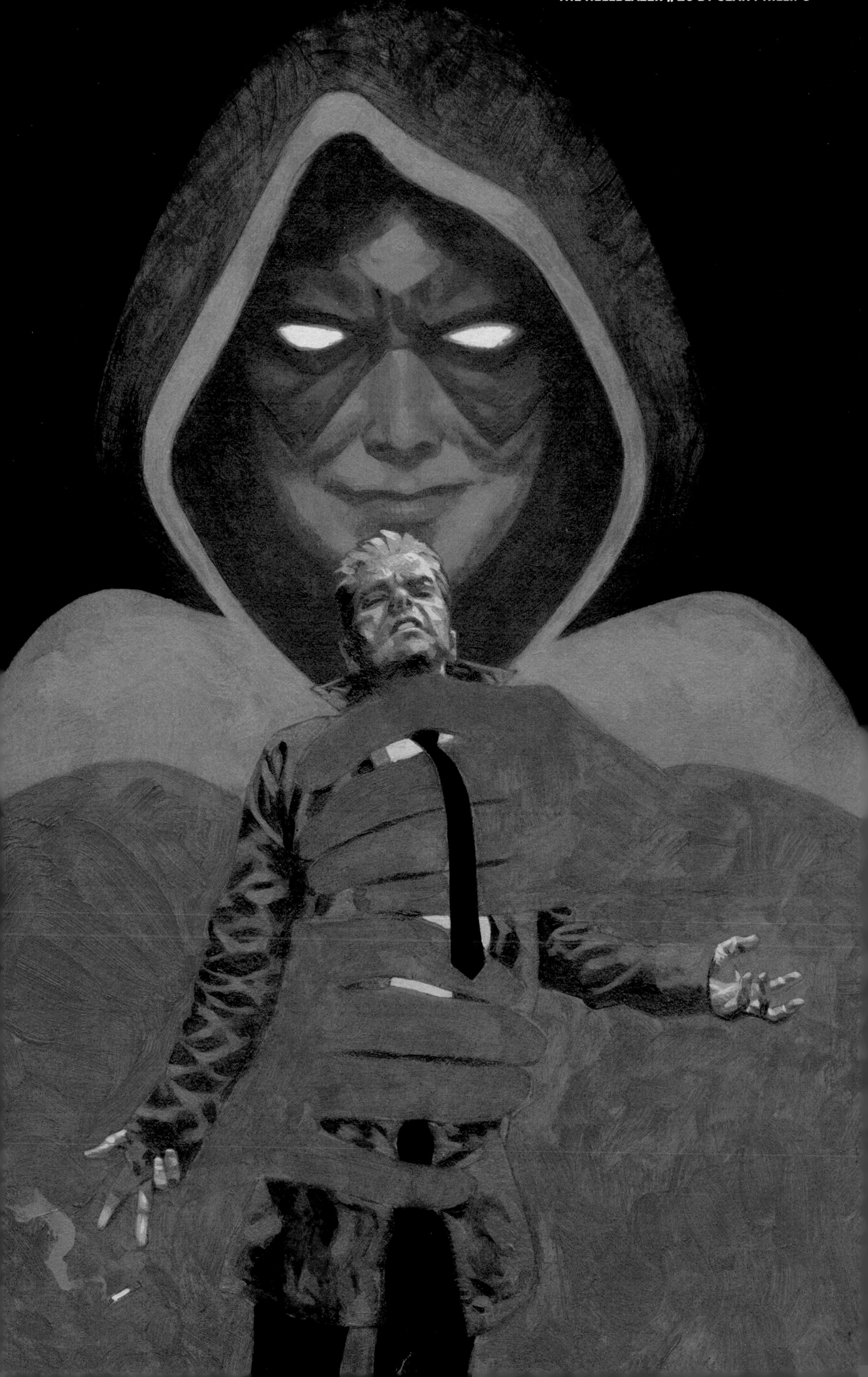

***THE HELLBLAZER* #21 BY SEAN PHILLIPS**

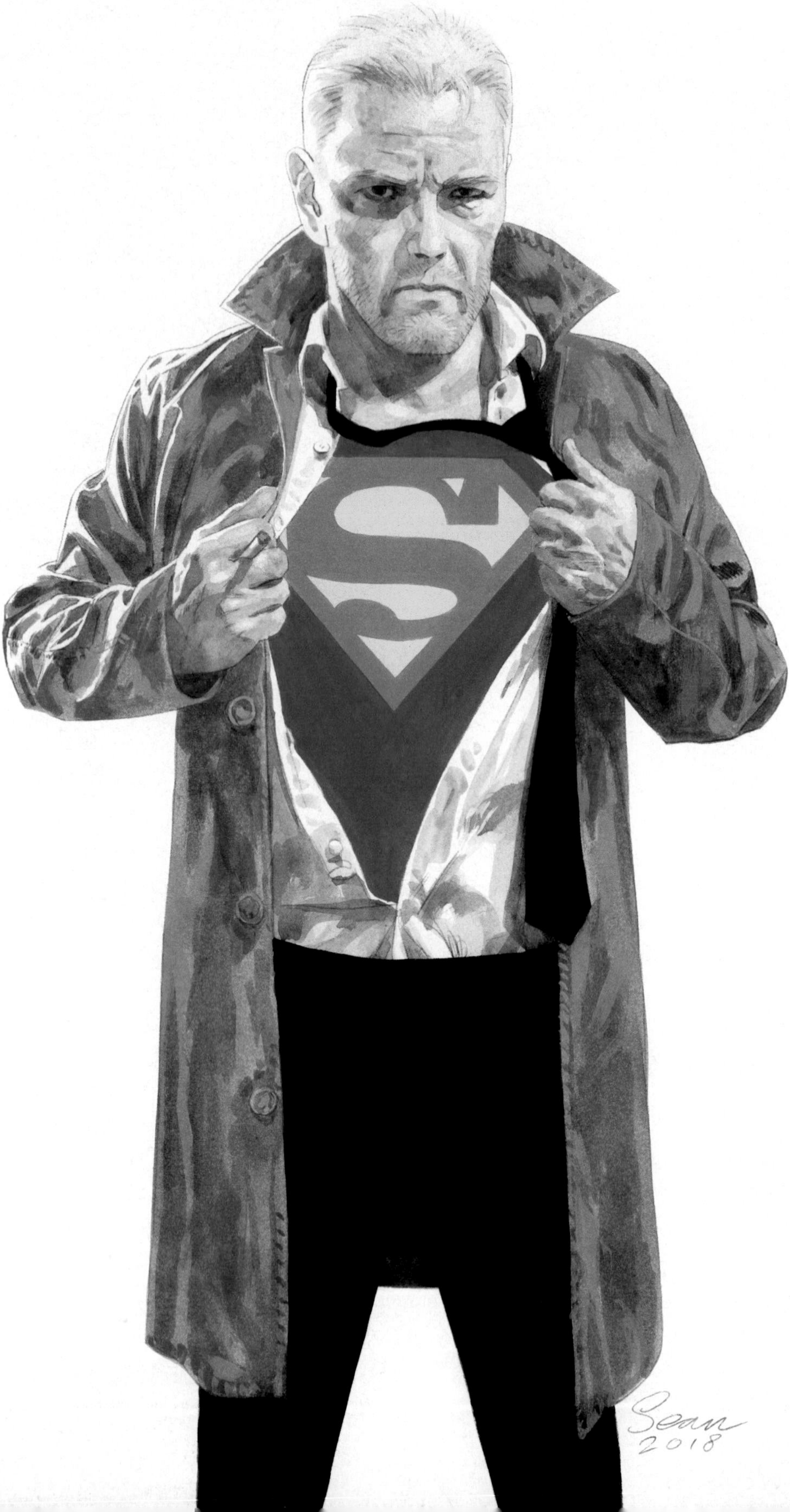
Sean
2018

THE HELLBLAZER #22 BY SEAN PHILLIPS

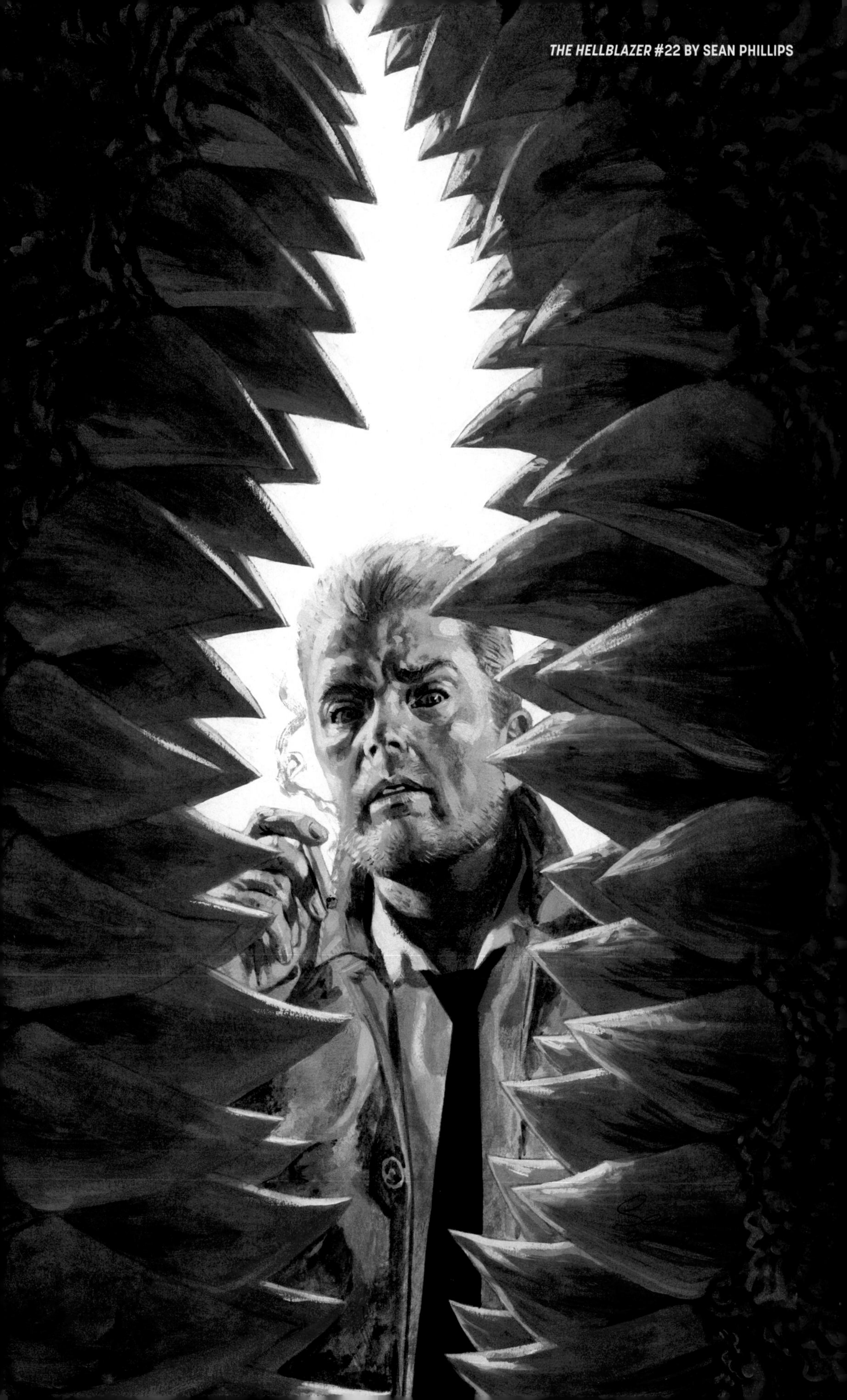

THE HELLBLAZER #23 BY SEAN PHILLIPS

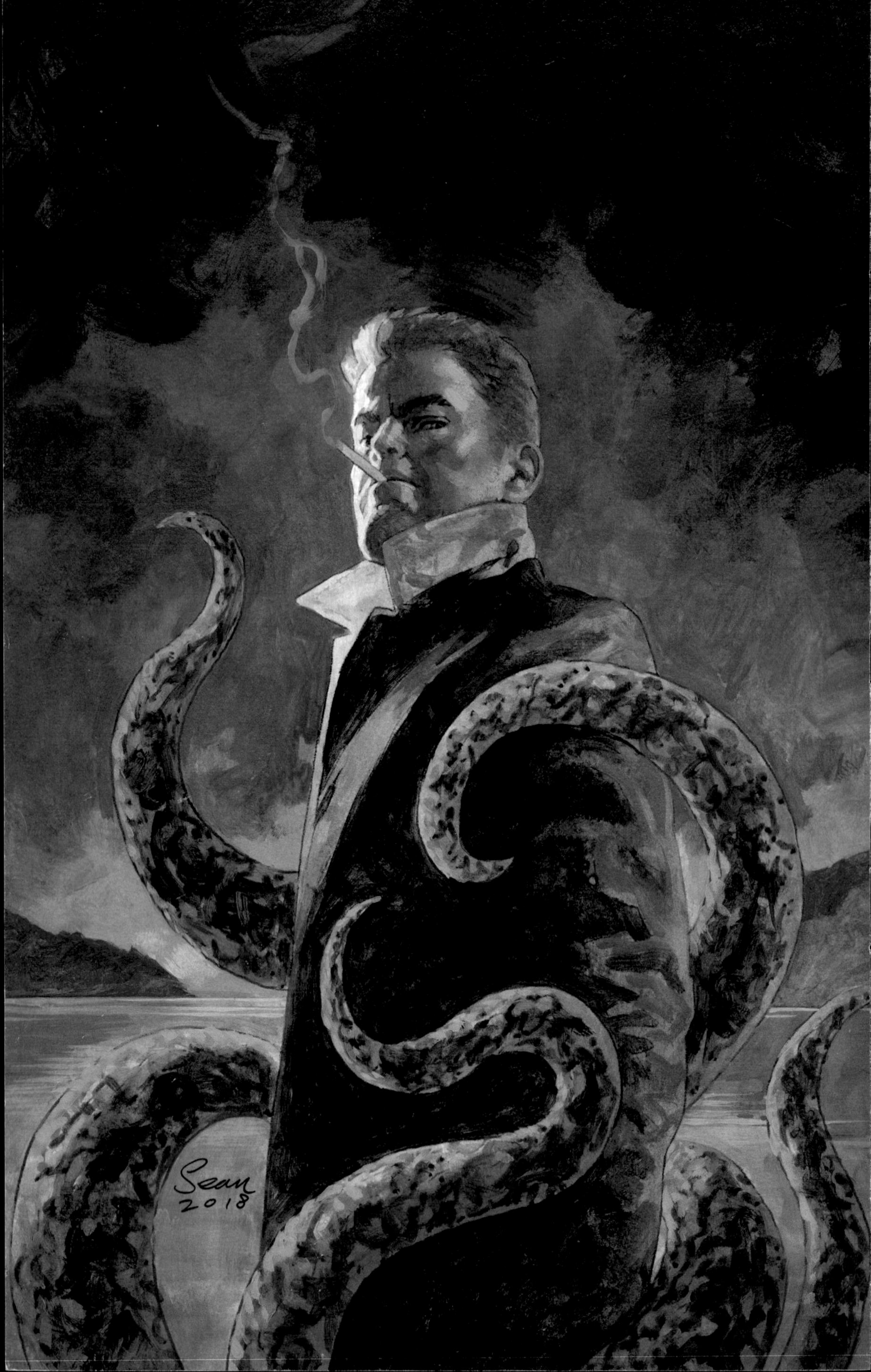
Sean
2018

THE HELLBLAZER #24 BY SEAN PHILLIPS

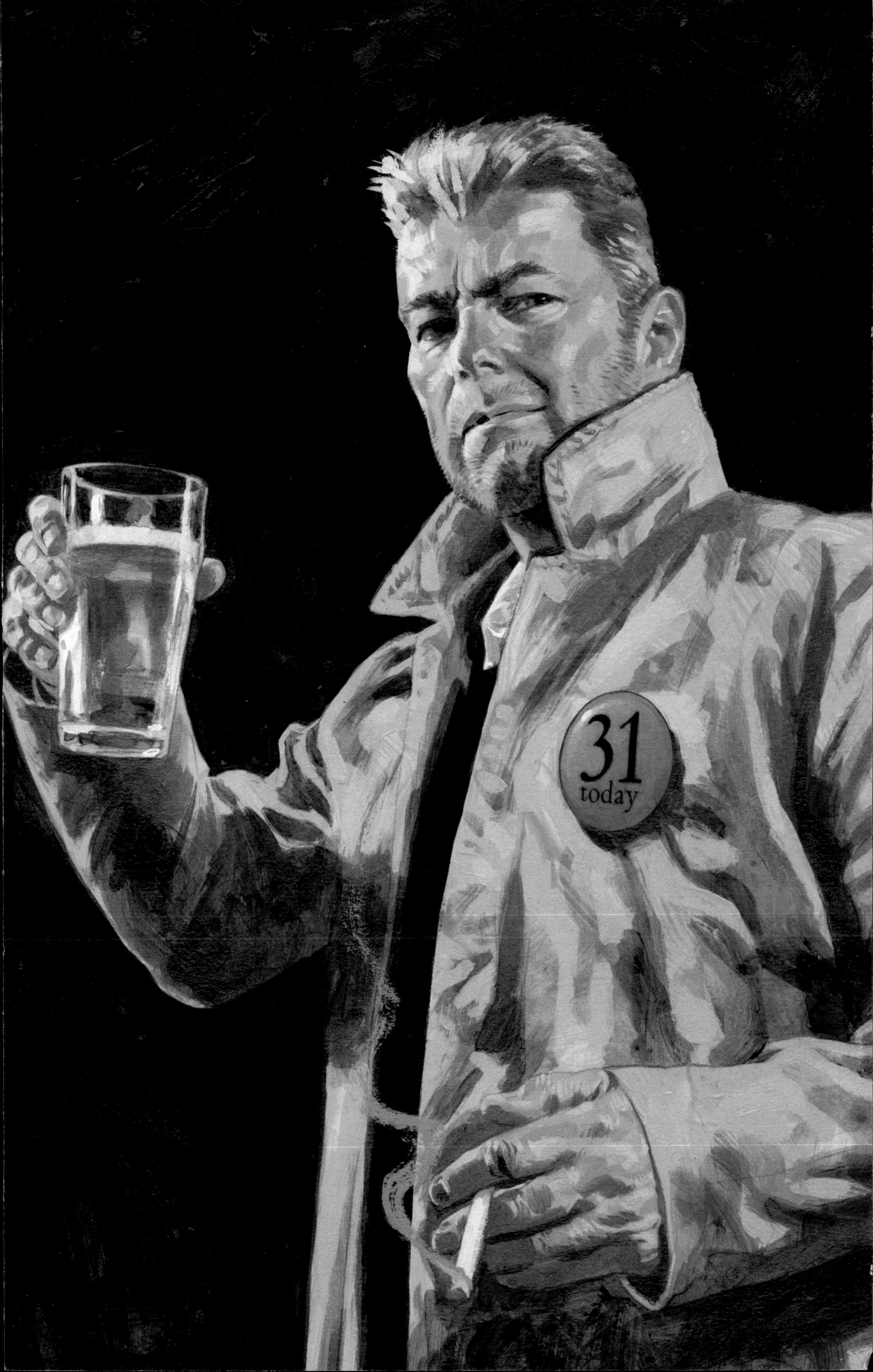
31
today

"It's nice to see one of the best comics of the late '80s return so strongly."
– Comic Book Resources

"It's high energy from page one through to the last page." **– BATMAN NEWS**

DC UNIVERSE REBIRTH
SUICIDE SQUAD
VOL. 1: THE BLACK VAULT
ROB WILLIAMS
with **JIM LEE** and others

VOL.1 THE BLACK VAULT
ROB WILLIAMS • JIM LEE • PHILIP TAN • JASON FABOK • IVAN REIS • GARY FRANK

**THE HELLBLAZER VOL. 1:
THE POISON TRUTH**

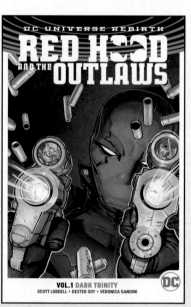

**RED HOOD AND THE OUTLAWS VOL. 1:
DARK TRINITY**

**HARLEY QUINN VOL. 1:
DIE LAUGHING**